DATE DUE			
FEB 2 3 1998			

Olympia Brown

The Battle for Equality

Olympia Brown

The Battle
for Equality

by
Charlotte Coté

Published by
Mother Courage Press

Front cover photo—*Schlesinger Library, Radcliffe College*
Back cover photo—*Wide World Photos, Inc.*

Library of Congress Catalog Card Number 88-60777
ISBN 0-941300-09-9 (paperback)
0-941300-11-0 (hardcover)

Mother Courage Press
1533 Illinois Street
Racine, WI 53405

This book is dedicated to the memory of Gwendolen Brown Willis who prompted my realization that the lives of women have been buried in the dust of marching feet and flying spears from the pages of the Bible to the present time.

Gwendolen Willis always felt that her mother's place in history had been overlooked by historians. And she was right.

This book has been written to correct that omission and to pay tribute to Olympia Brown, a dedicated, courageous campaigner for equal rights for women.

Acknowledgments

I would like to thank the following people for their help in obtaining information about Olympia Brown: Katharine Willis Hooton, Marcella Chalkley Holmes, Jane Ciarcia, Donald Towne Marshall and Elvera Belden of the Racine County Historical Society. I would also like to thank the following institutions for their permission to use their resources and quote from their material: The Arthur Schlesinger Library, Radcliffe College, Cambridge, Massachusetts; State Historical Society of Wisconsin, Madison, Wisconsin; University of Wisconsin-Parkside Archives, Kenosha, Wisconsin; Racine County Historical Society and Museum, Inc., Racine, Wisconsin. I also wish to thank Professors Kathryn Whitford and William Harrold of the University of Wisconsin-Milwaukee for their early help and encouragement; Elizabeth Olson for proof-reading; and a special thanks to both Barbara Lindquist and Jeanne Arnold of Mother Courage Press for their encouragement and painstaking editing of the manuscript. I thank my many friends and acquaintances who have so often expressed interest and encouragement in this project.

Contents

A bronze tablet in Atwood Hall at Canton, New York, commemorates the achievements of a remarkable woman who carried on a life-long struggle for equality, justice and voting rights for women.

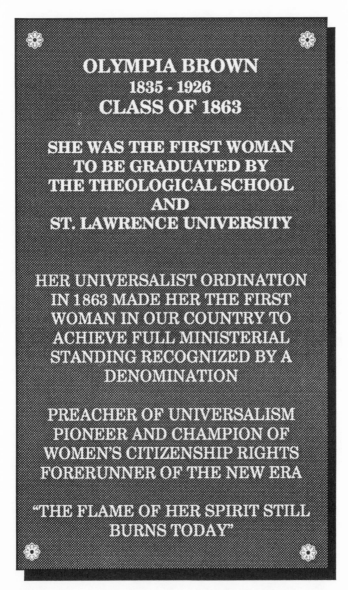

OLYMPIA BROWN
1835 - 1926
CLASS OF 1863

**SHE WAS THE FIRST WOMAN
TO BE GRADUATED BY
THE THEOLOGICAL SCHOOL
AND
ST. LAWRENCE UNIVERSITY**

HER UNIVERSALIST ORDINATION
IN 1863 MADE HER THE FIRST
WOMAN IN OUR COUNTRY TO
ACHIEVE FULL MINISTERIAL
STANDING RECOGNIZED BY A
DENOMINATION

PREACHER OF UNIVERSALISM
PIONEER AND CHAMPION OF
WOMEN'S CITIZENSHIP RIGHTS
FORERUNNER OF THE NEW ERA

"THE FLAME OF HER SPIRIT STILL
BURNS TODAY"

Prologue

The Flame of Her Spirit
Still Burns Today

Olympia Brown, a tiny, eighty-two-year-old protester, clutched her sign tighter in her hands as the wind blew a fresh blast of icy air down the street. It was a cold, raw day in early March of 1917. Clouds hung heavy over the scene and rain threatened to fall at any moment.

Mobs of men gathered along the way watching the lines of women march in front of the White House gates. Their cries of, "Go back home and take care of your children," and "You don't need to vote. We do that for you," rang on the chill air. The women ignored the taunts. Holding their heads high, they marched back and forth in front of the gates. Many of them carried huge purple, white and gold banners. Others carried signs that read, WOMEN DEMAND THE BALLOT.

Olympia saw a sudden scuffle in the street ahead. Several men had seized a banner from one of the women. "We'll show you what we think of this," they shouted, snapping the pole in two, then trampling the banner in the muck.

"You women belong in the home, not out here mixing in politics," they snarled. That act provoked more men to surge forward and begin wresting banners and signs from the marchers. Olympia saw one women stumble and fall. The next instant a man shoved another woman down. Although other women turned and hurried to their aid, the scuffle grew as more men tried to push some of the marchers down and break their banners and signs.

Her heart beat with fear and anger. She was afraid that the police would not come in time to prevent a serious injury, and she was angry that men could be so violent against women. When she saw a police car drive up, she felt a brief moment of relief. Several officers got out of the car and ran up to the scene of the struggle. Quickly seizing two of the women, they put them in the patrol wagon; then, as if amused by the conflict, they stood and watched the contention with apparent interest. Moments later a sudden stinging shower of sleet rained down on the crowd. The officers

1

leaped into action again. Hurriedly seizing several more women, they shoved them into the patrol wagon, locked the doors and quickly drove away.

Olympia stared after them, confusion washing over her. How could they drive away and leave the very people who had committed the violence? She turned to one of the women marching with her. "Why didn't the police arrest any of the men?" she asked. "They were attacking the women. They're the ones who should be arrested."

"Of course they are," the woman replied, "but President Wilson ordered the police to arrest the women—no one else. It's the women he wants to stop."

At those words, Olympia no longer felt the cold wind or the stinging rain although her teeth were chattering and her hands were numb. Didn't women even have the right to peaceful protest, to marching and picketing? Weren't they citizens of the United States? Or did men, for that matter, still view them as little better than slaves, still consider them as pieces of property?

The answer was obvious and the humiliation cut deep—even after so many years of reprobation. It seemed that by now she should surely have learned how to ignore or reject such acts of vengeance, but it was very hard.

The women continued to march hour after hour. Many had to peel off their wet gloves which had grown sticky and stiff from the varnish on the poles. Their hands quickly turned blue from the cold. Sometimes a bystander offered an umbrella or hat to the marchers, or a raincoat or shawl. Whatever items any of the women accepted, they shared with each other. Patrol wagons continued to come from time to time and take away more pickets. Occasionally one of the marchers fainted or dropped from exhaustion, and her companions helped her across the street to the National Woman's Party headquarters. Olympia, however, did not waver. She marched to the end of the day.

For the next two years, whenever she could, she joined the protesters picketing the White House.

In December of 1918, a month after the end of World War I, she joined thousands of women gathering in Washington, D.C., to protest President Wilson's visit to France as head of "the greatest democracy on earth."

"The United States is not even a democracy," she declared. "Half its citizens are not allowed to vote!"

On the appointed afternoon, women began forming a line and marching in single file past the White House, then along the edge of Lafayette Park to the foot of the Lafayette statue. Many of them were carrying large purple, white and gold banners, the symbol for woman suffrage, while others carried lighted torches. It was a magnificent scene.

Sensing the drama, a crowd began to gather at once around the statue. Somewhat awestruck by the scene, they watched intently as a young woman with a torch walked to the large urn at the base of the statue and set fire to the logs carefully stacked within. With the flames rising behind her, she sang in a loud, clear voice, the "Woman's Marseillaise."* The crowd cheered and clapped and cried for more.

Another woman stepped forward. She said that the women were burning the President's speeches and books on democracy, freedom and liberty because he did not believe these principles and policies applied to women. When she demanded that women be given the right to vote, a few hoots and jeers echoed on the evening air.

Suddenly, a hush fell over the crowd as a small, aged woman moved from her place in the shadows toward the urn in the brilliant torchlight. They recognized this veteran as the eighty-three-year-old Reverend Olympia Brown of Wisconsin, a friend and colleague of Susan B. Anthony and Elizabeth Cady Stanton. She held aloft a sheaf of papers. It was the speech Wilson had made on his arrival in France. As she thrust the papers into the flames, she cried out in a firm, clear voice vibrant with emotion, "I have fought for liberty for seventy years, and I protest against the President's leaving this country with this old fight here unwon!" A moment of silence—then with the suddenness of a thunderclap, the crowd burst into applause and continued to cheer as her companions helped her down from the base of the statue.

* See Appendix, page 208

3

Chapter 1

The Making of a Feminist

(with excerpts from Olympia Brown's unpublished autobiography)

Olympia Brown inherited her fortitude, perseverance and incredible tenacity from her parents, Lephia and Asa Brown, a young pioneer couple who set out for the west shortly after they were married in 1834. Traveling by team and wagon from the eastern slopes of the Green Mountains in Vermont, they arrived in the territory of Michigan several weeks later. The land they were seeking lay on the edge of the frontier.

Lephia, reluctant at first to leave her beloved mountains and valleys, fully realized that good farmland was scarce in Vermont. Most of the young people at that time were going east to the cities or west to seek new farmland. One of her own sisters and several other family members had already settled in Michigan territory in the village of Schoolcraft. They wrote back about the rich soil and vast stretches of prairie land available for farming, and Asa and Lephia decided to go there. It was an eight-hundred-mile trip which, although tiring, was looked back upon by Lephia in later years as a delightful adventure. She picked armsful of wildflowers and listened for hours to the song birds of the prairie as she walked beside the slow-moving wagon. They crossed the state of New York, the northwestern part of Pennsylvania, and the rolling hills of northern Ohio before turning north, heading for an area near Kalamazoo in the territory of Michigan.

Not long after they arrived in Schoolcraft, Asa Brown purchased a farm north of the village in an area known as Prairie Ronde. There was a small log cabin on the land, a small woods and a marsh, but most of the farm was unbroken prairie. The soil was rich and fertile which pleased Asa, who had spent most of his life helping his father till their thin Vermont soil. Lephia, in turn, was happy to be living so near her sister Pamela Nathan and her family. Having grown up in a large, close-knit family, Lephia soon missed the daily interactions which shaped her early life, and she looked forward to visiting and taking part in social events in Schoolcraft. When she learned that she was expecting a child, she began to feel, for the first time, that she was putting down roots in the new country.

As with most pioneers, the first job for the young couple was to try to make the home as comfortable as possible. Asa built most of their furniture himself—tables, benches, shelves and beds. He strung heavy rope slats across the bed frames while Lephia made the mattresses. She soon learned to sew heavy cotton ticking together, then stuff it with prairie grass that she had cut and dried in the sun. The stuffing had to be renewed from time to time, but the cost of a new mattress was minimal—involving only the labor.

From Olympia's later visits in the area, she recalled many frontier homes where the beds stood out in the open like any other piece of furniture. Her mother, however, had different ideas. She hung muslin sheets between the beds which were placed side by side at the far end of the little cabin. Hired men lived with the family from time to time, and she felt the need for at least a small degree of privacy.

Asa also built a small storage room onto the cabin for there was no room inside to store such staples as flour, sugar, coffee, beans and salt.

Olympia was born on January 5, 1835, in this tiny cabin that the young couple had repaired and made relatively comfortable. She was a healthy child, energetic and curious by nature. Her small, round face was soon framed by thick, dark brown hair which her mother worked into braids as soon as it was long enough. As the first-born child, she often had her own way in the household.

The contents of the storage room formed one of Olympia's earliest memories. Every frontier child learned early in life that the food in the storage room was not to be wasted under any circumstances. Olympia was aware of the importance of the food supplies but the temptation was too great for a small child. She clearly recalled running to the door, pulling it open, and calling out to her mother, "I mean to be good, I mean to be good," as she slipped inside the room for a finger-lick of sugar. She could not remember how often she slipped into the anteroom for the little treat, but she could not ever recall her mother reprimanding her. Candy was virtually unknown to frontier children, and a little finger-lick of sugar was their only substitute.

As a child, Olympia loved the little cabin with its surrounding farmland, wildflowers and tamarack swamp. Although life on the frontier was stark, Olympia's many fond recollections of it portray a warm and comfortable home and loving parents. Her first clear memory of the cabin occurred when she was only about two years old.

Her father and a group of men were sitting around the table playing cards. Card playing was an unusual activity in the Brown household. Lephia harbored a strong dislike for wasting time. Improving one's mind by reading was a far better activity then playing cards, she believed, and she voiced her opinion at every opportunity. Perhaps it was a rainy day and the men were waiting for the weather to clear before going back outside. Whatever the reason for the card game, they were enjoying themselves and Olympia was fascinated with the activity. She had never seen playing cards before and she stood by the table watching the men play, intrigued with the bright colors and the strange symbols. The quick talk, the joking, the loud laughter and, always, the slap-slap-slap of the colorful cards on the bare wood delighted her.

The men got up from time to time to stretch and to fill their coffee cups. This offered Lephia the opportunity to walk over to the table, gather up her apron, and quickly sweep the playing cards into it. Olympia watched her mother turn and walk back to the far wall. There she threw the cards behind one of the beds and then lay down to rest. Surprised and disappointed that the game was over, Olympia turned her attention back to the men. Her father, upon returning to the table, immediately began looking for the cards. Olympia scurried to help him, thinking that this must be a new game. Quickly gathering all of the cards from behind the bed, she handed them triumphantly up to Asa. When she turned to her mother, expecting a smile of approval, she saw Lephia's face was filled with reproach. Instantly, she realized that she had made a dreadful mistake and should have left the cards where they were. The memory of that betrayal etched itself deeply into her mind, and that one experience taught her much about her mother's philosophy of life.

Asa worked hard to increase their tillage and Lephia worked just as hard at all of the tasks a pioneer woman had to perform. She was a small, energetic woman and she cherished a fierce determination to do the best she could for her family. At times warm and fun-loving, she was also idealistic, proud and resolute. Olympia adored her.

A second daughter, Oella, was born in the little cabin in 1837. The children, parents and several hired men ate and slept in the one room. It was no different from other pioneer families, but Lephia longed for a larger house. She worked hard doing the cooking, cleaning, washing and other endless household tasks that women had to do in the mid-nineteenth century. Cooking three meals a day in an open fireplace, often for six or seven people, made her long for a new kitchen and a new stove.

Perhaps the hardest task was the laundry. She had to pump water at an outside well, carry it into the cabin in buckets, and heat it in a great iron pot over the fire in the fireplace. All of the water for cooking, dishwashing, bathing and laundry had to be heated in this way. Doing the laundry by hand in a tub of water with a washboard and homemade soap was both backbreaking and time consuming. Olympia, like most children, loved to play in the suds while her mother scrubbed clothes, and she soon learned to help with the small items. Her mother also taught her how to sweep and dust, wash dishes and carry in wood for the fireplace. As she grew older, she learned how to make butter and cheese, milk cows, spin flax and wool, make candles and soap, help bake bread, and salt down meat for the winter. She began to realize, even as a child, that there was a certain satisfaction in hard work and accomplishment, a lesson that remained with her all of her life.

The cabin was crowded now with two small children, and when Lephia learned that she was going to have a third child, she insisted that Asa build a new house. He finally agreed and set about building the new home as soon as the weather was favorable. Lephia drew up the plans. She insisted that there must be a parlor, a small sitting and dining room for the family, and a large kitchen with a pantry on the first floor. The bedrooms would be upstairs, and there would be a nice, closed-in stairway.

When the house was ready, Asa bought her a new stove for the kitchen. Although Lephia had many fond memories of the cabin, she was particularly happy to give up the old fireplace. The new house was, in reality, simply a modern farm home of the 1840's, but it seemed like a palace to Olympia. She was then four years old and newly acquainted with fairy tales describing large castles with long stairs and many rooms.

In this house, her sister Marcia was born in 1839, and her brother Arthur, four years later. With his birth, the family was complete.

Olympia continued to learn new tasks as she grew older. In addition to her regular duties, she helped with the smaller children. In the summertime, Lephia and the children often went out to pick wild raspberries and blueberries and, in the fall, cranberries. Besides the fun of a day spent picking and gorging themselves on the sweet fruit, these excursions were a welcome break from the tedious daily chores on the farm. Although her father had planted fruit trees as soon as the young couple settled on the land, the trees did not always bear a large crop. Many times Olympia's mother wished that they had more fruit trees, and she would talk about the wonderful orchard her parents had on the farm in Vermont. Listening to her, Olympia would envision row upon row of apple, plum and cherry trees, their branches touching the ground with the heaviness of the ripe fruit. She wondered what it would be like to see baskets of fruit ripening in the cellar and jars of jams and jellies on the pantry shelf. Sometimes families in the neighborhood bartered among themselves, exchanging butter, cheese, candles or fresh vegetables for fresh fruit.

Olympia's pleasure at watching plants grow and her loving care of them were put to good use by her mother. Their garden boasted beans, beets, carrots, eggplant, squash, potatoes, onions and melons. Olympia learned how to plant, care for and harvest all of the vegetables, as well as the very necessary skill of storing both vegetables and fruits for the winter. It was Olympia who loved gardening with a passion that lasted a lifetime.

She often wandered away by herself where she could watch birds and look for wildflowers—pink orchids, moccasin flowers and pitcher plants. Years later with the poignant memories still fresh in her mind, she wrote,

The common wildflowers, violets, wind flowers, columbines, hepaticas, grew in wonderful profusion around the house. I loved to watch the poplars which grew in a group at the north end of our house, as the wind blew their delicate green leaves and kept up their characteristic quivering motion. Birds built their nests in the form of long bags which hung from the branches of these trees, and I watched them all summer as they swung to and fro.

Olympia had a lively imagination and she delighted her younger sisters and brother by spinning tales of Indians slipping through the prairie grasses and into the swampland at night or gliding across the newly planted fields to the creek. She learned from her parents that the Indians had been moved out of the area only shortly before Asa and Lephia arrived in Schoolcraft, and she thoroughly enjoyed fabricating stories about them.

The tamarack swamp, a dangerous and forbidden area, fascinated the children. The parents told them they must never go there to play, but Olympia found herself drawn there by the dark, brooding recesses and she often led her sisters into the swamp on secret excursions. Stories about the deep mud holes and quicksand in which horses and whole wagons had sunk out of sight terrified them but drew them inexorably to the boggy land. They explored for hours, poking sticks and small logs into quicksand, watching birds and insects, swinging on wild grape vines, climbing trees and hunting snakes and turtles. Olympia killed a rattlesnake one time and, although proud of herself, never told Lephia or Asa what she had done. She knew that she would be confined to the house and yard if her parents found out about the escapades. It was years later when she finally confessed to the adventures.

Pamela Nathan, Lephia's sister, and her husband, Thomas, were dedicated abolitionists. When Olympia was still a small child, she learned that they were operating an Underground Railroad station in their home in Schoolcraft. As part of a network where runaway slaves could find food and shelter on their way to Canada and freedom, the Nathans hid the refugees until it was safe for them to travel to the next station. Their work was secret and dangerous but they were prepared to do anything they could to help the antislavery movement.

9

Olympia learned a great deal about slavery by listening to her aunt's stories and by talking with some of the ex-slaves when they were hiding in the Nathan home. She never forgot her astonishment when she first learned that many people regarded Negroes as inferior simply because of the color of their skin. She was equally puzzled and disturbed to learn that most slaves had never been allowed to go to school. Few knew how to read or write.

She learned firsthand about the life of one slave when a man named Morgan Elam came to the farm. He had run away from his former home in Missouri and was looking for work. Asa hired him and he stayed with the family for seven years, a faithful and dependable worker.

Olympia was particularly fond of talking with Mr. Elam. He would take the time to answer her questions or even tell her a story, something that her father rarely took time to do.

"Why did you come to Schoolcraft, Morgan?" she asked him when he first came to work for the family.

"Well, after my master died, I was afraid I'd be sold down in the deep south," he said. "There were lots of stories going around about slaves being starved or beaten to death down in Mississippi and Louisiana, and I didn't want that to happen to me. So one evening I decided to get up real early the next morning, find me the gray filly out in the barnyard, and just ride away. I didn't care where, so long as it was north. And that's how I finally got here."

Olympia turned his words over in her mind. She could almost see him wrapping up his few belongings, slipping out of the cabin in the dark, and riding quietly off into the dawn. Perhaps he even looked back a few times to see if someone was following him. He told her he had ridden for many days, never knowing when someone might try to capture him and send him back. A new thought struck her. "Was the horse yours, Morgan?" she asked.

"I reckon it must have been. I raised it," he replied. It was her first lesson on the philosophy that laborers are entitled to their products, a philosophy that she thought about many times during her life.

The issue of slavery troubled Olympia deeply. When her uncle wrote his autobiography many years later, she searched eagerly in the book for the story of the Underground Railroad and how his family had helped. She knew that the Nathans had helped nearly fifteen hundred ex-slaves escape to Canada, and she expected to find some mention of their experiences. However, she could find nothing about that work in his writing.

Disappointed and puzzled, she turned to her aunt and asked her why he had not included the story in his autobiography. He had, after all, helped save the lives of many people. Pamela Nathan, a pragmatic woman not given to philosophical discussions, replied, "Well, Olympia, I suppose your Uncle Thomas just plain forgot about it. And why shouldn't he? He didn't do any of the cooking or cleaning, or washing, either. Which explains why I remember it better than he does."

Why then, Olympia countered, hadn't he at least given Pamela credit for all of the work that she had done?

"Women get very little credit for what they do in this world," Pamela Nathan replied, "which is something you'll have to accept when you grow up and start making your own way through life."

Olympia, however, had been learning a very different lesson from her mother. Lephia believed fervently in the equality of the sexes and she instilled that principle in her children when they were still very small. She was their sole teacher for several years before a school was established in the area. Besides teaching them to read, write, spell and do arithmetic, she read poetry to them and taught them some of the basic Universalist tenets—that salvation is extended to all human beings; that God is kind and loving, not angry and vengeful; and that there is no such place as hell. This affected Olympia's life very deeply when she went away to school as a young woman and had to cope with the ardent tactics of zealous evangelists who were preaching hellfire-and-brimstone sermons and stressing the sinful nature of all human beings.

When Michigan became a state in 1837, the legislature adopted a statewide public school system. The citizens of each district or municipality, however, were responsible for building their own schoolhouses and hiring their own teachers. Many were in no hurry to do so. The process usually took considerably longer in rural areas than in towns or cities. Farmers had many other tasks to do besides getting together to build a schoolhouse, and many of them actually resisted the idea of "book-learning." There were more important things to do, they said, than read books. Why did anyone need an education to plow the fields and gather the harvest, milk the cows and feed the chickens?

Olympia's parents, however, felt differently. Her father decided, most likely at the prodding of Lephia, that he would build a schoolhouse on part of his land when the two older girls reached school age.

A schoolhouse on the frontier in the 1840's was rustic in every sense of the word. Usually built of rough logs with a door at one end and a fireplace at the other, it had only one or two windows along the side walls. The windows were very small so that the room would be easier to heat during the bitter cold winters in Michigan. Desks were simply flat boards fastened onto supports along the walls. Homemade stools or benches served as seats. A table, sometimes a desk, and a stool for the teacher stood at the front of the classroom.

11

Olympia watched the men build the little log structure, and her excitement grew as it took shape and neared completion. She particularly liked to go inside and smell the newly cut wood, play with the little piles of sawdust, and dream about the day when school would begin. She took the broom with her one day and swept off the desk tops and the floor. Then she swept the splinters and sawdust outside onto the bare ground. "I can't wait for school to begin," she said to her mother that night. Then she said a little more quietly, "I wonder how many children will come."

Lephia already knew of her daughter's eagerness to learn, but she also sensed her slight trepidation at meeting new children. Olympia was shy by nature, a trait that she would have to work hard to overcome. The children were somewhat isolated on the farm. The sheer amount of hard physical labor expended by pioneer settlers often excluded frequent socializing. Although they were well-acquainted with relatives in Schoolcraft, they knew few neighbors well, some not at all.

One day near the end of summer, Asa saddled two horses, one for himself and one for Olympia. Together they rode around the countryside visiting each neighbor. He had built a schoolhouse, he told them, and he was going to hire a schoolteacher. "She'll get a dollar-fifty cents a week and she'll stay with each family for a week or so, boarding around." He explained to them that was the way most school districts paid their teachers. Each family would contribute to her salary, he said. There was often a short discussion, sometimes an objection or two, but Asa prevailed. He collected the contributions and supported the little schoolhouse for many years.

A taxing system had not yet been devised so there was no money to buy textbooks, paper or pencils. Each child was told to bring a book from home. Many, of course, had nothing more than a Bible, an old hymnal or an almanac to bring. The children learned to read from those. Sometimes a child was unable to bring a book from home, and the students would have to take turns sharing theirs with the unfortunate youngster. Many times the books were reglued, recovered and passed down in families from one child to the next until the youngest was finished with it. Immigrant parents had a particularly difficult time providing books for their children. Some had only a Bible in their native language. People in the community were asked to donate a book or two for the school and one or two families would sometimes respond.

Each child had to provide a slate, chalk and cleaning cloth. Olympia remembered with special pride the new slate Lephia gave her when school started.

She soon learned that some of the school children had different customs and manners from those of her family. Like most children when

12

confronted with new ways of doing things, she began to wonder about her own family's customs and the reasons for them. Lephia decided that perhaps all of the children could learn from the questions Olympia brought home, and she instituted a family discussion period. Over the years the children discussed schoolwork and the problems they were having with any of the students or the teacher. Lephia soon turned the discussions to subjects of a broader nature. Each evening they read and discussed articles in *The New York Weekly Tribune* to which Asa had subscribed. They also read poetry and stories in some of the books that she borrowed from relatives in Schoolcraft. Besides helping the children gain a broader understanding of life, Lephia believed that the discussion periods would teach them how to think and speak effectively.

This may very well have been true. Olympia became a minister, Oella and Marcia, teachers, and Arthur, a lawyer. Theirs was a unique household in a time when most parents believed that children should be seen and not heard. Lephia not only encouraged them to ask questions and to seek answers, but she stood ready to help them in any way that she could. She was ever ready to "spend and be spent" for her children's education, in Olympia's own words.

Study became the first object of the household. The two older girls soon learned that their mother would not call on them to help with household chores if they were studying. Accordingly, both began exhibiting a great fondness for their books.

They studied reading, writing, spelling, the English language, arithmetic and "decent behavior." Since many children came from immigrant families and were unfamiliar with the customs of their new country, "proper" behavior became a required subject. There were always in every community, those vigilant citizens who felt it their duty to set the standards, scrupulously operating on their definition of propriety. No one seemed to object, and the teacher bore the burden of trying to decide which rules must be taught.

Classes were held in the winter when there was little farm work to do, and again in the summer after the crops were planted and before harvest. Usually, only girls and younger children attended school during the summer. Education ranked second to the plain struggle to survive on the frontier, and most children had to help with the planting and the harvest before they could attend school.

The New York Weekly Tribune brought news of national and world events to the family which was otherwise quite isolated. It also brought literature and poetry, subjects which Lephia considered even more important than news. When *The Tribune* arrived, Asa and Lephia spent several evenings reading and discussing the articles, and the children listened to them. After they had finished reading the paper, Lephia read some of the literary articles and poems to the children and they discussed them one by one. She then cut out and pasted the poems into a scrapbook to be read later by all the family. Olympia loved the very personal nature of the learning experiences that her mother provided and she absorbed some of Lephia's love of poetry through the discussions. As a young mother, Lephia had neither the time nor energy to write poems, although she had a talent and a deep yearning to do so. There was simply too much work to do to allow her to spend precious time writing verses, but she resolved that her children would have the time, and she would teach them to enjoy literature.

Early childhood passed swiftly in work and play. When Olympia was ten years old, her parents made a decision that markedly affected her young life. They gathered the children together one evening to make an announcement. Olympia sensed her mother's excitement and she and her sisters waited with bated breath for the surprise. When it came, she was almost speechless with the wonder of it. The family was going to Vermont for the summer, Lephia explained. "It's been eleven years since we came here, and none of you has seen your grandparents. The journey's too hard for them to make, so we are going there." She went on to tell them of all the wonderful things that they would see, the lakes and rivers and mountains. Both Lephia and Asa had talked often about the beautiful, rugged Green Mountains, the quiet valleys and picturesque farms, and the thought of going to see them was almost overwhelming to Olympia who had never been farther from the farm than the village of Schoolcraft. It seemed forever while they sorted, cleaned and packed for the trip.

Part of the trip would be by team and wagon, and part of it would be by boat, Asa explained. Few roads existed in Michigan or even in the more settled state of New York in 1845, and those roads were often virtually impassable much of the year. Whenever it rained, they became so muddy that horses could not pull wagons on them. When the roads dried in the summer sun, the ruts were so deep that people often had to bypass them, sometimes going miles out of the way. Lephia and Asa gave the two older girls a lesson on geography, showing them that the fastest way to travel from Detroit to Albany was to cross Lake Erie to Buffalo and go on to Albany by way of the Erie Canal. "It will take between two and three weeks to get there," Lephia noted, "even traveling on the canal."

Asa, having read newspaper accounts of the traffic on the waterway, told them about express boats. "They can go a hundred miles in twenty-four hours. It would take a team and wagon a week to go that far," he explained. Olympia did not care how long the journey took. For her, it was all a great adventure. Her excitement grew, and she, Oella and Marcia dreamed about the trip day after day. Arthur, only two years old, was too

14

young to share their enthusiasm.

At last, early one morning, they started out by team and wagon, following a track that led east from Schoolcraft. The route they took was an old Indian trail leading to Detroit. As countless other travelers had done before them, they followed the trail across the rolling prairie past farms and tracts of woodland. Near Detroit the trail crossed a dry lake bottom. Here the children stared in wonder. On either side of them rose the skeletons of abandoned wagons buried in the clay. Many had sunk to the axles, some even to the wagon bed. Broken timbers lay scattered about, mute evidence of the vain struggle to free the wagons from the muddy earth. The hot sun dried the clay, virtually baking the abandoned vehicles and timbers into the ground.[1] Olympia and Oella wondered if they would get safely through, or if the rain might come and trap them there with the ghostly relics.

At Detroit they boarded a steamship and set sail across Lake Erie for Buffalo. In all of her life, Olympia had seen only the great expanses of the Michigan prairie broken by a few groves of trees. Never had she imagined being out of the sight of land. The lake, blue as the feathers of the raucous blue jay back home, stretched in every direction. The sun scattered light on the water like handfuls of snow, dappling the surface briefly, then disappearing. She watched the ripples for hours and the foam that spewed out from the prow of the boat.

When they reached Buffalo, she was sorry to have to leave the steamship, but when she saw the canal boats, her excitement returned. They were shaped somewhat like long, narrow, oblong blocks. Each canal boat had a main cabin, a galley at the rear, and a small cabin for women and children forward. Olympia and her sisters began exploring at once. They found the main cabin with its tables and chairs. Here they would eat. Bunks lined both sides of the walls, and this was where they would sleep, she thought. She soon learned, however, that women and children were relegated to a tiny, dingy cabin forward.

"Why don't we have as big a cabin as the men?" she demanded, voicing one of her first protests against discrimination.

Lephia tried to comfort her. "I suppose it's because not many women or children travel, Olympia. I know it doesn't seem fair, but there are a lot more men on these boats than women."

Olympia chafed against the unfairness of the tiny cabin in spite of her mother's logic. It did not seem right to her.

The canal boats stopped at every town along the way, sometimes picking up new passengers and giving the children a chance to see other activities. There was little for them to do on board the boat except watch the scenery and walk around the narrow deck. On rainy days, everyone had to stay inside and time passed very slowly for the passengers, particularly the children. The cabins were uncomfortable in hot weather and most of the people stayed out on the deck during the day. Many of them slept out there at night. The children begged to be allowed to sleep out on the deck, too, but Lephia refused. The danger of losing a child in the canal was too great, she said.

Altogether it was a delightful journey for the older children, although tiring for Lephia and Asa. Each day was a new adventure. The scurry and bustle of the towns and cities enchanted the children who had never seen so many people before. Olympia's heart ached to explore the streets of the towns and absorb the excitement of each new place.

The boat journey came to an end at Albany, New York. Their destination, Plymouth Notch in Vermont, lay about a hundred miles east on the other side of the Green Mountains. They made the last lap of the journey by team and wagon. It was an exhilarating trip for the end of the long journey was in sight and spirits were high.

Olympia stared up at the rocky slopes as they rode eastward on the narrow road. How did the mountains come to be, she asked? Could she climb them? Were there wild animals hiding there? Settling down at last to gaze in silent wonder at the scenery, she sensed that life would never be the same for her. All the way to Plymouth Notch, she absorbed the astonishing beauty of the mountains, marveled at their rugged valleys, their clear-running streams. The world had expanded so quickly before her eyes that every day was an enchantment.

When they drew up before the large white farmhouse, Lephia's family was waiting for them. Nearly overcome in her joy, Lephia seemed to forget the long, exhausting trip. Laughing and crying, she went from one to the other of the family members that she had not seen for so long, embracing them, wiping her tears away, introducing the children. Olympia, sensing the deep feelings that flowed between her parents, grandparents and other family members, longed to be part of this great, warm kinship. Listening to the talk, wondering at the bursts of laughter, the frequent tears, she began to absorb some of the family history. As she listened to her parents telling about the hardships they had first suffered in Michigan, she began to realize how different life was for her grandparents. She looked about her at the house filled with comfortable furniture. Would her family ever have a home as fine as this one, she wondered?

Even after she went outside to explore the farm, she continued to compare the ways in which the two families lived. Staring, entranced at the fat cattle, sleek horses, plump ducks, geese and chickens, she turned to her grandfather. "You must be awfully rich," she said, unable to contain the thought any longer.

Her grandfather could only smile at such a thought, and he told her that

16

they had worked for many years before they had a comfortable home and well-fed stock. Then he said to her, "Someday, Olympia, your farm will be fine, too. Your father's land is much better than ours, and you will soon have many things you only dream about now." He showed her around the farm, and soon she was wandering along the neatly cultivated fields daily, following the fence lines to the pasture, or climbing the steep path that led up the mountainside. There she sat and listened to the roar of the stream as it tumbled down the rocks into the valley below. It seemed to her that she was in another world far removed from Schoolcraft, and she stored the sights and sounds away to be recalled later. Inexplicably, she began to feel that Vermont was as much her home as the Michigan farm. Perhaps she was a particularly impressionable child, or perhaps she felt the same strong family ties tugging at her that Lephia felt. Whatever the cause, she began to feel that Vermont was the land of her roots, and years later when she was grown, she referred to herself as a "New Englander."

Olympia was surrounded by "Browns."

She met many aunts and uncles in the area around Plymouth Notch, and cousins almost beyond count. Both of her parents' families had the surname "Brown" and lived just a short distance from each other, but they were unrelated. It took the children several weeks to sort out which Browns were their father's relatives and which were their mother's. Her mother came from a family of eleven children and Asa's family numbered twelve. There were relatives to visit all that long summer and stories to listen to as the families sat together in the soft, warm twilight, laughing and reminiscing. Olympia's kinship with the family grew with every story she heard.

"Did you know you were named after your mother?" her grandmother asked her one day. She was always ready to tell a story. Olympia shook her head, somewhat puzzled by such a question. After all, her mother's name was Lephia, wasn't it? "When she was born, we named her Relief Olympia Brown. It was a very popular name then, but we found it easier to shorten it to Liefie. That's what she was till she went to school. Then she wanted to be called Lephia. So we went along with that. But it was her middle name that was so special. She always said it was such a noble name, and that if she ever had a little girl, that's what she'd call her. And that's how you got your name."[2]

Olympia was pleased. She already felt strong ties to her mother, and this information only increased the feeling.

They visited Asa's parents and his family, too. Asa's mother, Priscilla Putnam Brown, was an independent and forthright woman who could tell exciting stories about her adventures as a young woman. Olympia listened breathlessly to her tale about riding a horse alone all the way back to

Connecticut. "I went there to visit my relatives from time to time," she said. "I could make the journey much easier than they could. And I liked to get away from the farm once in a while."

"How long did it take you to get there?" Olympia asked, visions of dark woods and lonely trails springing up before her eyes.

"Oh, several days," Priscilla Brown replied; then she would go on, describing the trip for the children. She had ridden south through the Green Mountain foothills, then on down through Massachusetts and into Connecticut. "There weren't any roads to speak of then," she said. "I just followed Indian trails," and her eyes brightened at the memory.

Olympia stared at her, recalling stories that she had heard about Indian ambushes and scalpings. "Weren't you afraid of the Indians?" she asked, breathless with wonder.

Her grandmother laughed. "No. The Indians didn't bother me. They were friendly. Sometimes, we even helped each other out. I never had trouble with any Indians."

All that summer Olympia absorbed the stories, the dreams, the great love that bound the families together, but she felt the current of restlessness underneath, too. One by one, her aunts and uncles were packing their belongings and heading in other directions. They dearly loved Vermont, but the opportunities were limited and they either went east to the large cities or west to seek farmland as Lephia and Asa had done.

All too soon the summer was over and the family had to return to the Michigan farm. A sudden sense of loss or being uprooted pervaded Olympia when they began the return trip. It seemed as if a part of her stayed in Vermont, and she would always look upon Plymouth Notch as her second home. The journey and the relationships with the extended family in the east had a profound impact on her life as she moved from one stage of development into another.

The girls went back to the little log schoolhouse in the fall. For Olympia, the world had expanded and she now began to feel the limitations of pioneer life. She often dreamed of going to school in town where there was a large schoolhouse with several classrooms and different teachers. Although she and Oella could walk the three miles in good weather, when winter came it would often be difficult to get to school. Lephia promised them that when they were older they could enroll in the public school, and Olympia was satisfied for a time.

Two cousins from Vermont came to live with the family when their mother was widowed. She came to keep house for an uncle in Schoolcraft, and the two boys went out to the farm where they learned to help with the farm work. The boys, Addison and Nelson Carter, were about the same age as Olympia and Oella. They were intelligent and sensitive and soon fit into the educational pattern Lephia had established in the home. All of the children went to the little log schoolhouse together. After chores were done, they still had time to explore the farm, woods and tamarack swamp, and the six children played well together.

It was not long, however, before they looked for another outlet for their energies and talents and decided to write a monthly newsletter. They settled on the name, *The Family Museum*. Its motto: "Tall Oaks From Little Acorns Grow." It was a project that continued for a year and a half. Each issue comprised four pages of articles, stories and poems carefully copied in pen and ink by the aspiring journalists. The first issue was dated July, 1849.[3]

The youngsters wrote according to their interests and talents. Oella excelled in poetry, Addison in adventure stories, and the others contributed news items, essays and puzzles. Each selected a pseudonym, preferring to remain anonymous. There were tales of Indian raids and distant California adventures, probably inspired by newspaper accounts of the 1849 gold rush. There were notes on the solitary life of a hermit and the invention of the mariner's compass, fantasies about the autobiography of a blackboard and the history of a looking glass. Olympia added essays with a strong moral flavor and saw to it that the pages of the paper were completely filled with each issue. Her first essay appeared in the July, 1849 issue.

YOUTHFUL ZEAL

How ardently it burns. How eagerly it grapples with almost insurmountable difficulties! With what unabated ardor does it ever press on! We see a young student grasp a proposition in Algebra perhaps which none of his predecessors could solve. Perhaps it is a cold winter evening. He soon becomes so wrapt in his problem that he heeds not the cold. Perhaps his chum comes in from a visit to some of his schoolmates. He knows it not unless fortune has favored him and the problem is solved; suppose it so. He soon retires and bright dreams reward his labors. He dreams of the approving smile and the highest credit mark. His sleep is refreshing and in the morning he gets up with a light heart and a joyful countenance and trips lightly to school.

On the other hand, he who gives up without a struggle gets up wearied from his sleep, goes to school with a troubled look, is cross. He gets no credit mark. It makes him surly and his schoolfellows detest him. Be assured he never made a scholar.

Her mother's teachings of idealism, hard work and reward are as clear as a handprint in this essay.

19

One day they all agreed to exchange writing duties, each envying the others' prestige. Olympia offered to write a poem and Oella, an adventure story. The boys agreed to provide the essays, puzzles and filler. Olympia soon found that she did not have her sister's talent for writing poetry. She struggled for many hours to complete a few short verses. Oella, in turn, began an adventure story describing an interesting family in her first chapter. She then wrote, "We will now pass over the events of a long and bloody war," and she wrote the final chapter, not even referring to the problems that she had raised in the beginning. The two boys did not have the tendency or disposition to write an essay, and they struggled to provide a few puzzles and proverbs. The next month all were happy to return to their regular writing assignments. Each youngster did learn the valuable lesson of respect for one another's talents in the exchange of duties, and they did not belittle or minimize one another's contributions after that episode.

The problem of continuing education surfaced in the fall when Olympia was fourteen. Asa was reluctant at first to send his daughters into town to school, citing the distance and even wondering if further education for the girls was necessary. "They'll only get married, anyway," he said. "Why do they need any more education for that?" The girls, however, had other ideas. They might not get married, they pointed out to him, so they should have some way to earn a living besides keeping house. Wouldn't he rather have them earn their own living than stay at home on the farm for the rest of their lives? Such an argument prodded him to a more favorable decision.

It was clear to Olympia that her father had given little thought to what his children would do when they grew up. He had worked very hard to establish a farm and it still absorbed most of his thoughts and energy. When he finally agreed to enroll them in the public school in the village of Schoolcraft, they embarked on what was at that time the equivalent of a high school education. They either walked or rode horses until winter weather descended, then they stayed in town with relatives. Asa went into town to get them on weekends, and they returned either on a Sunday afternoon or early Monday morning. It was a pattern followed by many farm children for the next several generations.

Olympia was delighted with the new school, most of all with her teacher who was, she said, "a true scholar." She devoted herself to her studies to please him. As an educated man, he presented a sharp contrast to the young country school teachers that she had known in the little schoolhouse on her father's farm.

It was with misgivings that she soon noticed girls were treated differently from boys in the school in regard to lesson requirements. She was used to the equality of elementary classes where girls and boys learned the same subjects together. There was no differentiation in their lessons or in their recitation and she had never given the matter a second thought. In the Schoolcraft classes, boys were required to give oral speeches and debate, but girls were only allowed to read from prepared manuscripts. She had yet to learn that society did not consider public speaking proper conduct for women. A few women were transcending the barriers, such as the Grimke sisters, Lucretia Mott and Elizabeth Cady Stanton. Some of them were beginning to discuss politics and demand equal rights, but Olympia had not yet heard of such things. She did, however, believe that girls should be treated equally with boys. That was what she had learned from her mother. She longed to participate in the oral recitations and debates; she had a quick mind and tongue. Feeling that it was not her place to argue the matter, she proposed to Addison Carter that he present a resolution at the literary class. This resolution was to allow girls to debate and give speeches the same as the boys.

Neither youngster was prepared for the consequences of this act. After Addison presented his proposal, the teachers looked at one another, surprise and disbelief settling on their faces. A long silence followed. Then, slowly, the teachers rose from their chairs en masse. "We will leave the class if the students persist in such a resolution," one of them said, utter contempt edging her voice.

Olympia was stunned. Did they really believe that public speaking was a dreadful thing for a girl to do? How could educated people like teachers actually believe that female and male minds were different? She struggled in the silence and tension of the room, watching her cousin sit down in his seat, dismayed at the reaction to his resolution. At last one of the teachers relented. "I guess Addison just wanted a little fun," she said. With that, they all sat down again.

The meeting continued and Olympia, temporarily subdued, said no more. Her first effort for the equality of the sexes was unsuccessful, but she would try again in every school that she attended.

When she was fifteen years old, she taught for a term in the little schoolhouse on her father's farm. She received a salary of one dollar and fifty cents a week and boarded with the families of the children she taught. The experience was crucial in helping her decide that, although she believed teaching was a noble profession, she wanted to do something else with her life. When the term was over, she returned to her classes at Cedar Park Seminary in Schoolcraft.

In the ensuing years, she began to make plans for furthering her education, but she was frustrated and angered to learn that no university would admit a woman as a student. Neither would any of the colleges to which she applied. She began to wonder where she could get a higher education, an ambition that grew with each passing year yet seemed unlikely of culmination.

Lephia, ever alert to educational news and opportunities for her daughters, read one day about a school near Mount Holyoke, South Hadley, Massachusetts, that admitted only women. Mount Holyoke Female Seminary, founded in 1836 by Mary Lyon, had grown rapidly in the ensuing years and was gaining an enviable reputation as a center of learning. Although Mary Lyon had not dared call the school a "college," the courses were considered by many as college level. This, Lephia decided, was where Olympia and Oella should go. A major problem remained, however. It would take money to send the two young women there.

Lephia had no money of her own. In those days when a woman married, all of her possessions became the property of her husband by law. She had no choice but to ask him for whatever she needed or wanted. This was a particularly galling task for such a strong and forthright person as Lephia, and she rarely asked Asa for anything unless it was an absolute necessity. Sending the two older girls away to school could scarcely be termed a necessity, yet it was vitally important to them and to her, too. As their mother, she had done all that she could do. Perhaps it was time for Olympia to take on the task of convincing her father that the two girls needed more education, she thought. Olympia was now nineteen. As the oldest, the responsibility should naturally fall upon her. Certainly it was time that she began making some decisions about her life. Since neither girl seemed interested in marriage yet, further education was a pressing matter if they were to go out into the world and find work. The opportunities for employment were severely limited with the level of education they now had. All they could hope to do was teach school somewhere in the countryside, and Olympia had already decided against such a career.

Asa Brown was a stern and practical man and did not share Lephia's dreams for the girls. He did not value education as highly as she, although he was merely reflecting society's general attitude in that period of time. Marriage was the accepted role for young women with teaching almost the only career open to them. There were no professional careers that women could enter such as medicine, law or commerce, and any woman who wanted to break down the barriers to enter such a sphere had to run a gamut of opposition designed to defeat such a perverse attempt. It was almost universally believed that only men needed higher education, and Asa subscribed to that opinion. He also believed that hard work was a prerequisite to a good life, and Olympia knew he would say that she and

22

Oella had enough education already. With this in mind, she began to prepare her arguments.

Having already learned that the timing of any request was just as important as the actual request itself, she waited until her father was in a good mood. Certainly the best time to talk to him was directly after supper on a day when all had gone well. Noting one evening that he was in a pleasant frame of mind, she followed him into the living room determined to explore the likelihood of winning his assent to go away to school. Her mind flew back to her daily long walks from Schoolcraft. How dusty her shoes had been when she got home! Involuntarily her eyes dropped to examine the toes of her slippers as she walked over to a chair and sat down. She breathed a great sigh. How many times she had made that walk over the last five years! Yes, it was time for a change.

"You have something on your mind, Olympia?" Asa asked, settling back in his chair.

"Yes," and she turned to him. "Oella and I have been thinking about our future and the kind of work we'd like to do. Neither one of us plans to get married soon, and the only work we can do is teach in a country school. That doesn't pay very well, but if we could teach in a city school, we'd be paid a lot more." She paused a moment, knowing these words would register interest in his mind. It was true that she did not plan to be a teacher herself, nor did she know just where her interests lay, but she decided to keep these thoughts to herself. Teaching was an appropriate argument to justify her drive for a higher education. It was a proper field for a woman, and that weighed heavily with Asa. "Cities are growing fast now all around the country, and schools are growing, too. They need teachers everywhere. But we need more education to teach in town or city schools."

She hesitated a moment, gathering her arguments together; then she launched her campaign. "We know of a school in the east that's just for women, and we could get good training there. It doesn't cost very much to go there because all of the students have to work for their board and room. We'd be doing all of the cooking, cleaning, sewing, washing, and ironing, right along with our studies. It's like a manual training school." Knowing that victory lay in stressing both the economic benefits and the work required at Mount Holyoke, she continued in that vein. "If we started studying right away here at home, we could pass the first year's examinations as soon as we get there. Then we could start with the second year's work. We'd be able to do the whole course of study in two years instead of three." She had her father's attention now. He nodded as she made one point after another. Then she delivered her final argument. "Neither one of us wants to go out and work as hired girls, and we don't want to stay here

23

on the farm and have you support us. The only way we can become independent is to train ourselves for better jobs. Don't you agree, father?"

Deep in thought, Asa fixed his clear, blue eyes on his daughter for several moments. There was little doubt that her final arguments must have awakened him to the fact that his children were nearly grown and that they would soon be leaving home. What they would do with their lives suddenly became important to him. "You mean that you girls would be doing all that work and still have time to study?" he asked, a trifle skeptically.

Olympia assured him that this was so, and with that she had won him over. She did not ever know if he honestly thought that she and Oella were attending a manual training school or whether he simply thought that plain hard labor should go along with higher education. Whatever his thoughts on the subject might be, she did not care. All that mattered now was that she was going to get the higher education that she so intensely desired.

Chapter 2

Mount Holyoke
and Its Limitations

Olympia and Oella completed their applications and began studying for their examinations to enter Mount Holyoke in the fall of 1854. Lephia, swept up by the excitement of the two girls and their dreams for the future, helped them make their clothes for the year that they would be gone. Little of their clothing would be purchased and there was much sewing to do.

Olympia, feeling that she was at last going to embark on a new life, plunged into the preparations with a heart full of gratitude to both parents, yet it was to her mother that she felt most appreciative. Without Lephia's early guidance and spirit, she might never have felt the passion, the determination to get a higher education. She might have simply become a schoolteacher somewhere in the Michigan countryside. Now the doors to a far different future were opening before her.

By the end of the summer, they were ready to leave. Their trunks were packed and shipped, and their traveling bags were ready. Another girl from Schoolcraft was going with them, and the three young women enjoyed celebrity status in the village, for few women even graduated from high school in the mid-nineteenth century. To go away to school was, indeed, a privilege.

Olympia, savoring the anticipation of her first breath of freedom from the close family ties, expected that the three young women would make the long overland journey to Massachusetts alone. She was nineteen and Oella seventeen. They were certainly not children any more. She had not reckoned with her father's reluctance to set his daughters free, however.

"It's improper for young ladies to travel alone," Asa said firmly. "I'm making arrangements for a merchant in Schoolcraft to go with you as far as Albany. He's going to New York to buy merchandise. He can put you on the stagecoach for South Hadley when you reach Albany."

Olympia protested vehemently, arguing that they could very well manage to get to their destination by themselves. However, the other girl's father joined Asa, insisting that they must travel with a chaperone because the distance was so great. Although Olympia continued to argue, Asa remained firm and she finally had to accept his decision. She consoled herself with the thought that by the end of the school year he would see the matter differently, and that in just two years she would be an educated and independent woman, free to travel wherever and whenever she wished.

When the time came for the two daughters to say goodbye, Olympia turned and saw tears streaming down Lephia's face. Only then did she begin to realize the change that this trip would make in her parents' lives, particularly that of her mother. It was the first break in the family. She and Oella would be gone for the greater part of a year, leaving only two children at home. Life on the farm would never be the same again. Their younger sister, Marcia, was already fifteen and would soon be teaching school. Eleven-year-old Arthur was hoping to go to school in the village soon. For Lephia, the busy years of childrearing were over. She was beginning to feel the first pangs of loneliness as her children grew up and went away.

Olympia's spirits soon began to soar again after the tearful farewells. The passing scenery and the anticipation of a year at Mount Holyoke made the journey pass swiftly and pleasantly. When they reached Albany, they took cheerful leave of their chaperone. Now, surely, they were free, she told herself.

The rugged Massachusetts countryside delighted her. She had not imagined they would be living amidst such breathtaking scenery. This was the culmination of all the hopes and dreams she had envisioned during her long hours of study and preparation. Everything seemed perfect!

The three young women were assigned a dormitory room together on the third floor of the single, large building that comprised Mount Holyoke Female Seminary. It had originally been designed to house two students to a room, but the school had grown very rapidly. There were over two-hundred-fifty girls to accommodate the year that Olympia and Oella arrived, and the building had not been expanded. The problem was temporarily solved by crowding three girls into each dormitory room. The rooms were fairly large, measuring eighteen-by-ten feet, but those measurements included a large, lighted closet about six feet square. The actual living quarters were only about twelve-by-ten feet.

Each room was furnished with a dresser, washstand, table, chairs, mirror, beds and an open Franklin stove.[1] Although the rooms must have been cramped and uncomfortable, Olympia paid scant attention to inconveniences. Single-minded and resolute, she reminded her sister that they were at Mount Holyoke to get an education, not to enjoy comfort.

It did not take long, however, for them to learn that life in a boarding school was far different from anything that they had previously experienced. Even before they were given their lists of rules and regulations, they learned that, "Young ladies are not allowed to stand in doorways, linger in the halls, or stand on the portico." Indeed, they soon discovered that even their conversations were to be closely governed, that their "quiet" times and "study" periods were to be monitored, and that they were to spend an inordinate amount of time in their rooms.

Olympia had not imagined that the students, many of whom were eighteen and nineteen years old, would be treated like small children. Each young woman was given a list of more than forty rules and regulations which were to govern her conduct. They were told that they must report any rules they broke or that they saw another student break.

Each afternoon the young women were called together. A section teacher read aloud all of the rules and regulations, one by one. She then asked for confessions. Olympia watched in silent amazement as one young woman after another rose and confessed to a minor offense. A teacher duly recorded the incident and gave the young woman advice. Occasionally, the principal would come into the room and give a lecture on morals.

The waste of time appalled her, but even more disturbing, the staff encouraged the students to watch each other and report any impolite or improper behavior. Most of the students did not conform to such a policy. Those who did soon found themselves in a somewhat hostile atmosphere.

The list of rules overwhelmed some of the students, many of whom had not realized that every minute of their lives would be so closely regulated. A letter written by one of the young women reveals just how strict they were.

It is against the rules of this Seminary to send papers–to throw anything out of the windows, to speak above a whisper in any of the halls–to stop long enough to count 10 in ditto, purchase any eatables anywhere else, to leave your room during study hours. To enter any person's room except at about three particular hours in a day (except recreation day), to make any communication *in the Seminary Hall, to get up before five o'clock or after 6 to go to bed after 10, to write anything on any part of the building... to be tardy a second at the table or any exam—(That's awful) ... Go not out of the house after tea without permission. Make no calls without permission. Check your lamps. Never sit on your bed. Never step in your chair without a paper in them, etc. etc. etc. ....*

We are not allowed to look out of the window, nor speak loud in any room but our own, if one of the teachers is present; we must rise

*when the bell rings, retire when the bell rings, work, and leave off
working; go to the table and take our seats there when the bell rings;
and from 10 to 12 a.m. and 2-1/4 to 3-1/4 p.m. we cannot speak to
anyone, they call them silent study hours.*[2]

Most of the students complained about not being able to look out of
the windows. It seemed such a senseless rule, but one of the students
explained it in this way. "Miss Lyon didn't want people to think this was
a seminary for young ladies when she opened the school. She didn't want
anyone to be seen sitting in the windows. But everyone knew it was a
seminary for young ladies. What difference did it make? And what
difference does it make now? It's like a prison if we can't go and look out
of the windows."

Olympia agreed. "But there really isn't much we can do about it," she
said. "They won't change any rules. We'll just have to learn to abide by
most of them."

She, who had been so accustomed to the freedom of life on a
midwestern farm, found that the regulations governing every hour of their
lives seemed at times almost unbearable. When she wrote home describing their duties and her surprise with the discipline demanded of the young
women at the institution, Lephia sympathized with her, offering advice
and encouragement. Asa, however, was pleased. His daughters were
learning discipline.

The three young newcomers were assigned their work schedules
shortly after their arrival. Their first assignment was laundry. Every
morning they got up at five o'clock, dressed and made their way down to
the basement. There they wrung out by hand three huge tubsful of table
linen that had been put to soak the night before.

"After three months you will be given a slightly easier task," the
supervisor said. The plan, Olympia decided, must surely be to give new
students the most difficult work to harden them. When the other two girls
were sick, and they often were, she did all three tubs of linen. Her reward
came by the end of the winter when the supervisor assigned her the task of
wiping tumblers.

Many of the students were divided into units of ten or twelve girls. A
leader organized their work. Those scheduled to prepare breakfast were
downstairs in the kitchen shortly after five o'clock. There were over two
hundred and fifty people to feed each mealtime, and the kitchen was a busy
place. One young woman started making fires in the kitchen stoves while
seven or eight set the tables in the dining hall. Three or four began peeling
potatoes and preparing the rest of the meal. Their work was finished when
everyone was served, and another group cleaned up after the meal. They

washed, wiped and put away all of the dishes before going to their first classes. The students followed the same procedure at each mealtime, different units working each time.[3]

The food served at Mount Holyoke was wholesome and nutritious by mid-nineteenth century standards. Graham toast with molasses, hot biscuits, warm rice, hominy or mashed potatoes comprised breakfast. The dinner menu was usually roast beef or codfish, dumplings, pies or puddings, and graham or Indian bread. Supper was a lighter meal such as bread and butter, sauce and cake, or sometimes boiled cracked wheat with milk and white sugar.[4]

One day each week, classes were suspended while all of the students helped clean the classrooms, dormitory rooms, dining hall and kitchen. They also washed clothes. It was a busy day and even the teachers worked. Olympia welcomed the interruption from class routine. She did not mind hard work although some of the young women grumbled at both the work and the regulations.

Bathrooms had been installed in the school just two years before Olympia and her sister came to the seminary. The girls no longer had to go all the way down to the basement with pails to get hot water for sponge baths. They did, however, have to go down to get the wood for their Franklin stoves, which provided the only heat in their rooms. There was a small elevator, also called a dumbwaiter, that they used for that purpose.[5]

When Olympia and Oella appeared before an examining board prior to being assigned to classes, they explained that they had been studying all spring and summer. "We are ready to pass all of the first year examinations so we can start with second year classes," Olympia announced proudly.

"But that's not possible," a board member said, visibly shocked at such an idea. "We never examine young ladies in Algebra or Latin. You have to start at the very beginning of the course of study. You are required to attend all of the classes and pass an examination on each subject. Those are the rules here at Mount Holyoke." The other members agreed. Olympia, taken aback at the unexpected barrier before them, argued and pleaded but to no avail. The board members simply could not deviate from the way in which Mary Lyon had laid out the course of study nearly 20 years earlier.

In spite of the inflexibility and seeming fatuity, Olympia and Oella decided to make the best of the situation. It seemed to them a dreadful waste of time, money and effort, but neither one wanted to return to Schoolcraft. Surely studying other books and reading in the school library could make the year worthwhile, they decided. Their course of study included such subjects as *Greene's Analysis*; Latin; History; (*Worcester's Elements* and histories of Greece, Rome, England and France); Algebra;

Euclid; Philosophy of Natural History; and Ecclesiastical History along with a class in gymnastics.[6]

They soon found time to organize a literary society where they could debate, give readings and practice public speaking. A number of young students became interested in such an audacious enterprise and joined the society. They worked hard and, as soon as they were ready to present a program, extended an invitation to the teachers to come to a meeting. The teachers chose to ignore the new little group at first. The weeks passed and they did not accept the invitation or even acknowledge the group. Olympia was finding both pleasure and challenge in the literary society. It was the one place on campus where the heavy restrictions did not hang over her head. But the day came at last when a committee of teachers announced that they were going to attend the next literary society meeting. Olympia and Oella, having had the most experience, chose to present a debate for their benefit. The program seemed to go well and the teachers listened in utmost silence. Not one of them voiced a word of criticism during the debate. When they left at the end of the meeting, they neither commended nor disapproved of the program, a matter which puzzled Olympia and her sister. Perhaps that fact alone should have given the young women cause to be suspicious, but they continued the literary society programs in high spirits.

The blow fell at the end of the term. All society members were ordered to appear before a committee of teachers. "The literary society must be disbanded," the leader said, "or you cannot continue to attend this seminary."

Olympia, momentarily stunned into silence, found such an attitude difficult to believe. At this point, Oella stepped forward. "What is your objection?" she asked. "Doesn't debate make us independent? Doesn't it teach us how to think for ourselves? That's what we are supposed to be learning here, isn't it?"

The answer came, "It makes you too independent. Were not you and your sister on opposite sides of the debate?"

Oella agreed that, indeed, they were. The teacher then argued, "If you spoke from conviction, that represents a division and antagonism between sisters which is both dangerous and indefensible. If, on the other hand, you are actually agreed in opinion, then one of you must have been arguing against your own conscience. That is inexcusable."

Olympia, concluding at once that arguing was fruitless, acquiesced to the decree. Did all institutions of higher learning have such narrow-minded instructors and rigid regulations, she wondered? Surely there must be other institutions where they could go to study, schools where the instructors were more interested in teaching than in maintaining outdated standards. It was a problem which she began to think about as the school year progressed, but an even greater dilemma, rooted in religious preference, began to grow for her at Mount Holyoke.

Every young woman had to classify herself in one of three categories when she enrolled at the seminary: "professing Christian," "hopefully pious," or "hopeless." Mary Lyon, a deeply religious person, felt responsible for the souls of the young women at the school, and she instituted that rule when she opened the doors to the institution in 1836. She then organized a plan of action whereby believers helped convert non-believers. It was a practice still in effect in 1854, although Mary Lyon had died in 1848. Nothing was changed. Teachers announced weekly prayer meetings and everyone was encouraged to attend the services. Immediately after the meeting, dedicated teachers and students talked to those who had not yet converted. Sometimes an evangelistic preacher came to the seminary for several weeks to preach and help convert errant young women.

Olympia and Oella, encouraged to attend one of the prayer meetings, finally accepted an invitation. It was a vastly new experience for them to hear someone ranting about hellfire and brimstone—and most alarming, too. Raised in the Universalist faith and taught its tenets by their mother, Olympia realized these teachings were far different from any that she had heard. Universalists do not believe there is such a place as hell and they believe that God is kind and loving, not a vindictive being brimming with jealousy and spite. Overwhelmed with a sense of uneasiness, she was dismayed when the evangelist approached them immediately after the service. After greeting them, he asked pleasantly but pointedly, "What are your religious convictions?"

At best an unsettling question, she could not give him a definitive answer for it was a question to which she had given little thought. Now she realized that, although she had read passages from the Bible, she had never studied it. There was no Universalist church in the area where they had grown up so the children had never attended Sunday school classes or even a church service. In trying to recall her mother's early religious teachings, she could not remember hearing any of the harsh doctrines that the evangelists preached. She and Oella, with their lack of knowledge, were ripe for religious conversion.

While attending several more of the prayer meetings, she and her sister heard one sermon after another on hell and endless punishment. The evangelists seemed to thrive on vituperation, and she began to wonder where they acquired such information and why they dwelt on an angry God. Was this information in the Bible? What was the truth? Most important, how could she find it for herself?

31

Deeply troubled by the conflicting arguments and testimony, she wrote to the Universalist headquarters in Boston for books to help her study the Bible. She must find out what the Scriptures said and what they meant. What she learned from these guides and her studies both astonished and comforted her. There were many interpretations of the Bible and good reasons why she need not believe the frightening messages the zealous evangelists were preaching. She learned how they lifted sentences out of context and put their own interpretations on them, how they used the threat of endless punishment to intimidate people.

Then she asked the question that was to guide her entire future life. "Why don't preachers dwell on God's love when that was such a motivating force behind Christ's teachings?"

Although she and Oella used the Universalist study guide to read and try to understand the Bible, the zealous teachers and students continued to wield pressure on the two young women to convert to their form of Christianity. Their crusading zeal shadowed Olympia's thinking in spite of her resolution to ignore it. Deeply troubled yet, she at last turned to her mother with her doubts and misgivings. Lephia's letter to her provided the strength and guidance she so desperately needed, and from this point on she was able to manage her ordeal and reject the teachings of the evangelists.

Tuesday, April 12, 1855

My Dear Olympia,

I have thought of you much since I received your last letter and with a feeling of anxiety and uneasiness unusual when you were the subject of my thoughts. The more I have reflected on the subject and tone of your letter, the greater has seemed its significance. You ask for commentaries and say you "do not wish to get fooled into the presbyterian church."

Allow me to say, my dear, that under the influence that surrounds you there, it would be impossible for you to come to any just conclusion upon a subject so mystified by creeds and theologians, particularly a person of your enthusiastic and impressible temperament.

While there is no faculty of the human soul so elevating, so delightful, as pure devotion of feeling, there is nothing so benumbing, so deadening, so baneful, as a narrow, soul-contracting creed. It is absurd to judge of the Almighty and his disposal of the human race from some text of scripture or peculiar wording of some phrase.

She went on to explain that the Bible was subject to misinterpretation through various translations and to alterations brought about by different superstitions and beliefs. Christ himself never once attended to either the probability or danger of a hell, Lephia wrote, but repeatedly assured the people that he came to save them from sin. She instructed Olympia to get her Bible and read Corinthians carefully so that she would understand the message that is there.

Then she wrote a final paragraph:

> *It would cause me the most poignant sorrow were you to become the dupe of superstitious bigotry—dismiss the subject of creeds for the present and be content with a pure heart, a conscientious discharge of duty, a resignation and trust in God. . . . I think a visit to Vermont will do you good both in mind and body. It will serve in some measure to break the thralldom that surrounds you—go and enjoy it. I would not have you stay there, their victim for no amount of money. Perhaps I do them injustice but I suspect the reason why they have you go so slow in your studies is that the mind unoccupied may more easily become their prey. My child, I feel as if much of the future happiness of your life depended on the present. . . I have great confidence in your excellent plain common sense. Use it. Don't regard the notion sometimes advanced that it is wrong to use reason in religious opinions—let me advise and entreat you to let the subject rest for the present. I am anxious only for your welfare and happiness. Let me hear from you soon.*
>
> > *Your affectionate Mother,*
> > *Lephia O. Brown.*

Written along the edge of one page is this final plea,

> *Do not throw my letter by carelessly but remember it is from the heart of your mother and its opinions, if not learned or well defended, are the result of years of reflection.*[7]

Clearly Lephia did not want her daughter to join an orthodox church. Such a crucial decision, she felt, would drastically affect Olympia's entire future life, hampering her education and curtailing her development. She would no longer be a free-thinking and open-minded person. What orthodox church would accept, without reservations and restraint, a woman who spoke openly and publicly about things "better left to the minds of men" as Olympia felt she had every right to do?

Olympia sensed her mother's alarm. Putting the letter away, she read it as the need moved her, drawing strength and comfort from Lephia's words. From that time on, she firmly rejected any efforts to convert her. Like seeds blown on fallow ground, those experiences lay dormant for a time. Later, they would germinate and provide direction to her life.

Olympia's essays reveal a great deal about her development at Mount Holyoke. In her first writings, she looked back with nostalgia on happy childhood days and bemoaned their passing away. Her concern for people's feelings, of primary interest when she first arrived, soon changed to a growing concern for their moral development. Moving from sentimental thoughts and observations, she began to acquire a more worldly view of human beings and their frailties.

In one of her last essays, she used strong words to describe people who are imbued with the passion for aristocracy, denouncing those who attempt to gain superiority over their fellow human beings. All such superiority is vanity and an illusion, lasting only a brief time, she declared. The very attempt to gain such superiority stifles independent thought and action and blocks self-improvement.

A deep and abiding commitment to self-improvement quickly became her first priority. She found that most of the teachers at Mount Holyoke were sincerely interested in developing the minds of the young women and teaching them independence, but guest lecturers who came to the campus from time to time often held different views. Some of them considered women dependent beings whose sole duty was to serve as assets to their husbands, fathers or brothers.

One such professor from Amherst came to lecture on chemistry. He opened his lesson with the comment, "You are not expected to remember all of this, but only enough to make you intelligent in conversation." Olympia, still too shy to speak out or challenge such a statement, could only ask herself how any college professor could believe that women's minds were somehow different from men's. Schools like Mount Holyoke were already proving that women could comprehend and master a college education. Weren't women already teaching Greek and Latin, mathematics and chemistry? How she longed to tell him that many of the students would not only remember his lecture, but some of them might even become chemists or chemistry teachers. Some might become doctors, lawyers, ministers or public lecturers. Such ideas were heresy in 1854 however, and she dared not speak out. "But someday no field will be closed to women," she consoled herself. "They will have to change their minds about us."

At the end of their year at Mount Holyoke Female Seminary, Olympia and Oella returned to the Michigan farm disappointed, angry, and frustrated. Olympia's disappointment reached so deep that she could not bear to return to Mount Holyoke. After relating the circumscriptions that bound them like invisible ties, the frustrations that hobbled them daily like shackles on the mind, and the slow pace of their studies, Olympia appealed to her parents for support. Where, she asked, could she go to gain a higher education, free from discrimination and restrictions, a school where she could get the knowledge she needed to determine her future life and work?

Asa, moved by his daughter's zeal for higher education and recognizing her resolution to somehow attain it, responded in a way that surprised her. "Olympia, I'll send you to any school of your choice. Find one that will admit you and you can go there," he said.

Overjoyed that her father at last wholly supported her in her quest, she began the search immediately. Over the next several months, she wrote letters to many colleges asking for admission. Only six replied in the affirmative. Four of those were connected with religious denominations and she refused to consider them. Oberlin and Antioch remained, both coeducational, both located in Ohio. Further inquiry revealed that Lucy Stone and Antoinette Brown, recognized public speakers, had graduated from Oberlin College, but neither had been allowed to read their essays at the graduation ceremony simply because they were women. She also learned that neither one could take part in any of the public exercises, either reading or speaking, while they were students there. Consequently, she dismissed Oberlin College as a choice. Antioch College remained. It was new and fast gaining fame as a liberal institution. The curriculum impressed her, as did the president of the institution, Horace Mann. Already famous for his educational work in the Boston schools, he expected Antioch College to be his crowning achievement. "The diploma at Antioch will be a certificate of character, not just an indication of work completed," he announced. Additionally, he said that there would be no religious instruction imposed on the students.[8] Olympia knew at once that this was the college of her choice. She wrote for admission and began her preparations to go there.

35

Chapter 3

Opening Doors—Antioch College

Olympia Brown was twenty years old when she set out for Ohio. This time she went alone. If she felt any apprehensions about the journey, she swallowed them and put her thoughts elsewhere. She had much to think about—her future, her studies and her enjoyment of the passing scenery.

Upon arriving in Yellow Springs, she found the campus lay among rolling hills laced with deep ravines. Smitten with the picturesque countryside, she soon found the time to take long walks along the winding roads and through the woods. It was only a short time before she struck up a number of friendships and soon joined the young women who were walking to the towns of Xenia, Clifton and Springfield on weekends when the weather was pleasant.

Most of the students at Antioch were mature young men and women. Many of them, she learned, had already made up their minds about their future life and work. This surprised her and she began to wonder when she could make that decision herself. Finding that she still lacked certain Latin and mathematical skills, she entered a preparatory class along with a number of other students preparing themselves for regular classes the following term.

A liberal spirit pervaded the campus, and here Olympia found the freedom and acceptance that made her studies a delight. Gone were the hours spent pouring over a Bible trying to untangle its mysteries. Gone were the daily section meetings of Mount Holyoke, the long lists of rules and regulations to read and obey. She wrote letters home singing praises of Antioch College, its curriculum, its teachers. Her parents were pleased; their daughter was happy at last in her studies.

During the first term, she studied algebra, Latin, Greek, drawing and designing. Her second term included English, geometry, Greek and the history of the Roman Empire. She made great strides in writing from the time she first entered Antioch until her graduation. Her earliest essay, dated January 5, 1856, entitled, "Life and Character of Louis the Eleventh of France," was one long paragraph written on a single sheet of paper.

There was little punctuation; the handwriting was small, cramped and difficult to read. Her teacher wrote a single notation at the top of the first page, "Many errors in punctuation. Please study that subject."[1] Olympia was quick to learn from her errors. Her next essays showed marked improvement in penmanship, punctuation and the organization of material. Several months later, another notation appeared on one of her essays, "Rather hurried and short." She soon remedied that fault. Her essays increased rapidly in length and content, some reaching more than fifty pages. If her professors wanted information, analysis and conclusions, she was happy to give them all that they could read.

Students and faculty alike quickly began to realize how serious-minded she was about her education. One schoolmate described her candidly:

> *When Olympia arrived at Antioch, she was a pale, slim little girl with a head almost too large for her slender body and crowned with a wealth of soft brown hair. She was eager to learn and let nothing stand in her way of gaining an education, and the students soon recognized the strength of her intellect.*[2]

Olympia did not expect to find discrimination against women at Antioch, yet it soon became evident to her in both subtle and manifest forms. Some of the professors simply assumed that the young female students would get married and use their education to help their husbands in their careers. Few professors encouraged them to study for a career of their own. Yet Olympia found many of the young women planned to work, write, teach or go into business when they graduated whether they married or not.

One of her first experiences with discrimination came when she attended several lectures on the Bible. It was a subtle form of discrimination but very clear to her nonetheless. The professor announced to the class that he had selected role models from the Bible for young people. For the male students, he chose Samson and Samuel. Samson represented the great physical strength of Israel, and Samuel, the spiritual strength, he said. Physical and spiritual strength were the ideals for the male students. He gave two long lectures on the attributes of the two men.

For the female students, he selected Ruth and Esther. Here his lecture differed sharply. "Ruth represents the plain prose of woman's life," he told them. In a short lecture he pointed out that Ruth did not go about trying to make a name for herself. Instead, "She followed Boaz. She followed him to the field. She married Boaz and that was all there was of it. That was the plain prose of woman's life." This lecture was followed by another one, equally brief. "Esther represents the poetry of woman's life," the professor continued. "She was willing to sacrifice herself for her people." He then outlined the story of Esther noting that, "She was willing to put herself in great peril," and he put special emphasis on her spirit of self-sacrifice. In the two lectures for the female students, he had extolled the traditional roles of marriage and sacrifice as ideal roles for women. Most of the young female students were indignant at such lectures. They were expecting to find work outside of the scope of marriage and housework and wanted to hear about some of the wise women of Biblical days.[3]

Olympia also found the same form of discrimination that she had encountered as a young student in Michigan. One day the English instructor announced, "Your next assignment will be orations and readings. All of the young men will be required to give speeches before the class. The young women must bring manuscripts to class and read from them."

Momentarily startled by the announcement echoing her Schoolcraft days, she did not argue with the instructor. She already knew what she would do. When her turn came to read, she rose from her chair and walked up to the chapel, her manuscript clutched tightly in her hand. She never unrolled it. Standing before the class, she delivered her oration from memory. The faculty, thrown into confusion, did not know what to do. Olympia adamantly insisted that she had done nothing wrong. "I did the assignment the same as the young men. What is wrong with that? Surely women can speak as well as men. Our minds are no different," she argued. They could not manage her. From then on, she did not ever *read* her manuscripts before the class but proudly, and perhaps a little defiantly, gave orations.

She began to write essays asserting the equality of the sexes and condemning the discrimination society imposed on the female sex. Discrimination in the education of the two sexes was one of her first targets. Even as little children, girls were treated differently from boys. She pointed out that they were not allowed to run, jump, climb trees, or, in fact, play in the same way as little boys. They must learn to act like little ladies long before boys were encouraged to act like little men. Additionally, when they reached school age, they were discouraged from studying mathematics and science. "Devote your minds to art, music and literature," society decreed. Young women's finishing schools continued the practice of discriminatory education, teaching needlecraft, good manners and the "finer arts." Rarely, if at all, did any of them stress education for a career. Could any of the graduates go out and get a job, she asked? Could any of them teach in an elementary school? "Young women are not taught to think for themselves as individuals, separate from men," she declared.

The first Woman's Rights Convention had been held only eight years earlier, in 1848, but the publicity surrounding it had sparked consciousness-raising among some women. Olympia believed that equal rights for women would be tantamount to equality of the sexes. Soon, she wrote, women will be able to get any job of their choice and will have the same rights as men. She little dreamed that American society was already moving into the Victorian period, a time when customs governing behavior and dress would become increasingly rigid and binding. She could not have imagined that the great movement for woman's rights was to be strangled for over sixty years. Only the possibilities of a new society danced before her eyes, a society where education would bring sweeping changes and opportunities to the female sex. Her heart beat with the hope and fervor of her vision.

Guest lecturers visited the campus regularly. Students heard Horace Greeley, Wendell Phillips, Edward Everett Hale, Ralph Waldo Emerson and other famous writers and speakers. Olympia listened to them reverently, little dreaming that she would come to know and work closely with some of them in a very few years. In time, she began to wonder why the lecture committee only brought men to Antioch. She decided to find out if women were ever invited. The chairman of the committee listened to her politely then he replied, "There are no woman speakers comparable to the men that we have selected."

"But there are. There is Susan B. Anthony, Elizabeth Cady Stanton, Lucy Stone, Antoinette Brown, Lucretia Mott, Pauline Wright Davis, and Abby Kelley Foster. They are well educated women and well known. Some have spoken at Oberlin College."

The committee members remained adamant. "We can't consider a female speaker. Who would come to hear a woman lecture?" they asked and refused to change their minds.

Olympia decided that if she wanted to hear a woman speaker, she would have to find one and help organize a committee to bring her to campus. The young women students quickly joined her in the effort. They raised money, selected the Reverend Antoinette Brown as their speaker, and Olympia offered to write the invitation to her.

Antoinette Brown (unrelated to Olympia Brown's family), had completed the theology course at Oberlin College in 1853, but the administrators refused to ordain her. There were no ordained women ministers at the time, and few people thought it a field suitable for women. Antoinette Brown, however, did find a pulpit in a small Congregational church in South Butler, New York. The congregation enjoyed her preaching and decided to ordain her, but the denomination never recognized her ordination. Within a year she gave up the Congregational ministry and became a Unitarian. In 1856, she married Samuel Blackwell and devoted herself to raising a family for a number of years.[4] These facts are important as they relate to Olympia's choice of a career.

Several years earlier, when she was still going to school in Schoolcraft, an article had appeared in the newspaper about a woman who was preaching in a church in the east. The news had electrified Olympia, who was still young and impressionable. A woman preacher! Antoinette Brown had broken barriers! She was a symbol, an ideal toward which she could work. The vision remained, and she still remembered the excitement with which she had read the news, the flood of hope and aspiration that set her spirit afire. Now she was writing to her heroine.

After inviting her to come and lecture at Antioch on a Saturday evening, a new thought struck her. Since Antoinette Brown would be staying in Yellow Springs following her lecture, perhaps she would not mind staying over a little longer and preaching a sermon for them on Sunday morning. Accordingly, she extended the invitation.

Antoinette Brown accepted both invitations. In high spirits, Olympia began at once to make the final arrangements for the program. This was her first opportunity to take full responsibility for organizing a public event and she soon learned there were numerous complexities involved in such work. She had expected Reverend Brown to give her sermon in the school chapel, but an Antioch professor was already scheduled to speak there on that particular Sunday morning. When she asked if he would relinquish his time to Reverend Brown, "who is coming at a special invitation to preach to the students," he refused. Dismayed but undaunted, she set out to find another place for the service. She found a church in Yellow Springs available for that particular time, but she had to get formal permission from each one of its trustees. This task involved a long walk out in the country to each trustee's home. Never one to delegate work, she undertook the job herself. Having received full permission at last, she returned to the campus to await her heroine's arrival.

Antoinette Brown's visit to Antioch College was a marked success and proved to the lecture committee that women could speak as well as men. Her sermon the next day in Yellow Springs also drew a large crowd. The local newspaper aroused the curiosity of many citizens with its story of her impending visit, and they seized the opportunity to hear a woman preach.

Olympia was profoundly moved by the experience. "The sense of the victory lifted me up. I felt as though the Kingdom of Heaven were at hand," she said of Antoinette Brown's sermon.[5] The seed, scattered so fortuitously in her early years and at Mount Holyoke, was beginning to germinate.

On June 30, 1857, she received a letter from Horace Mann, then president of the College. It was the end of her first full year at Antioch and he wrote a testimonial letter in which he noted, "She behaved herself well and made great proficiency in her studies while here." He admitted her as a member of the Freshman class, apparently a formality, and certified her as a school teacher.[6] Olympia, however, was determined to continue her studies and receive a degree.

Lephia and Asa Brown, pleased with their daughter's glowing descriptions of Antioch College, decided to buy a house and move to Yellow Springs. "It's an opportunity to educate all of the children," Lephia said, "and we'll all be together again." This may have been her primary motive, for strong family ties bound her to her children. However, higher education loomed as vitally important, too. Accordingly, Oella enrolled in college as soon as they moved, and Marcia, a short time later. Their home became the center for many student gatherings, particularly among the young radicals. Olympia delighted in the discussions and debates on politics, education and many controversial issues as did her mother, who must surely have felt some twinges of regret that she had never had the opportunity to engage in such activities when she was young.

Olympia was popular with her classmates and had many friends. Although she did not encourage romance, she had several suitors during her years at Antioch.[7] Perhaps the Civil War interfered with any long term romance or perhaps her first priority was getting an education. At any rate, marriage did not appear to interest her at this time.

The Amelia Bloomer Dress came into fashion when she was a student at Antioch. It was very popular on campus and among many woman's rights leaders as well. The skirt was short, reaching halfway between the knees and ankles, a startling change from the long, heavy, floor-length skirts and numerous petticoats that women were wearing at the time. Underneath the skirt, women wore long pants gathered about the ankles. Olympia found the dress was comfortable and practical, as did many of her classmates. They could walk, run, go up and down stairs and play games with great ease. They were enjoying a freedom of movement that they had never experienced before and they encouraged women everywhere to adopt the style.

Men, however, began to ridicule the dress and the women who wore it. Soon, even small boys on the streets were imitating the jeers and taunts of the men. Newspaper articles derided the fashion and other women began to join in the general mockery. When they should have asserted their right to wear a comfortable dress of their own choice, most women succumbed to societal pressure and abandoned the fashion. Olympia and her friends chose to continue wearing the style until they graduated from

Antioch College in spite of its unpopularity in the general public. How could they give up that wonderful freedom from swirling skirts and petticoats that brushed the ground, tangled their feet when they climbed staircases, or impeded them when they ran?

No athletic classes were scheduled for female students at Antioch College, and they soon began to take long walks in the area to get their exercise. When Horace Mann first learned that the young women were walking to the nearby towns to visit and shop, that they were seen running, laughing and talking noisily among themselves, he decided that he must do something about it. "Someone has to teach them more ladylike behavior now that they are away from home. I think we had better send to Boston for a chaperone," he announced.

His words brought a chorus of protests from the female students. He was discriminating against them, they said. After all, he hadn't hired a chaperone for the male students. It was all in vain. A chaperone arrived on campus in spite of their objections. They were prepared for her, however.

"Let's have a party for her," one student suggested. "We'll invite all of the German students. No one can speak in English. Everyone has to talk in German."

Accordingly, when the chaperone arrived at the party, a chorus of German greetings fell on her ears. "Oh dear, I have forgotten my German," she murmured to the delight of her tormentors, and they continued teasing and joking about her among themselves. Her discomfort grew throughout the evening. All of the following week and for sometime thereafter, they continued their raillery at her expense, always in German. At last she gave up, packing her bags and returning to the more conservative atmosphere of Boston. Mr. Mann made no further attempt to find a chaperone for the female students. "I believe he has arrived at the conclusion that we are quite able to take care of ourselves," Olympia noted, and her classmates agreed. They had learned that they could successfully respond to restrictions on their freedom. It was a small victory, but a victory, nonetheless.

Horace Mann was a popular president at Antioch. Tall and dignified in his bearing, he struck Olympia as a "most noble looking man." A brilliant and innovative educator, he also inspired respect and confidence. "He gave the students many inspiring ideas," she noted. She best remembered his lesson, "Be ashamed to die until you have won some victory for humanity." At the same time, he seemed to be unable to adjust his habits of thought to allow for differences of opinion. "As time went on, he seemed actually to dislike anyone who held advanced opinions varying from his own," she complained, noting that some of the students challenged him in the classroom, making him uncomfortable and defensive.

43

He spoke often of the "Great Experiment" of female education. Although he seemed to be pleased at the number of women enrolled at Antioch College, and of their work and grades, he sometimes expressed his ambivalence by calling a group of women students into his office to talk. There he discussed coeducation at some length; then he asked them, "Do you believe that the education of women will lead them to enter the professions?"

Olympia, thinking it a strange question for the head of a coeducational institution to be asking, replied, "Of course. Why else would we be getting an education if not to prepare ourselves for our future life and work? We do not all plan to get married and raise families, and we ought to be able to support ourselves, don't you think?"

Mann frowned and his eyes clouded at such a bold answer. He appeared to be distressed at the idea. "If that is the case," he said, "perhaps I am wrong to remain at the head of a coeducational school."[8]   The discussion ended there, but his answer troubled Olympia. Surely he did not believe that women were seeking an education for the sake of their fathers, brothers or future husbands? Mann's ideas had affected female education in the United States to a marked degree, helping to raise it to the same level as male education. Was it possible that he was having second thoughts about educating women? Perhaps he would discourage talented women from choosing a professional career. She could almost see the door through which she had walked beginning to close, and the vision distressed her. She was learning that no human being, even one held in great reverence such as Horace Mann, was the great, noble ideal that she had envisioned when she was a young girl. All were subject to human frailties. It was a lesson that helped her through many difficult experiences in the years ahead.

Horace Mann may have been reacting to another problem, however. The college was in deep financial trouble. In 1859 it was sold to clear its debts. Fortunately, a group of Mann's friends purchased it and insisted that he retain his position as head of the school. The strain was too much for his health, however, and he died that spring, the year before Olympia graduated. In spite of her reservations about some of his remarks and attitudes, Olympia admired him profoundly and felt that his death was a great loss to Antioch .

She was developing strong moral, religious and political ethics as she matured. An ardent abolitionist, her anti-slavery feelings harkened back to her days in Schoolcraft when she visited with runaway slaves at the Underground Railroad station her aunt and uncle operated. She had changed, though, broadening her outlook. "Slavery is a terrible wrong, but so, too, is the subjection of women," she wrote in one of her essays.

"Negroes and women are considered inferior beings and, as such, fit only to do what white men want them to do. They have no property, political or even personal rights. Their own children do not belong to them. These wrongs must be rectified. This nation cannot continue under such conditions."

The words flowed from her mind so fast that she could not get one thought down before another took its place. Her handwriting, round and firm at the beginning of each paragraph, was almost illegible by the end. She wrote as she would speak, not bothering to go back and organize her work into a more orderly and cohesive whole, but making point after point as a speaker would do.

Her graduation essay was strikingly different from much of her other work. It was almost a sermon by contrast, and was considered one of the best in the graduating class.[9] By this time, she had given much thought to what she wanted to do with her life. The field was limited, for men still decreed that women could not be doctors, lawyers, leaders in business or government; that their mentality was inferior to men's and their sphere must be the home or the teaching of children. Olympia did not accept this limitation. Her experiences at Mount Holyoke left a deep impression on her, and she began to consider ways in which she could counteract the evangelistic fervor that had nearly swept her off her feet. How could she tell people the truth about the doctrine of endless punishment, that it was false and there was no such place as hell? Surely people would rejoice to hear such words, she thought, little knowing how tenaciously they cling to old beliefs. The answer, clearly, was to become a minister. This idea had grown slowly during her years of study at Antioch, and when she graduated, she was ready to face her parents with her decision.

"You're wondering what I'm going to do now that I've graduated, aren't you?" she asked them after receiving her diploma.

Her father nodded thoughtfully. "That we are. You decided you want to teach, after all?"

She shook her head and smiled down at her father, seated comfortably in his chair. "No. I've decided I want to be a minister."

"A minister!" he exclaimed, gazing up at her in astonishment. "A preacher? You want to be a preacher?"

"Yes, I do. More than anything else. But it will take two more years of school to do that. I believe I have a calling for the ministry. That's the only way I can explain how I feel."

"Two more years of school," he echoed, rubbing his chin thoughtfully. "And where might that be?"

"I don't know, yet. I'll have to find a theology school that will admit me. Not Oberlin. They won't ordain women so I won't go there. But there

45

must be one somewhere, and I'll find it. I've believed for a long time that women should be in the ministry. They'd make good preachers and they'd be better than men at working with parishioners. Women try to help each other, not outdo each other like men. All I want is a chance to prove myself."

Asa studied her for a time, then he shook his head again. "It won't be easy, Olympia. I don't know if most men will want to go and hear a woman preach."

"I know that, but I want very much to try," she replied.

It did not take her long to convince her father that she would not consider any alternative, that she was determined to become a minister. At last he agreed to support her and she began at once to locate as many theology schools as she could so that she could write to them requesting admission.

She spent most of the next year at home in Yellow Springs, writing letters, studying and preparing sermons. Dreaming of a future where she would teach people about God's great love for them, she visualized large crowds flocking to hear her preach. She was totally unprepared for the reality that most people are reluctant to consider anything new. It was well that she had no idea of the difficulties that lay ahead, or of how strong the prejudice was against women preachers. She might not have had the courage to set out on that road had she known. But she was young and ready to sacrifice to reach her goal.

Her letters requesting admission to theology schools brought nothing but rejections, one after another. "We do not believe ladies are called to the ministry," appeared more times than she cared to remember, yet she continued her search.

Another great passion consumed much of her time during the winter of 1860-61. Her thoughts turned toward the tragedy of discrimination against women in almost every walk of life. She wrote countless pages detailing her frustrations and resentment. Her words fell across the pages so closely that it was difficult to tell where one word ended and the next began. Little trails of blots ran along the lines. Like twigs thrown onto a bonfire, her words seemed to fuel her fervor.

In one essay, "Politics and Piety," she accused women of being ignorant and sentimental. Women are more concerned over "the sigh of a disconsolate lover than the moans of a dying country. They weep more bitterly over the last farewell of a faithless suitor than at the sound of the death knell of liberty," she wrote. "Even though they cannot vote, they should know what the issues are and be able to discuss them intelligently. They should have solutions for the problems in this country. They should help make improvements instead of sitting back and excusing themselves for their ignorance."

She was equally emphatic in her assault on teachers. "They are the very people who mold the young and pliant mind; yet they ignore the great problems of the day. Teachers are so preoccupied with their own little world of duties that nothing else seems to matter. They possess more knowledge than any other class of people. Their morals are universally unexceptionable and the whole succeeding generation is subject to their influence." She believed they should be teaching the young that education is to be used in working for the country and in helping the oppressed, not just for individual advancement. "They ignore politics," she charged, "or do they fear that they, too, will become corrupt if they involve themselves in governmental policies?"

In another essay she accused novelists of portraying women as vain, foolish, insipid and vacant-minded. "Women appear to be incapable of doing anything with their own lives or influencing other people. Can this be so?" she asked. She then charged women with letting men dominate their lives. Why did they not get an education so they could make intelligent decisions about themselves? How could they just let themselves drift through life without any fixed purpose in mind? "They live on, guided by the caprices and whims of others, their thoughts and opinions controlled by those of whom they obtain their daily support and they only mindful [sic] of what they shall eat or what they shall drink or wherewithal they shall be clothed," she declared. "Women let men make all their decisions for them and have little or no interest in their own development or fulfillment."

Sometimes she attacked from a different vein. "I have been told that not one woman in ten has ever read the Constitution of the United States; that beyond a vague notion that Columbus discovered America and Washington was the father of his country, they are entirely ignorant of our history; that their interest in politics is confined to looking at a torchlight procession or in presenting a flag to some political club. They waste their time and energies on trifles; a pet dog or cat, a bird or a rabbit assumes a wonderful importance in the eyes of these exceedingly refined damsels. The emancipation of three million slaves is as nothing compared with some of these little fancies."

In her essay, "Female Education," she attacked the practice of teaching little girls that they must act like little ladies. "Girls are simply children," she wrote. "They should be allowed to run and play the same as little boys, to climb trees and ride horses, to play ball." Perhaps she was thinking of her own girlhood and the freedom she had enjoyed on the Michigan farm. Young women's boarding schools, she noted, were only continuing women's ignorance by teaching them "frivolous pastimes" instead of encouraging them to develop their talents. It was no wonder that women became bored, melancholy and subject to hysterics. They had nothing to think about but themselves. They existed just to please men. Why could they not see themselves as persons separate from men instead of in relation to them as wives, mothers or sisters?

"Women fear failure in any effort they might make to gain more freedom, so they rarely try to do so," she said, but men were to blame, too. They had to learn that "all mankind are born free and equal, and this includes women as well as Negroes. Certainly reformers must work for that principle, even though there is immense opposition against such an idea."

She was surprised by the hostility of many women to the idea of equality. Their ignorance not only blinded them to the concept of equal rights, but it raised a fear that they might lose certain benefits and privileges they were presently enjoying.

Olympia was not acquainted with any working women and knew virtually nothing about their living conditions, particularly those who worked in the textile mills or clothing factories in the east. Textile workers were laboring twelve to fourteen hours a day at that time, and their children, who should have been in school, also worked in the mills. Everyone in the family had to work in the sheer struggle to survive. Little publicity was given to their plight, however, to their long hours and low wages; and few reformers were even aware of their problems. If the leaders had known about them and been able to organize them, the history of woman's rights would likely have been very different. Concentrating their energies on middle and upper-class women, most reformers perhaps believed that only those women had the education, time and money to bring about social change. It was a mistake that cost them many years of futile work and delayed equal rights for women untold years. The movement needed to include farmers, factory workers and domestic laborers, as well as the middle class and wealthy women in the work for equal rights and voting privileges.

During the Christmas holidays of 1860, former schoolmate Mattie Tilden invited Olympia to visit her in Cleveland, Ohio. Olympia accepted, and soon found herself enjoying the warm hospitality of the Tilden's busy household. After a few days, Mattie's mother brought out a property rights petition and showed it to Olympia. "I've been asked to take this around the city for signatures," Mrs. Tilden said, "but I'm much too busy to do that. You're so interested in woman's rights, Olympia, that I thought you might like to go out and see if you can get some names on it for me. It would be your chance to do something for women."

Olympia's heart leaped. A property rights petition! She read it eagerly. Addressed to the Ohio State Legislature, the petition asked that married women be allowed to control their inherited property, their own earnings and the guardianship of their children. All of these benefits were denied them. "I'll go out the first thing in the morning," she cried, scarcely able to control her excitement. It was an opportunity she had never dreamed would fall into her hands, and early the next morning she started out on her adventure. By the time evening came, she had eighty-nine signatures on the petition. The Tildens were astonished. "I've only begun," she said to them, and went out again the next day and the next after that. She worked every day except Sunday, often losing all track of time and coming home after dark. The Tildens had all they could do to convince her to give up the task on New Year's for just that one day.

"It's a holiday, Olympia," Mrs. Tilden insisted, "and we have social calls to make. We want you to come with us."

"I've hardly had a chance to visit with you since you took on this task," Mattie interceded. "Come and enjoy the holiday with us."

"You can go out with the petition again tomorrow," Mrs. Tilden assured her, and at last she reluctantly acquiesced to their request.

Filling the petition was a task to delight her soul. Most women, she found, were willing to sign it as soon as she explained it to them. Most men, however, were prepared to argue with her. "Let women have money in their own names and the guardianship of their children?" they laughed. "That's impossible. Women can't handle money. They know nothing about it. And what about the children? If the women have guardianship of them and the husband dies, they can squander all of the inheritance. No, they know nothing at all about handling money."

That women can learn these matters very easily and that they have minds and native intelligence was her primary argument. She did, in fact, suggest that men could teach their wives such basic information themselves. Some men, however, refused to listen to her. There were those who believed that their wives and daughters were their property, and that they should have full control over all of their affairs. They could not believe that women had brains the same as men, but Olympia argued, sometimes an hour or more.

"Why should women have to rely on men for everything?" she asked. "They have only to be educated to take care of themselves and their property. Shouldn't they learn to assume some of their own responsibilities? Isn't it time we taught young girls how to earn and manage money?" The petition continued to grow.

Occasionally, when she returned to the Tilden home in the evening, a terrified or angry woman was waiting to talk to her. "Take my name off that list," the women usually demanded, followed by the cry, "My husband laughs at me. He says I'll be wanting to vote next!"

Was that such a dreadful idea, Olympia asked? Weren't women citizens of this country, too? She then began to explain, quietly and logically, the petition and the principle of property rights. She talked about a woman's right to her own children, and what it meant to have their guardianship. "Women do not need to have someone else do their thinking for them. We are human beings with minds the same as men's and we should have the same rights as they do. Our own property, our wages, our inheritance, should belong to us—not to our husbands or fathers or brothers. And women, not men, should have the guardianship of their children. It's the women who bear the children. Why should they be forced to give them up? The law must be changed, and this petition will help do that."

Most women, convinced that they had been right to sign the petition after all, left well-prepared with new arguments to use against their husbands.

Olympia was constantly dismayed to find so many women who saw themselves only in relation to husbands or fathers. It was a cultural failing, an educational fault, she believed. How could they be taught to view themselves as separate human beings with their own lives, hopes and dreams? Could it be done in the schools, she wondered? "Girls should learn different roles and traditions, and I don't think they will ever learn those in the home. Society must somehow change the way it views women. It will be a monumental task and I'm not sure where we can begin, but I do want to try."

The property rights reformers in Columbus, Ohio, soon learned that Olympia had obtained many hundreds of signatures on the petition she took around the city of Cleveland. "She went into business offices to get men to sign the petition," the women said to each other in shocked undertones.

"Refined ladies never go into business offices unless they are accompanied by a man," came the frequent retort. The more enlightened and progressive sisters, while lacking the courage to follow Olympia's lead, nevertheless admitted to having a grudging admiration of her. "Perhaps," some of them suggested, "Miss Brown can come to Columbus and canvass our business district." None of them had dared venture into those offices, but they were willing to enlist the aid of someone who would.

Olympia accepted the invitation. How amusing it was, she thought, that adult women with husbands and families should fear going into a place of business. She spent an entire week in Columbus getting signatures from businessmen there; then she helped paste all of the petitions into one long, continuous roll. At last it was ready to present to the State Legislature during the spring session.

"Miss Brown, would you like to come with us when we present it?" Mrs. J. E. Jones, the apparent leader of the reformers, asked her. "You've spent so much time on this petition, and you did get so many signatures, we thought you might like to come with us when we present it to the State Legislature."

"Of course, I would," she cried. "I would love to come with you," and so she accompanied the reformers to the State Capitol on the day of their scheduled appearance. When they entered the front door, the group paused. Mrs. Jones, who was carrying the large roll of names, handed it to Olympia. "You deserve the honor of presenting it to the Senate," she said, "for you did more work on it than any other one of us."

Olympia caught her breath in surprise, then reached out and took the roll almost reverently. Together, the women walked to the front of the assembly chamber. There, she handed the large roll of names to one of the senators. Taking it from her hands, he carefully unrolled it. By the time he had reached the end, it stretched all the way through the chamber and out into the corridor looking like a long, narrow, white carpet. Awed silence settled over the senators for a few moments as they contemplated the number of names on the petition; then they broke into a cheer.

The little group of reformers were led up to a platform in front of the legislators for the presentation. The older women gave speeches but Olympia had to remain silent. "You are too young yet to give a speech before the Legislature," Mrs. Jones told her prior to their trip to the State Capitol. Appreciative of at least accompanying the group for the presentation, she had not argued the point, but she chafed under the restriction.

"I had to content myself with listening to them," she said later, "although I really had a great deal I wanted to say on the subject."

She later learned that the petition helped women secure important property rights in Ohio, and she was proud of her part in that victory. She had learned many lessons during her canvass of Cleveland, but she began to realize that more than one generation might pass before she saw any great changes in the way in which women viewed themselves.

A letter arrived in March from St. Lawrence, the Universalist Theological School in Canton, New York. As with the many others she had received, she opened it, fully expecting another rejection. This letter, however, was different. As she read the words penned by Ebenezer Fisher, president of St. Lawrence, her heart began to race. "You will be admitted into the school and have all of the opportunities that the school affords .. you must bring satisfactory testimonials as to your moral and religious character, believe in the Holy Scriptures, and you must have a fixed determination to devote your life to the Christian Ministry," he wrote. These conditions were required of all divinity students, he noted. Olympia knew she would have no trouble meeting those requirements, and her spirits soared. "Tuition is free. Board costs $2.25 per week including washing. Students supply their own bedding and room furniture." He suggested, as an afterthought, that she might wish to board with a private family.

She immediately arranged for testimonials to her character and also for room and board with a family near the theological school in Canton. Her dreams were about to come true! Then another letter came from Mr. Fisher. In this one, written in June, he warned her of the many problems that she would encounter as a student at an all-male theological school, pointing out to her that there had never before been any female students there. "It is unlikely that there will ever be any others," he wrote. "However, if you feel that he [God] has called you to preach the everlasting gospel, you shall receive from me no hindrance but rather every aid in my power." Olympia saw at once that he was having second thoughts about admitting her. He went on to state, "I do not think women are called to the ministry, but I leave that between you and the Great Head of the Church."

"That is exactly where it should be left," she thought to herself. She could ask for nothing better.[10]

Chapter 4

Breaking Barriers

Olympia Brown arrived at Canton, New York, in the fall of 1861. She made her way to the campus of the St. Lawrence Theological School with mixed emotions. She was already twenty-six years old and knew that she had two years of study ahead of her. There was no doubt in her mind that she could complete the course of study, but what about ordination?

She walked across the grounds, a small, resolute figure. Weighing scarcely ninety pounds, she exuded great energy and spirit. Her thick, dark hair, parted in the middle and pulled back from her small, round face, was fastened into a large bun at the back of her neck. She had a high, broad forehead, wide-set eyes under straight brows, and a firm mouth and chin. Her air of determination generated respect; she wore it like a cloak.

Intensely aware that she was the only woman student on the campus, she walked quickly toward the main building. How would the faculty greet her, she wondered? Would they welcome her or resent her? How would the young men feel about a woman studying to be a minister?

Arriving at last at the office of President Ebenezer Fisher, she raised her arm and knocked on the heavy, dark door. She did not quite know what to expect, but she had prepared herself for almost any contingency. When the door opened, she gazed up at a very tall man with a white beard and a stern face. "Yes?" he said, looking down at her quizzically.

"I'm Olympia Brown," she announced in a firm voice. "I've come to begin my studies for the ministry."

He stood for a moment, wearing the baffled expression of a man caught by surprise. "I see," he said at last. "Yes. Olympia Brown. I really was not expecting you, Miss Brown. I thought my letters would discourage you."

"No, they actually encouraged me," she replied. "I want very much to become a minister."

A brief smile touched his face. "It won't be easy. As I told you, you'll be the only female here on campus."

"I know, but that won't bother me, and it shouldn't bother the other students if they are serious about their studies."

Mr. Fisher raised his eyebrows, then allowed a brief smile to cross his face again. "Well, Miss Brown, I'll help you as much as I can." He then invited her to come with him and meet some of the professors.

She agreed at once and found that they were not only friendly but supportive of her. Subsequently, she learned that it was the faculty wives who were a problem. Some were simply cool toward her, but a few were openly hostile. As the weeks passed, she tried to keep her mind on her studies and to ignore the wives who were unfriendly. When they saw how serious she was about becoming a minister, they would surely change their minds, she told herself. But why were they so resentful of a woman who was trying to better herself? Why did they think that only men could be ministers or doctors or lawyers?

In time, this plan did appear to work to a certain extent. Some of the wives began to invite her to their homes. At first they were primarily curious about her, but after getting to know her, they became sympathetic with her goal. Some of them soon became her staunch supporters and they prevailed upon the other faculty wives to support her. Their friendship meant a great deal to Olympia because there were no female students to give her support and her family was far away.

There were times when she felt isolated and lonely; the atmosphere was very different from that at Antioch. Some of her male classmates were friendly and helpful, but two of them were quite the contrary. They delighted in belittling her simply because she was a woman.

"What church will hire a woman preacher?" they taunted. "Who would ever go to hear a woman preach?" One of their favorite strategies was to get beneath her window at night and mimic her voice, which was soft and high-pitched. This practice grew increasingly painful to her because she knew of no way to improve her voice. She realized that there must be ways to lower the pitch and increase the volume and that she would have to learn elocution and voice control someday. How could she be a good preacher unless the congregation could hear her in the back of the church?

Her decision did not lessen the pain, but it did help her ignore the two young men. She did not respond to their teasing or show any anger at them, and they soon lost interest in that form of torment. They found another, however, to which she could respond. Each student prepared one sermon a week to read before the class. Classmates then criticized each other's work. This exercise was designed to help them learn their strengths and weaknesses. The two young men, however, found that it was another opportunity to disparage Olympia. They took turns making derogatory remarks about her work. One of the nicest remarks they ever made about one of her sermons was, "Well, it was very good but I should hardly call it a *sermon*."

Olympia, of course, soon responded to their sermons in her own way. Her tongue was sharp and she aimed for their weaknesses with a stinging accuracy. There are times when the Biblical injunction to turn the other cheek can be ignored, she told herself. In this way, she managed to cope with life at St. Lawrence.

She had prepared herself to find some discrimination against women at the college but the faculty members were all patient and understanding, and they treated her as an equal with the male students. The students, however, were not as understanding and their prejudice against women soon became quite clear. The Civil War had begun in April of 1861, and the intensity of feeling it aroused among the students surprised her. The campus, after all, was small and located far from the scenes of conflict. Yet young students delivered fervent speeches against slavery. "There must be freedom and liberty for all," they declared. Their words echoed across the campus grounds reaching the ears of virtually every student and faculty member. Olympia, thinking that their speeches included freedom and liberty for women, too, complimented the speakers on their progressive attitude. The young men, however, were appalled at the idea of freedom and liberty for *women*. "The Negro man is the one who has suffered," they declared. "He has no rights of any kind, no voting rights or property rights. He has to do everything the slave owner wants him to do."

"So does the Negro woman," she said. "You demand freedom and liberty for *all*. Those were your words. Negro women need freedom as much as Negro men. They have no voting or property rights, either. Don't you think women are human beings the same as men? Women are as much citizens of this country as men are." But it was too soon for the students to cope with such an outrageous idea. As far as they were concerned, women were hardly considered to be human beings with any rights, and they continued to harangue the same as before.[1]

She attended a speech one day by a visiting lecturer. He also spoke on liberty and justice for the "lowest and poorest," particularly stressing his points on justice several times. Olympia was impressed with his speech, and pleased that so many students were attending the lecture. She believed that it was just the kind of speech they needed to hear. This man is so broad and liberal in his sentiments that he is including women in his program of reform, she thought.

She wrote a letter to him afterward, thanking him for his inspiring speech. "Your remarks are precisely what other lecturers should be saying to help bring about equality and justice between men and women. If more people felt as you do, there would soon be justice among all peoples, not just among men." She ended her letter by saying that she hoped he would continue to support woman's rights.

A reply from the "great orator" came by return mail. He could not wait to set her thinking straight. Indignant at her assumption, he wrote, "You have put the wrong interpretation on my words. I have no sympathy whatsoever with the woman's movement."[2]

Olympia, stunned by his reply, had to conclude that he was just like all of the others who claimed they were ready to die to help the Negro gain his rights. At the same time, they were bitterly opposed to rights for women. Why did men have such a fear of losing power over women that they would not even consider the idea that women had basic human rights? Why, in fact, did they feel they had to control women? Pained by every act that defined her as less than a man and feeling a deep sense of humiliation threatening to envelop her, she realized that there was little she could do personally. She was far too busy with her studies to give any time to woman's rights work. That would have to wait until she graduated. Even then she would have to find a church that would accept her as a minister before she could devote time and effort to woman's rights work. The road ahead seemed long and bleak.

She had a natural flair for oratory, and she worked hard to develop her speaking abilities. Words that lay at the tip of her tongue flowed in smooth, logical order into sermons. Her teachers, recognizing her talent, encouraged her to go out and preach in the surrounding communities. It would give her the experience she needed, they told her. By the time the Christmas holidays approached, she felt that she was ready for just such an experience. It was too long a trip to go back to Yellow Springs, well over five hundred miles, and she decided to spend the time between semesters studying and preaching wherever she could find a pulpit in the Canton area.

A church in the village of Ogdensburg, about twenty miles northwest of Canton, agreed to hire her. She packed her valise and took the stagecoach there. After getting settled in the local hotel, she began to consider her Sunday service and made some inquiries to see if there might be a choir available to sing. The proprietor of the hotel, a spirited and independent woman, gave her the names of the regular choir members and Olympia set out to visit each one. All of them agreed to sing for her service until she came to the last woman. That woman refused to sing. The news spread rapidly in the little village, and all of the other choir members notified Olympia that they would not sing, either.

Olympia was astonished at such a turn of events. "But I must have music for my service. Surely there are other people who can sing," she said to the proprietor who then gave her several more names. It did not take her long, in such a small town, to get another choir together. She returned to the hotel late that afternoon. The proprietor met her at the door, her eyes twinkling.

"The woman who refused to sing in your choir doesn't like the idea of a female preacher. She's a Universalist herself, and a business woman, too. The only other one in the town besides me," she laughed. "I just cannot understand some women."

The evening before the service, the businesswoman apparently had a change of heart. She appeared at the hotel. "I would like to see Miss Brown," she said to the proprietor.

The hotel proprietor shook her head. "She's not here right now, but you can leave a message. I'll give it to her."

"You may tell Miss Brown that our choir has decided to sing after all, to make the service respectable," the woman said.

"Miss Brown will preach whether your choir sings at her service or not," the proprietor retorted, evidently pleased that she could strike a small blow for Olympia.

The next day Olympia had two choirs for her service. The congregation, pleased with her preaching, asked her to stay for the several weeks of her winter vacation, and she accepted.

Her second term at St. Lawrence went much more smoothly than the first. The two young men who had bothered her so much in the beginning now left her alone. Good reports of her preaching at Ogdensburg followed her to Canton, and she was able to get as many appointments to preach as she wished. She was beginning to enjoy her life at St. Lawrence.

Part of this change came about of her own volition. She was determined to overcome her acute sensitivity and began developing a stoic attitude as a defense against psychological pain. She would have to harden herself, she realized, if she were to complete her theological training and go out into the world and preach. The prejudice against women ministers was far stronger than she had realized, but that knowledge only increased her determination to achieve her goal. She would help other women by breaking down barriers, whatever the cost.

As soon as classes were over for the summer, Olympia went to Yellow Springs to visit her family. While she was there, she was invited to speak to the Literary Society at Antioch College, the group to which she had belonged when she was a student there. What message could she give them, she wondered? Should she tell them about her experiences at St. Lawrence, the disparagement, the criticism, the pain? It had helped her grow. In the end, she did relate some of her more painful experiences to them, showing that these events could be turned into opportunities to practice perseverance and patience.

"Go out into the world and do your best in whatever job you might find," she encouraged them. "Maintain your rights at all times and never compromise your principles. You can succeed in spite of great difficulties. You must put your minds and talents to work and maintain a spirit of determination and independence."[3] She ended her talk by wishing them well in whatever work they might undertake. This philosophy had stood her in good stead and she was pleased to pass it on.

After her visit in Yellow Springs, she journeyed to northern Vermont where she would be spending her summer filling the pulpits of vacationing ministers. She stopped to visit her grandparents at Plymouth Notch, but these visits were always too short. She would have liked to spend the entire summer hiking the mountain trails, walking the meadows and visiting relatives, but she had work to do. She must gain experience preaching and what better place, she asked herself, than in the state where her parents were born and raised?

Olympia preached wherever she could find a pulpit that summer. She was determined to return to classes in the fall with the added advantage of several months of practical experience. This was an opportunity to preach many different kinds of sermons and to see what kind of responses she would get from conservative New Englanders. Knowing that most of the people in the congregation did not believe that women should be ministers, she preached sermons on justice, stressing the dignity and worth of every person, male and female. She tested many of her ideas on her audiences, soon learning the best ways to phrase words and evoke responses. When she returned to St. Lawrence in the fall, she knew that she had made the right choice in deciding to become a minister. Only in the ministry would she be able to get across many of her ideas.

Her second year at the theological school was pleasant and virtually trouble free. The two young men who had annoyed her during her first year did not return to classes. They had evidently decided that the ministry was not their calling. The other students accepted her completely and she was able to devote her full energies to her studies. The year slipped past quickly.

Early in 1863, she decided that it was time to begin steps toward her ordination. She knew that she was a good preacher because Mr. Fisher often commended her on her sermons. Seeking ordination, however, would be a different matter. It was a move that would likely cause strong opposition among faculty members, including Mr. Fisher. She had already broached the subject with him earlier in the year, and he had spoken strongly against it. When she learned that the Northern Universalist Association was meeting at Malone, New York, in the spring, she decided that she must go there. Malone was only fifty miles from Canton, an easy journey. She would go and ask the ordaining council to ordain her. It was, she felt, her only chance.

When President Fisher learned about Olympia's plan, he was surprised and somewhat dismayed. He tried very hard to dissuade her, but she would not change her mind. "You do not want to ordain me here at St. Lawrence because I am a woman, and you do not think it is appropriate for women to be in the ministry. You do not want to be responsible for being the first theological school to ordain a woman. I know that I will be left out of the class of students who are going to be ordained. I know that most of the professors oppose my ordination. But you must consider the fact that I have completed the theology courses here and I am as well qualified as any of the other candidates in my class. I am a woman and that makes all the difference. I won't change my mind about going to Malone."

She faced strong opposition in her quest, not only at St. Lawrence but also at Malone. After she arrived there, none of the professors would support her and several spoke out against her. She did not let that bother her. She fixed her eyes on her goal, argued her own case before the ordaining council, then waited for the outcome. At the end of her argument, she asked only that the board members be fair and impartial, and that they judge her solely on her merits, not on her sex. It was to her advantage that she had preached in the church in Heuvelton, New York, the week before. A member of that church was a delegate on the council. He had heard her preach, and he was well aware that the congregation in Heuvelton had asked her to be their minister. He was duly impressed with her qualifications and her appeal before the board. The council members knew that they would be setting a precedent if they agreed to ordain Olympia Brown. Never before had a denomination ordained a woman, and the decision was fraught with a degree of risk. There would be many who would condemn the action.

Olympia awaited their decision, wondering what she would do if the council rejected her request. What step would she take next? Renew her arguments with St. Lawrence officials? Go to Boston to plead her case before the president of the Universalist Association? She did not know, and she hoped that she would not have to continue the struggle. Fortunately, she did not have long to wait for her answer. When the council called her in for its decision, the chairman said simply, "Miss Brown, we have agreed to ordain you. Let us set the date now for your ordination ceremony." They agreed on the date, June 25, 1863, and Olympia, rejoicing in her victory, returned to St. Lawrence with the news.

Mr. Fisher may have been shocked by the council's decision, but he overcame his opposition to her ordination and magnanimously took part in the ceremony. His wife, however, expressed her personal opposition in strong words. "You will see now the consequence of this. Next year there will be fifteen women in the class and then women will flock to the ministry," she said disapprovingly, insinuating thereby that women would lower the quality of the profession.

Olympia hoped that women would, indeed, "flock to the ministry," but she learned that others did not share her enthusiasm. Another woman at the ceremony complained that the profession would soon be swamped with women and this would bring down the price of preaching. One young male student commented, "If Miss Brown seeks an appointment to preach, there will be a gradual turning up of noses."[4]

The practice of belittling and begrudging any woman's achievements was so ingrained that women responded without even questioning such an unfair attitude. That women needed encouragement from members of their own sex was a thought that did not seem to enter their minds.

Perhaps women were simply envious of her accomplishments. Most of them had never had the opportunity to make choices in their own lives. Now they suddenly glimpsed possibilities that would never be theirs. Their education was limited. They had married and centered their lives on their husbands and children. They could not hope to reach a different goal in their lifetime, and resentment and envy came to the fore. There was no immediate answer to the dilemma, but higher education for women would solve the problem, Olympia believed.

Having received her ordination, it was only natural that her thoughts turned to Antoinette Brown, the woman who had inspired her ten years before. Olympia was momentarily dismayed to learn that she had married Samuel Blackwell and given up her public work to devote herself to her family. Although Mrs. Blackwell had broken barriers by completing the theology course at Oberlin College and by accepting the pulpit of a church in South Butler, New York, she had resigned after only a year and changed her affiliation from Congregational to Unitarian. In doing so, she had failed to set a precedent because she did not return to the ministry. Nevertheless, Olympia held her in high esteem.

Now, however, Olympia believed that she herself must set the precedent of serving in a church as faithfully and steadfastly as a man. Perhaps, then, other denominations would take note and follow the lead of the Universalists in ordaining women ministers. Perhaps too, women would see that it was an ideal field of work for them.

After she received her diploma from St. Lawrence University on July 9, 1863, she turned her attention to finding a church. One of the professors, Mr. J. L. Lee, told her that she might find a parish in northern Vermont. "I understand that the Reverend Eli Ballou of Marshfield wishes to go to the northern part of the state. His congregation is looking for a pastor. Would you be interested in applying for the post?"

Visions of the Green Mountains sprang up before her eyes. She could visit her grandparents, aunts, uncles and cousins. She could walk her beloved fields and trails again, renew old family ties. She could ask for nothing better! "Of course. I would love to go to Vermont," she said.

When she arrived in Marshfield, the trustees of the church were astonished to learn that the Reverend O. Brown was a woman. She smiled at their consternation and assured them that she was an ordained minister and had preached many sermons. Their reply, however, was terse, reflecting their staid dispositions and giving her cause for second thoughts. "You can preach a sermon on Sunday. If the congregation likes you, they will hire you. If not, you will have to find another church."

Her sermon must have been more than adequate for the people in the church voted to let her fill the pulpit. Pleased that she now had a church, at least for the summer months, she set out the next day to find a place where she could board and room. She made her way around the entire village but to no avail. It seemed that no one wanted a woman minister as a boarder. Their response stunned her. How could they accept her as a teacher and spiritual guide yet deny her a place to live among their own families? Perhaps she had been wrong in coming to Marshfield after all. What was she to do?

Troubled and disillusioned, she was on her way back to the hotel when a buggy suddenly drew up beside her, dust billowing up behind the rig. "Is this Miss Brown?" a woman called out as she brought the buggy to a halt.

Olympia looked up in surprise. "Yes," she said, staring up at the first pleasant face she had seen in Marshfield.

"I'm Mrs. Smith. My husband said you wouldn't get a boarding place in town. Would you like to board in the country with us?"

"I would love to board anywhere!" Olympia cried, and she climbed gratefully into the buggy. She found Mr. Smith to be as good-natured as his wife. He was known in the neighborhood simply as "Barefooted Smith" because he wore no shoes in the fields. Theirs was a congenial family and Olympia stayed with them the entire time she served the Marshfield pastorate.[5]

Olympia soon realized that she had time to prepare more than one sermon a week, and she began to wonder if there was another village nearby where she could preach. "I suppose you'd find a willing congregation in East Montpelier," Mrs. Smith suggested. "We could drive over there and find out. It's only eight or nine miles." When they went to investigate the possibility of holding services there, Olympia thought that it would be worthwhile and she made the arrangements. Throughout the summer and early fall, the two women drove by horse and buggy to East Montpelier early every Sunday morning and waited for the congregation

61

to gather there. Olympia preached her sermon and then they drove back to Marshfield where she preached her second sermon. Both congregations were small, but she found that serving two churches satisfied her for a time.

Although the people came to hear her preach, they remained personally aloof and unresponsive, and she worried that she was, somehow, failing them. The thought that they might be failing her did not seem to cross her mind at the time. Doubtless, their aloofness was due to the fact that she was a woman minister, and they could not adjust to such an anomaly. Although she was disappointed in their response to her, she tried to make the best of it.

During her ministry in the Marshfield area, she received several letters from Susan B. Anthony asking if she could help in woman's rights work. The letters stirred a conflict within her. She wanted to work for woman's rights, but she had studied long and hard to become a preacher. Her first duty, she felt, lay with the ministry, and so she declined until a later time.

Many changes were taking place in the Brown family since she had left Yellow Springs two years before. Her sister Oella had married and moved to Chicago. Marcia, after graduating from Antioch in 1862, went away to teach school. She eventually settled in Kansas. Arthur graduated the very year that Olympia was ordained, and he had already enrolled in law school at the University of Michigan in Ann Arbor. Her mother wrote and told her that they had decided to sell their house in Yellow Springs and move back to Michigan. They bought a house in Kalamazoo where they could be near their old friends and family members still in Schoolcraft.

When fall came, Olympia received an urgent letter from her mother. Arthur had suffered a severe attack of inflammatory rheumatism and Lephia had hurried to Ann Arbor to take care of him. She asked Olympia to come and help her. Alarmed at the news of her brother's illness, Olympia immediately resigned her two pastorates and prepared to go to Michigan. Both congregations asked her to return when her brother was well, but she declined, saying that she wanted to serve a larger church.

While she was busy helping her mother care for Arthur, Olympia's thoughts often turned to the problem of finding another parish. She decided to write a letter to Antoinette Brown Blackwell telling her about some of the discrimination she had experienced in Vermont and asking her for advice. Olympia wrote, "People do not readily accept a woman minister," a truth which Mrs. Blackwell must have agreed with at once, "but I thought perhaps you might know of a church where I can preach."

Mrs. Blackwell's reply, while warm and encouraging, was not quite what Olympia expected. "You do not need to preach in a Universalist pulpit," she wrote. "As long as you have oneness of general views and well-grounded convictions of your own, you can preach wherever you find a pulpit." Mrs. Blackwell encouraged her to go out and preach to people no matter what their faith. "To be forever talking to those who believe precisely as we do may be to edification, but it was not Christ's way who was always seeking to save the lost."[6]

Olympia did not completely agree with Mrs. Blackwell. She was determined to preach and serve in a Universalist church. Preaching to the general public or to those with a differing philosophy may be challenging, she felt, but she had many new thoughts to cast before members of her own denomination. She would have to wait until Arthur was well before seeking a parish, but she decided to read and go to lectures at the University in the interim, for she could not bear to waste time.

One day she attended a lecture by a Dr. Dio Lewis of Boston. His views on physical education for women were new and considered quite radical. Why did women need physical education, people were asking? Understandably, men needed such exercises to help them build strong bodies, but women? Women were frail by nature. It was the customary argument of the upper classes who completely ignored, or perhaps were ignorant of, the millions of women working in factories or on the land— the farm women, the homemakers without hired help.

Many young women attended the lecture, Olympia noted, pleasantly surprised. Dio Lewis had a gymnasium in Boston where he taught exercises which not only made women feel better but improved their health, he claimed. Many young women were entering his program. He described some of the exercises and Olympia listened closely, so impressed that she went up and talked to him afterward.

"I've been told that my voice is too soft and high-pitched for public speaking. I am a minister, and I must find a way to improve it. It seems that people in the back of the church have difficulty understanding what I say. Would your exercises help?"

Dio Lewis smiled. There was no doubt in his mind that he could improve her voice with his exercises. "Of course," he said. "We have exercises that will develop your chest and lungs. We can teach you how to breathe so that you can lower your voice and learn how to project it. And we have elocution teachers who can help you."

Olympia had her next goal. She would go to Boston as soon as Arthur was well. The winter months passed slowly for her because Arthur did not improve quickly. Although he never completely recovered from the effects of the illness, he was able to renew his studies in the spring. Lephia returned to Kalamazoo and Olympia set out for Boston.

The city delighted her with its noise and bustle. Every day became a new adventure for her. She enrolled at once in Dio Lewis's gymnasium classes and began the exercises that were to develop her shoulders and chest. When she was not at the gymnasium, she was exploring the city. On Saturdays, the students had to attend a lecture, the purpose of which was to "help stimulate your intellect," they were told. The lecture was invariably delivered by some prominent man. Most of them, Olympia found, were garrulous and boring. She learned to sit through the talks in silence, then leave to pursue her own interests.

One Saturday, however, she behaved in a most irregular manner. It happened after a Mr. A. Bronson Alcott, renowned New England intellectual, gave a speech. She noted that he seemed to be much more concerned with his appearance and mannerisms than with what he was saying. He began his talk, "Men and Women," speaking in a slow, authoritative voice—"apparently his idea of how a philosopher should speak," Olympia wrote later in telling the story. She prepared to listen carefully to such an interesting subject.

"Men are all thought and women are all sentiment," Mr. Alcott said, then he immediately pointed out that there were many exceptions, of course. "There are as many masculine minds in feminine bodies as feminine minds in masculine bodies," he declared, and he tried to explain this theory to the class during the rest of the lecture. At the end, he invited questions from the students. No one seemed to want to ask any and Mr. Alcott appeared to be genuinely disappointed. "My lecture must have been a failure if no one has any questions," he said. "Surely you have one or two."

Olympia, smiling to herself, raised her hand at this point. "How did you arrive at your belief?" she asked. "If there are as many masculine minds in feminine bodies as feminine minds in masculine bodies, isn't it possible that the principle is wrong since there are so many exceptions?"

The great man stared at her a moment, frowned, then shuffled his papers together. "Some women like to argue and that proves the rule," he said. "I think I have talked enough." With that he turned and left.[7] She had aimed her point so precisely that Mr. Alcott was left bewildered and exasperated. Cutting to the heart of a speech was already an art with Olympia.

Mr. T. F. Leonard, a noted elocution teacher, became her favorite instructor. Although most people ridiculed elocution lessons, Olympia firmly believed in them. "The voice can be improved as well as any other part of the body," she argued. "All it takes is instruction and practice."

She well remembered what the Reverend Eli Ballou of Marshfield wrote about her the year before. "Her voice is now pleasant & distinct but lacks for volume or bulk & does not seem to fill the room although everyone understands her," he noted.[8]

How his words had stung! "Some day," she vowed, "I'll be heard in every corner of a church or hall. People are going to hear and understand every word I say." She worked every day practicing diction, doing breathing exercises and practicing voice control. Thus she began her program of developing a voice that gained her national renown as an orator in a few years.

Olympia decided to visit with the Reverend A. A. Miner, head of the Universalist Association headquartered in Boston. Perhaps he could help her find a parish, she thought. He welcomed her and they had a pleasant visit, but when she asked him if he knew of a church that needed a minister, he responded in a most negative manner. "I do not believe that it is in the nature of women to become preachers," he said. Of course, he did not oppose them, either, he assured her.

Olympia urged him to reconsider. Women were particularly well-suited to the ministry, especially in their roles as homemakers and mothers she pointed out. The ministry led to a life of usefulness and holiness such as she had not anticipated when she first began studying for the profession. She had expected to find some prejudice against women's preaching, but it had been far stronger than she anticipated, she told him. "We must change that attitude, and I believe it will change as more women become preachers." Reverend Miner had given little thought to the matter, she could see. Now, however, with the opinion of an ordained woman minister to consider, he might come to reconsider his views.

Reverend Miner relented and told her that a church in the little town of Weymouth Landing just south of Boston had been without a minister for many months. Perhaps she should go there and apply for the position, he suggested. Olympia made arrangements at once to go to Weymouth Landing and give a sermon. The trustees of the church were as brusque as their counterparts in Vermont. "You can preach one Sunday on trial," they told her. "If the congregation likes you, you can stay." Although somewhat taken aback by this abrupt proposal, Olympia prepared and delivered a fine sermon. The congregation voted overwhelmingly to hire her and offered her a salary of five hundred dollars a year. She was pleased with this offer and delighted to have her own church at last. The formal installation ceremony was on July 8, 1864, a memorable day for her and for her mother too, who had put so much effort and hope into her children's education.[9]

Olympia was to remain in Weymouth Landing for five years, a busy, happy time for her.

After the installation, newspapers across the country carried the story since there were still no other ordained woman ministers in the United States. In Vermont, the Montpelier newspaper carried an article noting that she had served two parishes in that area, one at Marshfield and one at

65

East Montpelier. Both parishes had asked her to stay, the reporter wrote.

She possessed good talents and acquirements; and her energy, conscientious faithfulness, and perseverance in the discharge of duty, give her the elements of success in her chosen vocation. She has no enemies in this section, and is deeply respected and beloved on account of her kind, amiable disposition, her deep sympathy with bereaved mourners and sorrowing hearts, and her many excellent qualities and Christian virtues.[10]

Olympia read the article with some surprise. How could the people who had been unwilling to take her into their homes as a boarder now claim that she was "respected and beloved"? It was true that they had been willing to accept spiritual comfort from her, but they had given virtually nothing of themselves in return. She was fast learning the eccentricities of human beings.

She was learning other lessons, too. One day she solemnized a marriage, and the next day the townspeople were complaining that the marriage was not legal. The reason? It was performed by a woman. Disgusted by such complaints, she petitioned the Massachusetts legislature asking that marriages performed by a women be made legal and learned that marriages solemnized by women were already legal.[11] She put that information in the local newspaper. There were no further complaints.

The former minister of the church still lived in town, and Olympia soon heard that he was involved in spiritualism. He held regular seances in his home and claimed that he communicated with the dead. Several former church members attended the sessions regularly. Olympia began to wonder if she might be able to bring the former members back into the church if she went to visit them, and so she tried. They, however, were not to be swayed. "We could never belong to an established church again. Spiritualism is our religion now," they insisted. Their fervor was so ardent that she began to wonder just what they saw in the practice. Although she did not personally believe in spiritualism, the practice was enjoying a sudden popularity in the nation and she recognized its strength. Perhaps, she thought, she should attend some of the seances and see if communication after death really did take place. More likely, she thought, the people were being duped.

She asked the former pastor if he had any objection to her coming to some of their meetings. When he appeared to hesitate, she assured him, "I am very liberal in my ideas." He thereupon extended an invitation to her, perhaps thinking that he might be gaining another convert. Olympia was surprised to find that all of the people who came appeared to be honest, sincere individuals, most of whom truly believed in the phenomenon of communication with the dead. Trying to keep an open mind so that she could take part in their spiritual communication, she found that she could not believe any such thing actually took place during the seances. The matter troubled her deeply. She thought that the people were being duped by the medium, but nothing she said would change their minds. It was a fad that had to run its course, she decided. Few people can be logical about such an emotional issue, particularly those who have recently lost a loved one.

Aside from this problem of spiritualism in the community, she was happy with her church work. Her parishioners were broadminded, charitable people, many of whom often traveled to Boston to attend lectures. Olympia soon began to consider the idea of bringing lecturers to the church. "We could invite the townspeople to come and hear them. It would be good for the church and the community," she argued. She won her point. The church soon became widely known for its intellectual programs. People came to hear Maria Chapman, William Lloyd Garrison, Wendell Phillips, Henry C. Wright, Ralph Waldo Emerson and many other well-known speakers. It was a time of great joy for her. She felt that she was accomplishing something, making a difference in the community.

On occasion Olympia could be candid, perhaps even blunt. Some people called her totally outspoken, others labeled her frank, while a few claimed she was sometimes just thoughtless. Perhaps she was a combination of all three traits. One particular incident revealed her typical response to questions she felt should not even be asked.

Ralph Waldo Emerson had given a lecture at the church, and he stayed overnight at his cousin's home in Weymouth Landing. Olympia was invited to tea there the next day. He was a noted conversationalist as well as lecturer and Olympia looked forward to the visit. Mr. Emerson held the guests spellbound for most of the afternoon. At length the talk turned to woman suffrage, and he remarked that he believed in the principle. "But I'm puzzled to find that the women whose opinions I most value and respect are opposed to it," he commented thoughtfully. He then turned to Olympia. "Have you not found this to be so?" he asked.

She had not yet mastered the arts of tact and diplomacy, and her words rushed forth, "I should not value the opinion of any woman who was opposed to woman suffrage." Audible gasps of surprise followed her remark. Too late she realized that her statement was regarded as heresy by the group, yet in her heart she knew that she had spoken the truth. She gave everyone in the room something to think about that afternoon, including the esteemed Mr. Emerson.[12]

President Lincoln was assassinated on April 14, 1865, less than a year after Olympia was installed as pastor of the church in Weymouth Landing. The ministers of all the Weymouth churches met to organize a united memorial service. Early in the meeting, several of the ministers said that they had changed their minds and excused themselves from the group. Olympia suddenly realized that these men of God did not wish to unite in a service with a woman minister. With consummate composure, she rose from her chair and faced the group of men.

"The Universalist Church will hold its own memorial service," she announced, and without another word left their meeting. She had not expected such prejudice among *these* ministers of Weymouth Landing, many of whom she knew. Again, she saw that these men did not necessarily believe what they preached. How long would she have to cope with such behavior, she wondered? Years? A lifetime?

The Weymouth congregation increased her salary to six hundred dollars the following year. Then, after finding that the "subscription for preaching" (the pledges by the members of the congregation) brought in more money than they expected, they offered her an additional hundred dollars.

She was happy in her work and enjoyed the intellectual atmosphere in the village. Here for the first time, she could develop her own ideas, for nothing else divided her time and energy. She enjoyed a freedom that she had never had before. Her family was far away and made no claims on her. Here too, she first met John Henry Willis, a member of the church and the board of trustees—and the man she later married. Olympia had no thoughts of marriage at this time for she was wholly occupied with her ministry and she was becoming involved in woman's rights work.

During the Civil War years, women had given up their equal rights efforts and put all of their energies into war work. They had fully expected to be rewarded by being given the ballot as soon as peace came, but that did not happen. Many women were bitterly disappointed when Congress continued to ignore their demands, and a new movement for woman's rights began.

Susan B. Anthony was in the forefront of this new movement. The group organized a woman's rights convention to be held in New York City in 1866. Miss Anthony wrote a letter to Olympia inviting her to attend the convention. There would be many famous speakers, she wrote, and Olympia might think about giving a speech herself. It was an exciting prospect and Olympia decided that she must go.

Turning to her wardrobe, of which she normally gave little thought, she stared at her clothing in dismay. She was looking at it as if for the first time. Most of the dresses appeared to be old and shabby. "Just like a minister's clothes," she mused. If she was to go to New York City, she must have something new to wear. A shopping trip to Boston was the only answer.

Olympia's favorite color was a dark plum red—a family tradition, she claimed—but it was not a suitable color for a minister. She lovingly fingered the bright fabrics, then turned aside and selected an appropriately drab-colored dress of crepe-marette, a silk and wool material much in fashion. She also found a cape and bonnet that matched the dress in color. The bonnet had a little pink rose on one side. Perhaps it looked all right for someone attending a woman's rights convention, but she knew she would have to take the rose off when she got back home. Ministers did not wear frills. Then, at the last minute, she spied a little silk umbrella. Although the price was twelve dollars, she must have it. Having spent that much money, it seemed only fitting that she buy a new traveling bag to go with her new outfit, so she bought a twenty-five dollar valise. It was well beyond her means, but what was money when preparing for her first woman's rights convention!

The date of the convention arrived at last and Olympia took a train to New York. She had never been to New York City before and she had no idea of where she should stay. Looking over a listing of hotels, she selected one that sounded literary and distinguished, the Irving House. Fortunately, it was both comfortable and within walking distance of the Church of the Puritans where the woman's rights meeting was to be held.

She rose early on the morning of the convention and enjoyed a leisurely breakfast before walking to the church. When she arrived, there was no one about the building yet, so she walked around to the side of the church. There, spread across the wall in big letters, she saw the sign, WOMAN'S RIGHTS CONVENTION HERE TODAY. She stood several minutes, staring up at the sign, overwhelmed with the thoughts that ran through her mind. How long would it be before women had equal rights, before they could vote or hold jobs that now only men held? Surely justice would be done soon now that women were demanding equal rights, now that they were bringing their problems before Congress. She could not believe that Congress would refuse to grant them voting rights—and after voting rights, the other rights would surely follow.

Turning slowly away from the church, she walked to a little park across the street where she could sit down and think. She knew that educating people was the answer. Few realized the subordinate position of women. Even women themselves accepted it. It was their lot, a position reinforced by the Bible, and therein lay its great strength. At this time however, she could not foresee that the church would be one of the major antagonists women would have to face in their long battle for equality.

It was a momentous day for her. She heard many speakers whose

69

names she had often seen in newspapers: Susan B. Anthony, Elizabeth Cady Stanton, Henry Ward Beecher, Theodore Tilton, Parker Pillsbury, Wendell Phillips, Frederick Douglass and many more. She would come to know them well some day. Perhaps Elizabeth Cady Stanton, who gave the main talk the first day, impressed her the most. Although Mrs. Stanton read her speech from a manuscript instead of speaking extemporaneously, her convictions and eloquence held the audience spellbound.

In the afternoon, Olympia met with a group of reformers. Together they organized the American Equal Rights Association founded to work for both women and Negros' rights. On the second day, Olympia gave her first woman's rights speech. She was beginning to realize now how much work lay ahead and that it would not be an easy victory. Nevertheless, she remained optimistic and believed that change would come quickly.

After she returned to Weymouth Landing, she thought often about the convention, the people she had met, and what they had said in their speeches. Many times she recalled those speakers who had carried only a few notes up to the platform and delivered a fine, well-organized address. Why couldn't she do that? She was writing two sermons a week and sometimes a speech in addition to that, and it was taking too much of her time. She must learn to speak extemporaneously, she decided. Accordingly, she began writing her sermons in notes, half-phrases and partial sentences, and she practiced speaking from them for hours. She worked on her ideas, diction and voice control. In a few months she had mastered the techniques. After that she did not have to write out her sermons or speeches before giving them, but she did continue to write articles and essays for publication.

A woman's rights meeting was held early in the summer of 1866 in Albany, New York. Olympia went to this one, too, eager to meet new reformers and learn more about the movement. It was here that she met Lucy Stone, who was already a noted activist. Although Lucy Stone was married to Henry Blackwell, she refused to adopt his name. This was a most unusual act and Olympia was curious about her reasons. She found Lucy Stone to be a spirited, independent woman eager to talk on the issues of customs and woman's rights.

When Olympia asked her why she had kept her own name, she replied quickly, "My own name is part of my identity and I won't give it up or change it. There is no law requiring a woman to take her husband's name. It is a matter of custom going back to the time when women were considered property, much like slaves were before the war. Taking the husband's name means ownership. I won't bear such a stigma," she said.

She did not stop there. She also told Olympia that she opposed the custom of calling unmarried women "Miss." "A woman should be called

'Mrs.' as soon as she reaches maturity," she said. "Unmarried men are not designated by such a prefix. Why should we do so to women and not men?" Olympia found that just conversing with Mrs. Stone was a singular, consciousness-raising experience, and she had to agree with much of her philosophy.

During that summer and fall she attended several other such conventions and found herself being drawn further into the cause. When Susan B. Anthony asked her to accompany a small group of reformers on a six-week campaign for equal rights in New York State, Olympia asked for a short leave of absence from her church and joined them. This was her first campaign for equal rights. She would get to make many speeches and even arrange some meetings, Miss Anthony promised. The four people in the group were Susan B. Anthony; Parker Pillsbury, a noted activist; Francis Remond, a Negro reformer; and herself. Lucy Stone and Henry Blackwell began the campaign with them, but left to start work in Kansas for an equal rights amendment.

The group gained wide publicity in the newspapers. A headline in *The World*, December 8, 1866, reads:

SHALL WOMEN VOTE. THE GREAT EQUAL RIGHTS MOVEMENT—MEETING OF THE ASSOCIATION YESTERDAY. ADDRESSES BY S. B. ANTHONY, H. B. BLACKWELL, MISS (BESSIE) BISBIE, MRS. STONE, REV. OLYMPIA BROWN, AND OTHERS.

Olympia Brown's speech was fervent, the reporter stated, and she was in favor of the *rights of colored women*.[13] Olympia noted that, although she did say those words, she said much more. She was including all women in her speech, but the reporter failed to mention that. She was fast learning that reporters took statements out of context, sometimes deliberately altered the meaning of words, and usually wrote in a style most likely to gain readers' attention. They seldom wrote to educate people, she noted ruefully.

She slipped easily into her role of reformer. This was her forte. It did not take her long to start educating women as to their state of subjugation and telling them to start developing their minds and talents. They were, she said, independent persons, not an extension of their husbands. Such an idea was revolutionary to many in the audience, and distressing to both men and women. She had so much to say on the subject that she had difficulty limiting her speeches.

It was not long before she discovered that she and Mr. Remond disagreed on a number of points. He believed implicitly that there was far

71

more injustice done to the Negro man than to women. Olympia challenged that belief. A far greater injustice was done to Negro women because they were subject to Negro men as well as white domination, she claimed. She and Mr. Remond debated the issue a number of times, but they never did reach an agreement. Both, however, agreed that lack of education was a major problem for many people, and as long as the white male considered himself superior to women and Negroes, there would be problems.

The public meetings were arranged by Miss Anthony most of the time, but Olympia found opportunities to arrange a few herself. She met many interesting people as they traveled and spoke in the various towns, but the highlight came when they reached the northern part of New York State. "We are going to spend a few days visiting Elizabeth Cady Stanton," Miss Anthony told her. "I find her a great help to me in this work. Whenever I have an idea, I share it with Elizabeth. She thinks about it, sounds it out, then gives me her opinion or else sets about developing it. Sometimes I take care of her children so she can go off upstairs and work on it." Olympia realized, in that brief visit, how well the two women worked together. They would surely make a formidable team. Perhaps someday she could work with them. She was already learning many practical steps in the campaign, and her hope was to be able to organize and conduct campaigns on her own.

The group was still touring New York State when a letter arrived from Lucy Stone. She and her husband were campaigning in Kansas for women's voting rights. "An impartial suffrage amendment is going to be submitted to Kansas voters in the fall election!" she wrote in a hurried scrawl. This news electrified the small band of reformers. Mrs. Stone also described some of their experiences and the frontier country through which they were traveling. She ended her letter with the comment, "We have promised to send a speaker from the east to help the Kansas workers during the summer months and into the fall."

If the amendment passed, both women and Negroes would be allowed to vote in Kansas. It would be the first state in the nation to pass such a law. Miss Anthony, excited about the prospect and what it would mean to the equal rights movement, mused about the work that lay ahead in Kansas. Although she speculated on what speaker might be available to tour the state during the coming summer months, none of them dreamed that the adventure would fall to Olympia Brown, least of all Olympia herself. She could not have imagined that in six months' time she would be criss-crossing a frontier state where Indians still fought battles on the open plains and raided homesteading families.

72

Chapter 5

Kansas Campaign—
A Frontier Adventure

Lucy Stone went to Weymouth Landing in the spring of 1867 to visit Olympia Brown. It was shortly after she and her husband returned east from their Kansas tour. Olympia was pleasantly surprised and honored by the visit, but she could not help wondering if Mrs. Stone hoped to engage her in another campaign or ask her to assist in organizing a convention somewhere. Lucy Stone, after all, was a dynamic reformer.

She was a handsome woman. Her dark brown hair, parted in the middle and pulled back over her ears, was fastened in a soft bun at the back of her neck, a popular fashion at that time. The style accented her oval face, large eyes and firm chin. Olympia wore hers in much the same style.

Mrs. Stone talked in great detail about her Kansas tour. She and her husband had spent weeks traveling and organizing suffrage campaigns around the state. Two amendments to the Kansas Constitution were being put before the voters in the fall election, she said. One of them would allow Negro men to vote; the other would enfranchise women.

Mrs. Stone, believing that the voters would ratify the amendments, said, "The mood is right. Kansas is a new country. Every day more pioneer families pour into the state. Women face the same dangers as men. There are Indians, wolves, storms, prairie fires, sickness and death. How can men refuse the vote to them when they risk their lives right out on the prairie beside them?"

Olympia's excitement grew as she listened to her describe the Kansas prairie and life as a pioneer out on the plains. The country was a great sweep of rolling grassland, Mrs. Stone said, with hardly a tree to be seen except along river banks. Most pioneers built sod houses because there was so little wood. The sod houses proved to be remarkably well-suited to the climate, warmer in the winter and cooler in the summer than frame houses. Cooking meals and keeping warm were particularly difficult

73

because the only fuel they had was buffalo dung, called "buffalo chips." Mrs. Stone explained that the women and children went out on the prairie with a wheelbarrow or small wagon, sometimes walking for miles before they filled it with dried dung.

Traveling in Kansas was an adventure, she laughed, and went on to tell of some of her experiences. There were almost no roads and travelers had to find their own way around the country. Unfortunately, most of the residents were vague about directions and many people became lost, sometimes for hours out on the prairie. At night, travelers often had to stay with a homesteading family. The weather was unpredictable. When it rained, streams filled up so quickly that it was often dangerous to try and cross them. With no bridges, travelers forded rivers and creeks as best they could.

As Mrs. Stone talked about the frontier towns and villages and the families in the lonely little settlements and homesteads, Olympia began to recall her own early days on the farm in Michigan. She could almost see the land, feel the wind on her face, smell the freshly turned earth.

At last, after her carefully orchestrated introduction, Lucy Stone came to the crux of her visit. The Republican party wanted an experienced speaker to travel around the state of Kansas during the summer and campaign for woman suffrage. None of the women workers in the east could go, she said. They all had families or commitments of one kind or another. Then she asked the question. Could Olympia go to Kansas and campaign for the cause?

Olympia had been longing to do something significant for woman's rights. Clearly this was a wonderful opportunity, but could she spend an entire summer out on the Kansas prairie and away from her church duties? She could not answer at once. Certainly she would have to think about it, and she would also have to get permission from her church. Perhaps they might grant her a leave of absence, she said, but she did not know.

Mrs. Stone now advanced her final argument. The Republican party had promised a conveyance and a traveling companion for the prospective speaker. Miss Bisbie, with whom she had already campaigned in New York State, was to be the companion. "There will be a ten to fifteen-mile ride between meetings, and there is beautiful countryside to see. The speakers' names will be advertised, and churches or halls will be ready when you arrive. Friends will receive you in each place," she said. The two women would only have to speak and keep the issue before the voters during the summer months. In September, Susan B. Anthony and Elizabeth Cady Stanton would come to Kansas to campaign. "Then," Mrs. Stone assured her, "you will only speak at the Republican meetings around the state."[1]

Mrs. Stone made it all sound so easy. Four months was a long time to be away from her church, but perhaps her congregation would allow her a vacation, especially if she was to work for such a worthy cause. She could not go until July, even though the Republican party had asked for a speaker to come out in June. "I'm scheduled to speak at Antioch during graduation ceremonies the last of June. I couldn't do anything until the first of July," she said, shaking her head.

Lucy Stone brightened. "You will be over half way to Kansas when you are in Yellow Springs, Olympia. It just might be that you were meant to campaign in the west," she affirmed.

In the end, Olympia agreed to talk to the trustees, and they granted her permission to go. Over the next few weeks, both Lucy Stone and Henry Blackwell sent letters to her brimming with news and advice about the climate, what she should eat and drink, and the kind of clothing she should take. Mrs. Stone was a practical traveler and she wrote, "Take only two dresses, a dark one in which to travel and lecture, and one nice dress to wear when you are in the cities. Kansas women and men are plain. The women come to lectures in calico gowns and Shaker bonnets."

Henry Blackwell's advice was more specific. "Drink as little water as possible in Kansas. Drink tea or coffee instead." He was giving her good advice because there was the ever-present danger of typhoid fever from polluted water. He also told her to eat fruits in moderation, pies and cakes sparingly. "Stick to meat & bread & potatoes—avoid much grease & don't get *chilled* at night & morning & avoid as far as possible direct exposure to the hot sun. Kansas is a very healthy country & traveling is more conducive to health than settling in one place."

This was rather unusual advice, but Olympia surmised that Mr. Blackwell was probably trying to reassure her that traveling was healthy and she had no need to worry. He had begun his letter with frank and sincere advice to her, but she sensed a change as she read through the letter. It seemed to her that he was beginning to have second thoughts about sending a Universalist minister on a political campaign.

"And now let me say a word in regard to the nature of the work you are undertaking," he wrote. "It is different from any you have hitherto done. It is *political*—your business is to *win votes for women*."

Such remarks did not set well with Olympia, and she could not but resent his assumption that she did not know the goal of the campaign or how to conduct it. She had spent six weeks working in the state of New York for woman suffrage just a few months earlier! She understood the issues very well.

The voters are Methodist, Baptist, Presbyterian, Congregational, Catholic—hardly any of them Universalist or Unitarian. Many of your strongest friends are orthodox ministers & orthodox people. By getting women a vote, you will do more to destroy sectarianism and emancipate the human soul than by any other means under heaven. But to do this, don't allude to theology—don't preach—don't call yourself a minister at all. You are Olympia Brown, an American Citizen—a woman and a human being.

Olympia was dismayed at such advice. She was proud of being a minister and she would let people know that she was prepared to preach whenever and wherever they wished, in addition to carrying on the campaign for suffrage, no matter what Mr. Blackwell's advice might be. His letter continued in the same vein.

Remember that our enemies are numerous & unscrupulous. Every liquor seller & drinker in Kansas will seize any opportunity to raise the cry of 'infidel' & this they ought not be allowed...Again, we want the vote of the Democrats . . . to offset the vote of those Republicans who think a negro better than a woman. Therefore don't attack Democrats as such. But show the right of every citizen to vote, white or black, man or woman, & ask the people whether they are willing that their own wives & daughters should be ranked politically below the negro.[2]

It was obvious to Olympia that he did not know her well at all. He had written her in detail about matters that she already knew and understood. She was considerably more politically astute than many reformers and she had no intention of following his advice. She could not agree with his final comment, either: "The issue will never be submitted to the people anywhere again if we fail to get the vote in Kansas."

Olympia did not let these things bother her, however. She packed her valise carefully, keeping Lucy Stone's advice in mind. She would be traveling almost daily and the less clothing she packed, the easier her journey would be. The Weymouth Landing newspaper published a brief announcement stating that she had been granted a leave of absence for several weeks to work in Kansas "under the auspices of the Universalist Suffrage Society." Her congregation did not realize at the time that she would be gone for more than four months.

When she set out for Kansas, Olympia's heart was full of hope. There was no doubt in her mind that once Kansas led the way, other states would follow suit. She was convinced that she was going to help change history, that this would be the first step on the road to equal rights for women nationwide.

Her stop at Yellow Springs, Ohio, was brief. She visited old friends and then gave her speech, "Diversities of Gifts." It was the kind of speech that Olympia most liked to give, a speech in which she questioned her audience's attitudes and basic beliefs, challenging their preconceived ideas about life and how it should be lived. Many changes were coming, she said, and people must learn to accept new ideas.

Inhabitants of remote places become rigid in their beliefs when they have little contact with outside sources. They think that their customs and beliefs are the right ones, and that their own little community is the model for the world, the hub of the universe. They fear change. They are shocked when any of their young want to leave and seek their fortunes elsewhere.

Although she was addressing the graduating class and their families, she was also remembering her summer in Vermont and her tour of upper New York State. She had visited isolated villages and met individuals so rigid in their beliefs that they could not accept change of any kind. It was an unsettling experience for her, coming from an open-minded, liberal environment where change was an accepted fact of life.

She urged people to try and understand and absorb new ideas during their lifetimes.

There is great diversity among people. Many individuals, freed from hard manual labor, have time to read and think, to develop new talents and interests. They are no longer bound to a particular business or occupation simply because their father was; they can seek the work which they most enjoy... Women, too, have a diversity of talents which are going unused. They are as suited to work in the library, to study, to engage in business as they are to the parlor. They must be allowed to do these things. Both women and negroes must be allowed to develop their talents, to gain an education, to serve in the legislatures and the learned professions. All ... must be given a fair and equal opportunity to solve the problem of their own identity.

After her speech, the college presented her with an academic degree of Master of Arts, an act which gave her a profound sense of appreciation and a deep joy that her work was recognized.[3]

She was soon on the train once more, this time headed across Indiana, Illinois and Missouri bound for Kansas. It was the first time that she had seen any country west of Michigan and Ohio. She marveled at the vast landscapes. Rolling hills, flat prairies, wide rivers and patches of forest followed one another as far as her eyes could see. When she grew tired of the scenery, she turned her attention to reading or to contemplating the forthcoming campaign in Kansas. She knew her arguments well; there was little reason to worry about what she was going to say. Instead, she dreamed about all of the country that she was going to see. She had already heard about the tall prairie grass that sometimes grew well above peoples' heads. How did they find their way about the land? Would she see any Indians? She had read about entire tribes being relocated to the state of Oklahoma, but she had also read about massacres along the frontier. Perhaps, she tried to reassure herself, there weren't any Indians left in the state.

Olympia arrived in Leavenworth, Kansas, on July 1, 1867. The weather was hot and dry and the streets were dusty, but she had too much on her mind to pay attention to minor discomforts. She went immediately to see Colonel Coffin, who, she understood, was in charge of her speaking engagements for the summer. Fingering her letter of introduction from Susan B. Anthony carefully tucked in her pocket, she introduced herself.

"Olympia Brown?" Colonel Coffin cried, obviously astonished to see her. "Why did they not send Anna Dickinson? Anna Dickinson is the one we want here."⁴ Miss Dickinson, a noted orator and reformer in the east, had not been able to undertake the Kansas campaign.

Olympia, understandably disturbed at such a reception, retorted, "I am the only speaker available from the east and I am well prepared to canvass the state for the next four months. I am ready right now to begin. Have you arranged any meetings for me here in Leavenworth? I would like to see how the people respond to my message."

Faced with her quick response and overwhelming determination, Colonel Coffin hurriedly assured her that he had arranged several meetings. She soon had the opportunity to speak on voting rights for women and found the audience interested and attentive. The meetings were well-attended, indicating not only an awareness of but a concern for the issue. Her spirits rose. It was time to move on to her next engagement.

When she asked Colonel Coffin about the promised conveyance and traveling companion, he shook his head. He knew nothing about such an arrangement, he said. "You will have to take the train to Lawrence. I'll give you the names of some people there. Go and see them. They're the ones to talk to."

Puzzled by his response, nevertheless she took the next train to Lawrence. As soon as she arrived, she went to see the minister of the Unitarian Church. He and his family greeted her cordially, the first real act of friendliness that she had met in the state.[5] They held a successful meeting in the church. Then she asked about her conveyance and traveling companion so that she could continue on her way. The minister knew nothing about either and suggested that she take the train to Topeka. "I'll give you the names of some people there," he said. By now, Olympia was beginning to wonder where she would eventually find her conveyance and companion, and how many more times she would have to ride the train to the next town.

When she reached Topeka, she found it too was as hot and dusty as the other two had been. There she met Sam Wood, the man who actually was in charge of her tour. An energetic, rough, frontier man, he welcomed her cordially and immediately invited her to stay at his home. He told her many stories about his activities in the border- ruffian fighting along the Kansas-Missouri border a few years earlier. Pro-slavery men had ridden in, destroyed whole towns and killed entire families. Sam Wood had led fights against them.

Startled to realize that she would be campaigning in an area that had been under siege just two years before, Olympia asked Mr. Wood if it was safe to go out and hold meetings in the towns and villages near the border.

Mr. Wood laughed, pointing out that the Civil War was over and Kansas was civilized now. Hundreds of families had arrived and settled down on farms and in the towns in the area. New businesses were starting up, new houses were being built, and most towns already had a school. Noting that she was a minister, he told her that churches were being built, too. "Our people are friendly, Reverend Brown. You won't have any trouble finding a place to stay or a meal to eat."

Perhaps Olympia should have realized that something was amiss with that statement, but her thoughts were focused on her speaking engagements and the publicity for the coming campaign.

"All of the plans have been made," Mr. Wood assured her. "Posters have been printed and sent out all over the state. Newspapers have printed notices about when and where you will be speaking, and you will have good crowds." He also suggested that she could preach, too. There were few ministers in Kansas. Occasionally a circuit rider preacher would stop for a day or two, but people usually just got together to read the Bible and sing hymns. They would be glad to hear a sermon by a real preacher, he said. He then helped her arrange several meetings in the Topeka area. They, too, were well-attended and she was now feeling more confident and optimistic about campaigning around the state. The people appeared to be warm and friendly and eager to learn.

She now had her speaking schedule and it was time to leave for her next engagement. "Is my traveling companion here?" she asked. "And

I've been told you have a conveyance ready for me."

Mr. Wood did not answer her at once. Instead, he talked about other things, about people and the futility of human expectations, the failure to accomplish certain things no matter how well planned. At last he seemed to have gathered the courage to confess to her that the Republican party could not furnish either a traveling companion or a conveyance. They had run out of money, he said, but she was not to worry. He had personally written letters to many fine people where she would be traveling. They would provide meals for her and a place to sleep. There would also be someone to take her on to her next meeting place. All of the plans had been made, he reiterated, as if to assure her that all was well. She would have no problems.

Olympia listened to him in disbelief. Shock settled down over her like falling snow—cold, quiet, numbing. What was happening to her? She was a lone and inexperienced young woman fourteen hundred miles from home in an unsettled country where Indians still rode the western plains and raided frontier homesteads. She was at the mercy of the inhabitants of a strange land, and she had no idea of how the people would accept her. Was she to eat and sleep in their homes? Why had Lucy Stone told her such a different story? Was she among friendly people or would she face hostility, perhaps even violence?

It was an act of courage on her part that she did not simply turn around and go back to Weymouth Landing. However she may have felt, she decided that she would stay and campaign. It was a matter of honor with her. Besides, if Lucy Stone and her husband could canvass the state, so could she. She recalled then a letter in which Henry Blackwell mentioned that some of the Republican party leaders in Kansas had wanted to drop the issue of votes for women and work only for the Negro vote. "But Lucy and I carried our point," he had assured her. "All you have to do is enlighten and arouse the people."[6]

It looked, she thought, as though they had not carried their point after all. She began to suspect that the Republican party leaders were afraid to support a woman speaker and the ballot for women, in part because they feared the liquor interests. The cry was already sounding that woman suffrage would bring prohibition. Olympia could see that her campaign was going to be difficult at times, perhaps marred by antagonism and even hostility.

Sam Wood was true to his word. He provided a team of horses, a carriage and a driver to take her to her next meeting place. People were expecting her, he said; they would take care of her and drive her to the next meeting. "You have nothing to worry about," he assured her one more time.

80

She thanked him as best she could as the driver started the team toward the open prairie and they left Topeka in a cloud of dust. The hot dry season was already on the plains. Days and nights were often sweltering. Long skirts and petticoats added to the discomfort, but Olympia tried to ignore the heat and concentrate on her speaking schedule.

In only a few days, she realized that Sam Wood's schedule was going to be very difficult to keep. He either did not know or had forgotten how far apart many of the towns were. Often she had to get up at four o'clock in the morning, eat a hasty breakfast, then set out on an eight or ten hour drive to get to a meeting forty or fifty miles away. There were times when she had to ride in an open wagon with no springs. The hot wind blew across the prairie whipping the high, tough grasses, some reaching over her head, and bending them like fragile flower stems. Marveling at the vast sweep of grassland stretching as far as her eyes could see, she wondered how people could find their way when there were no roads or trails to be seen.

She soon learned that people simply drove in the general direction of a settlement, often not sure how far they had to go or even if they were going in the right direction. If they saw someone along the way, they would stop and ask directions. Many times her drivers became lost and they arrived late at a meeting. At first she worried, but she soon learned to accept the timelessness of the prairie. No one seemed to care when she was late. When she finally arrived, she found the people amusing themselves by singing, putting on their own program or just visiting. "Everyone gets lost on the prairie," they would laugh and then settle down to listen to her speech.

Kansans were hospitable people. There was always a family ready to give Olympia a meal and a place to sleep. Sometimes she had a room and a bed of her own; sometimes she had to share it with a child. Usually she slept on a bed with linens, but sometimes her hostess spread blankets on the floor for her. She slept in the loft of a log cabin and considered herself fortunate. There were times when she shared a bed in a family dugout or a sod house. Olympia learned that dugouts were common and the quickest means of shelter while the family waited to build a sod house. She listened to the stories of their arrival on the prairie. They simply looked about for a small hill. When they located one, they dug out an area large enough for living space, much like digging a cave. When the farmer could afford the time and money, he got a wagonload of wooden planks, then used them to line the walls and ceilings of the dugout. This kept the dirt from sifting down onto the floor and furniture. If they could not afford the wood, many pioneers tacked up blankets or pieces of muslin to help keep the dirt in place. The dugouts were cool in the summer and warm in the winter.

Olympia found their way of life fascinating. Her heart warmed to the pioneers and their resourcefulness. She always received a welcome wherever she went and an offer of a ride to her next meeting. "Strange as it may seem," she wrote, "I never failed to meet an appointment during the whole campaign."[7] She rode in many kinds of conveyances. Her drivers were farmers, frontier men, Indians, Negroes, businessmen, and sometimes families visiting relatives. Occasionally apprehensive, she tried to be practical and logical about her experiences.

She soon grew to love the rides as she criss-crossed the eastern half of the state. One day, however, she faced a long journey across the prairie in a lumber wagon with an Indian driver. The local townspeople assured her that he was an honest and reliable man. Nevertheless, she felt a chill of apprehension as she climbed into the back of the wagon and they started off across the great tract of land. She looked about her at the bright metallic sky and the yellowish-brown grass turning dry in the hot wind. She could not see a tree, a field or a house anywhere. The only sound was the creak of the wooden wagon, the thump of the horses' hooves on the sod, the hiss of the wind through the grass. Did the Indian know the way? Could he be trusted? She stared at the straight, dark back of the figure seated before her in the front of the wagon. What had his childhood been like? Had he ever been a warrior, perhaps scalping an enemy? What kind of life did he lead now? Suddenly, as if he could feel her eyes upon him, he turned around and looked at her. "Why don't you get married?" he asked abruptly.

Olympia turned away, startled and a little angry. Why should she discuss the subject with him? "I could see that his idea of woman's sphere was precisely the same as Colonel (Theodore) Roosevelt . . . and other refined men of our day," she remarked later.[8] When she didn't answer, he turned and drove the rest of the way in silence. Relief flooded through her when they topped a low rise, and there before them lay the town where she was scheduled to speak. Never did the dusty road and a scattering of buildings look so sweet to her as they did at that moment.

Another time, an old gentleman asked her to hold a special meeting in his home. He promised to drive her on to her next appointment afterward, so she agreed. He invited all of his neighbors to come and hear her. The house was full. True to his word, he hitched up his horse and a rickety old buggy and drove her to her next meeting. They reached the village at nine o'clock that night. No one there could take her on, so he stayed. The following day he drove her to her next engagement. He worried about his chores back home, but he worried even more at the idea of leaving her without a driver, so he continued to drive her around for several days.

"Go back and take care of your sorghum," she finally begged him. "You left it boiling in the kettle. These people will find a driver for me."

She finally persuaded him to go, assuring him that someone would take her on to her next meeting rather than have her stranded upon them. Reluctantly, he turned his horse around and trotted back across the prairie, his buggy rattling plaintively across the sod.

She had sincere words of gratitude for her many drivers during her tour. "There was not one instance on the part of those men of rudeness or discourtesy or anything but utmost kindness and apparent interest in the success of the campaign," she wrote.

Olympia was traveling primarily over the eastern section of Kansas because the central and western parts of the state were at best only sparsely settled. During the previous two years, Indians had attacked and killed over two hundred people along the frontier, claiming that the white settlers were taking land and game reserves that belonged to them—and this was often the case. Yet homesteaders continued to push westward. Indians also attacked workers building the Kansas Pacific Railroad, which was being extended across the state to Denver, Colorado. Olympia heard people talking about the attacks, saying that many of the men were wounded or killed, yet the work went on. One day when she was in the town of Salina in central Kansas, she saw a carload of wounded soldiers traveling east on the train. "Where were those men wounded?" she asked a local resident.

His reply startled her. "There was a big Indian fight about fifty miles west of here. They're going to a hospital somewhere in the east."

It was frightening to realize that she was so near actual Indian forays. The townspeople told her that there were thousands of Indians only a few miles to the west. Stories of raids, killings and kidnappings spread rapidly, yet the settlers pushed steadily west, determined to build homes and communities in spite of the reprisals. Indian resistance, sporadic and bloody, was slowly crumbling, and Olympia could visualize rapidly developing farms and towns across the state in the coming years.

She found that most of the people were genuinely interested in what she had to say. Occasionally, however, she met hostility from some men who feared that women might gain a disproportionate share of power if they were allowed to vote. One of her first encounters with such a group of men came when she was campaigning with Joel Moody and his family. Mr. Moody was editor of *The Border Sentinel* of Mound City. He strongly supported Olympia's campaign in his editorials and articles, and he invited her to travel through southeastern Kansas with his family on a campaign tour. Olympia accepted, delighted with the luxury of a comfortable carriage and the prospect of pleasant sleeping accommodations.

One evening as they rode down the street of a bustling little town where they were scheduled to speak, a rain of sticks and stones greeted their carriage. Loud shouts and jeers followed them all the way to the schoolhouse where they were to speak. At first Olympia thought there must be a mistake. Nothing like this had ever happened to her before. She got out of the carriage in front of the schoolhouse while Mr. Moody drove off to make their sleeping arrangements. Pushing her way through the crowd to the door, she saw that it was dark inside. She turned and faced the mob.

"Who is in charge here?" she demanded, wondering if their hostility might be directed at her.

Several of the men in the crowd shouted back, "No one."

"Is there a minister present?" she asked. A man stepped reluctantly forward. "Will you open up the schoolhouse and put a light inside?" she asked. In a few minutes he managed to light a few lamps and a crowd of people rushed in, seating themselves as best they could. She began her speech at once. All went well for nearly half-an-hour, then a sudden clatter of stones rattled against the door and windows. Loud jeers followed. Olympia paused a moment, then called out loudly, "Do any of the opposition want to speak?"

Immediately a young frontier lawyer burst through the door followed by his cohorts. He pulled off his hat and rolled up his shirtsleeves as he made his way up the aisle to the speaker's platform. The air was hot and still, and sweat ran down his face in rivulets as he spoke. Olympia listened in astonishment as he attacked woman suffrage with the zest of a crusader, beginning with Queen Elizabeth. He assailed every other woman he could think of who had ever tried to bring about enfranchisement or any other kind of right since that time. Olympia watched him pound on the table, flailing his arms like a scarecrow. Was this the kind of speaker these people liked, she wondered? Her mind was soon put to rest on that subject. Some of the women in the front row began muttering among themselves, "You had better shut up. We've no use for you." The speaker, however, ignored them and continued his tirade. When he finished, he stepped down from the platform, apparently well pleased with himself, and pushed his way outside. Olympia heard the wild cheer that greeted him and she felt a sudden pang of disappointment. What kind of people could such a man have rallied to his side? How could she possibly reach them with her message?

Joel Moody went up to speak as soon as the lawyer disappeared outside, but a loud rain of sticks and stones clattered against the door again. Shouts and insults pierced the air. Unable to give his talk against the noise, he held up his hands at ten o'clock and announced that the meeting was over. They hurried outside to their waiting carriage and left town immediately, fearful that they might be followed. "We lost our supper, a

84

night's rest, and breakfast the next morning," Olympia noted, "but we were glad to get safely away."

On another occasion, she arrived in the town of Oskaloosa and discovered that posters announcing both herself and another speaker for the same time and at the same place were posted all over town. She and Judge Sears, a formidable opponent, had inadvertently been scheduled on the same day. People were milling about wondering what to do when the humor of the situation struck Olympia. She brushed the dust from her dress and walked purposefully toward her opponent. This, she realized, could be the most exciting meeting of her entire campaign. "Let us share the meeting," she suggested to him. "We don't want to disappoint all of these people. You take the first hour of the evening and I'll take the second if that is agreeable with you." Her strategy was simple. She excelled in debate; she would hear his arguments and she would have the last word.

Judge Sears graciously accepted her offer. She could see that he considered her an easy victory, for how could a woman possibly present arguments comparable to those of a man?

News of the pending debate spread rapidly and by evening a large crowd had gathered inside the biggest church in town. The debate first appeared in the *Kansas State Journal* but was soon carried nationwide by other newspapers. The language is colloquial and the feeling it generated was intense and genuine.

> *The largest church in the place was crowded to its utmost, every inch of space being occupied. Judge Gilchrist was called to the chair, and first introduced Judge Sears, who made the following points in favor of Manhood Suffrage:*
>
> *1st. That in the early days of the Republic no discrimination was made against negroes on account of color.*
>
> *He proved from the constitution and charters of the original thirteen states, that all of them, with the exception of South Carolina, allowed the colored freeman the ballot, upon the same basis and conditions as the white man. That we were not conferring a right, but restoring one which the fathers in their wisdom had never deprived the colored man of. He showed how the word white had been forced into the state constitutions, and advocated that it should be stricken out, it being the last relic of the "slave power."*
>
> *2nd. That the negro needed the ballot. He fought with our fathers side by side in the war of the revolution. He did the same thing in 1812, and in the war of the rebellion. He fought for us because he was loyal and loved the old flag. If any class of men had ever earned the enjoyment of franchise the negro had.*

85

4th. The Republican party owed it to him.

5th. The enfranchisement of the negro was indispensable to reconstruction of the late rebellious states upon a basis that should secure to the loyal men of the South the control of the government of those states. Congress had declared it was necessary, and the most eminent men of the nation had failed to discover any other means by which the South could be restored to the Union, that should secure safety, prosperity and happiness. There was not loyalty enough in the South among the whites to elect a loyal man to an inferior office.

"Upon each of these points, the Judge elaborated at length and made really a fine speech, but his evident discomfiture showed that he knew what was to follow. It was expected that when Miss Brown was introduced many would leave, owing to the strange feeling against female suffrage in and about Oskaloosa; but not one left. The crowd grew more dense. A more eloquent speech never was uttered in this town than Miss Brown delivered; for an hour and three-quarters the audience was spell-bound as she advanced from point to point. She had been longing for such an opportunity, and had become weary of striking off into open air; and she proved how thoroughly acquainted she was with the subject as she took up each point advanced by her opponent, not denying its truth, but showing by unanswerable logic that if it were good for certain reasons for the negro to vote, it was ten times better for the same reasons for the women to vote.

The argument that the right to vote is not a natural right, but acquired as corporate bodies acquire their rights, and that the ballot meant 'protection,' was answered and explained fully. She said the ballot meant protection; it meant much more; it meant education, progress, advancement, elevation for the oppressed classes, drawing a glowing comparison between the working classes of England and those of the United States. She scorned the idea of an aristocracy based upon two accidents of the body. She paid an eloquent tribute to Kansas, the pioneer in all reforms, and said that it would be the best advertisement that Kansas could have to give the ballot to women, for thousands now waiting and uncertain, would flock to our state, and a vast tide of emigration would continually roll toward Kansas until her broad and fertile prairies would be peopled. It is useless to attempt to report her address, as she could hardly find a place to stop. When she had done, her opponent had nothing to say. He had been beaten on his ground, and retired with his feathers drooping. After Miss Brown had closed, some one in the audience called for a vote on the female proposition. The vote was put, and nearly every man and woman in the house rose simultaneously. Men that had fought the proposition from the first arose, even Judge Sears himself looked as though he would like to rise, but his principles forbade. After the first vote, Judge Sears called for a vote on his, the negro proposition, when about one-half the house arose." [9]

Olympia treasured the newspaper accounts of this debate. She had seldom had such an opportunity to use her gift of argument. One of her great delights in later years was to recall this event and to relish once again Judge Sear's humiliation and defeat.

As her tour progressed, she was eager to see what each new day would bring, what new people she would meet, what new country she would see. Her enthusiasm never flagged. "I soon learned to ignore the discomforts of travel," she said, and there were many. She was unable to bathe, one of the luxuries she missed, for there simply were no facilities on the frontier. Those people who lived near a stream could swim and wash their clothes along the banks, but most people had to pump their water from wells. Olympia, however, was traveling and speaking seven days a week. She may have been able to take a sponge bath on those rare instances when she was given her own sleeping room with a basin and pitcher of water on the dresser. She may even have been able to rinse out some of her clothing and hang it up to dry in the room. The days often reached well over one hundred degrees in the summer and the nights were not much cooler, so laundry dried quickly. Occasionally she stayed overnight in the home of a wealthy family and enjoyed the comforts of civilization once more, but for the most part she traveled over a land that was not yet settled and into towns that had just been carved out of the prairie. She slept on mattresses made with dried prairie grasses, ate plain boiled meat and potatoes, cornbread and cornmeal mush, and drank black coffee.

"I didn't dare get sick," she laughed, "for there was no one to take care of me. Most towns didn't even have a doctor and there were no hospitals for hundreds of miles. I was careful what I ate or drank and never had any problems."

She looked forward to the times when she traveled with other campaigners like Governor Robinson and his family, and the John Hutchinson family, who were well-known singers and suffrage workers. They always had a comfortable carriage and stayed in hotels or were guests in the homes of influential families. At these times, Olympia was able to relax and enjoy the companionship of educated and knowledgeable people. These experiences made her realize once again the importance of education. Little sod schoolhouses already dotted the prairie, and pioneer children were learning the fundamentals of reading, writing and arithmetic, but it would take years to establish a good school system in the state.

For Olympia, as for her mother, education was a primary concern, and she was pleased to find that it was making progress in Kansas.

Prairie fires terrified her at first. She had never seen any before she came to this plains state. The fires occurred in late summer or early autumn when the grass was parched and dry. The first time she saw one, she found herself riding directly toward it with a nonchalant driver who seemed oblivious to the danger. She recalled her schoolbook pictures showing horses and other living things running wildly before the leaping flames, and she clung desperately to the sides of the carriage, convinced that they would be devoured by the fire. However, as they drew nearer the flames, she saw that it was only burning in patches and they passed safely around one side and found themselves on burned-over ground. "I learned that this, like many other of our difficulties in life, was more imaginary than real," she noted philosophically.[10]

She did not experience any of the great prairie fires started by lightning, sparks from a passing train or a careless farmer. Such fires could destroy settlers' homes and livestock and hundreds of acres of grass and farmland. Sometimes homesteaders themselves were trapped and died. The pioneers soon learned methods of fire-fighting however, where prairie fires were stopped by back-burning and plowing strips of ground wide enough so that a fire could not jump the strip. Olympia passed over some of the areas where farmers were already practicing this type of containment, so the fires were not as extensive as the more spectacular ones whipped by high winds and propelled for many miles.

As the hot summer drew to an end, she began to realize that the Republican party had, indeed, betrayed the suffragists and was openly opposing the ballot for women. She saw the circulars the party workers posted in the towns, read the notices that they placed in the newspapers, and heard about the speakers the party sent out over the state warning voters that the presidential election was drawing near. The question of Negro suffrage was the only issue before the voters, they said. Workers were told to concentrate upon that and ignore all other issues.

Other anti-woman suffrage speakers campaigned besides Judge Sears; some were unequivocally hostile and rude. The noted Negro orator Charles Langston appealed to the bigotry and ignorance of his audiences in his crusade for the Negro vote. During one of his speeches, when Olympia was sitting in the audience, he asked pointedly, "Do you want every old maid to vote?" The next day, after she gave a talk at a picnic, he took the platform and charged men in the audience with "preferring every *thing* that had a white face to the negro." Shocked and angry at such a display of prejudice by a well-known Negro orator, she began to question her own speeches. She had been including the Negro in her campaign for enfranchisement, but now she wondered if she should start speaking solely for the right of women to vote. When she remembered how Mr. Langston's brother had received much help and kindness from Susan B. Anthony, she grew even more troubled, and it was hard to suppress her resentment. Mr. Langston was preaching intolerance in a new country where all should be working together for universal suffrage. His personal attacks pained her deeply. How had this issue come to divide the Republican party and the workers, she wondered? The voter were actually being encouraged to choose between the ballot for women and the ballot for the Negro male instead of voting for universal suffrage.

Newspaper reporters were biased, too, she soon learned. One reporter working for *The Atchison Champion* accused Olympia Brown of saying that, "The negro is an ignorant, stupid being, unfit to exercise the right of suffrage, that the only safety for the nation was in putting the right to vote into the hands of the women, to act as a counter-balance—a check on the negro ignorance, bigotry and superstition." She was appalled to find her words misquoted and the meaning changed to make her look prejudiced and malicious.

She had her supporters, however. Relief mingled with satisfaction as she read an article in *The Kansas State Journal* of Lawrence. The writer accused *The Atchison Champion* of making degrading and false remarks. The reporter, they wrote, "evidently introduced and sandwiched his own ideas for those of Miss Brown."[11]

Her co-campaigner, Mr. Moody, editor of *The Border Sentinel* of Mound City published a journal of her meetings in Kansas. A short biographical sketch was followed with this comment:

> *With her talent and education, she has great physical power of endurance, lately speaking two or three times each day in hottest weather, travelling from twenty to fifty miles each day with only an average of about four hours sleep, and her speeches from one to two hours in length, without apparently the least fatigue, and weighing only ninety-one pounds ... Eloquent, hopeful and brave, with religion as the basis of all her actions, and piety her leading trait, she is the best pleader for woman that we have yet seen before the public.*[12]

Other local newspapers covered her campaign too and were generally supportive. *The Humboldt Union* praised her

> *... grand and lofty aims, burning eloquence and undisputed logic ... for soundness of argument, clearness of thought, and eloquence of expression, Miss Brown is fully prepared 'to travel' without fear of*

contact with the sterner sex. . . Miss Brown will surely teach every
woman to think and act for herself, and to open up new fields of work
and education for women.[13]

While she was campaigning near Osawatomie, a few miles from the
Kansas-Missouri border, Olympia met friends and relatives of the mar-
tyred abolitionist John Brown. Although he had been hanged in 1859 in
the state of Virginia, the people in Kansas still revered him. He had helped
many slaves escape through Kansas on the Underground Railroad. Olympia was curious about him, because there were many conflicting stories
about his life. "What was he like?" she asked some of the people who had
known him.

He was a deeply religious man, many of them said. He believed that
God had called on him to help free the slaves and he let nothing stand in
his way.[14] She listened to their stories about him; then she went to see the
cabin where he hid with the slaves he was leading north. Walking around
the little ramshackle building, she peered in the windows; then she turned
and looked at the wide sweep of prairie. Glancing at the sky, cloudless in
the summer sun, she could not tell where the sky and prairie met in the
distance. Ever mindful of her situation, she made note of the patches of
bare ground because she knew rattlesnakes could lurk anywhere. How
lonely it must have been to live in such a place. She wondered about the
slaves that John Brown had hidden in the log cabin. How many had he led
to safety? Would anyone ever know the truth about his life, his ideals and
dreams, or would he be forever shrouded in mystery?

It was disheartening to think that the truth of a life could be so easily
distorted or lost.

Her thoughts turned to the Kansas campaign, and she began to wonder
how history would treat *that* story. If the only record of it was based on
newspaper accounts, the truth would never be known. How many
interesting things had happened to her and how many people had helped
her! She began to think about writing down her experiences, for surely no
man would tell about the heroic women pioneers who worked on the land
alongside their men, who could shoot a buffalo or wolf with equal aplomb,
and who fought raiding Indians with unmatched fury. Many of the women
had survived border-ruffian attacks when abolitionists and slave holders
were trying to get political control of the state. Some of the attacks were
so ferocious that whole towns were burned to the ground; the men and
older boys shot in the streets or their homes. Many pioneer women, despite
losing husbands, fathers or brothers in those attacks, stayed in Kansas,
built homes and raised their families. Olympia had met and talked with
them. She had listened to their stories of survival, learned how they had

lived for weeks out on the open prairie. She ate at their tables, slept in their homes. Most had come west to find a new life, build a new community and raise a family. Fine, hard-working, intelligent people, they had as much at stake as the men. Why then, should they not vote, she asked? It was not long before these points became arguments in her campaign speeches.

Olympia campaigned through July, August and into September never missing a meeting. The heat and long, tiresome journeys did not daunt her. Indeed she seldom thought about the weather until one day in early September when she came across a newspaper article about the Honorable Sidney Clark. Clark was running for Congress and had just started campaigning that month. He had only canvassed a small portion of the state, spoke but once a day and rested on Sundays. He owned his own private conveyance and his sleeping and eating arrangements were all taken care of for him. Yet he had broken down in health and had to give up his appointments, the newspaper account noted. The Republican party was quick to excuse him. "It was not strange," they reported, "as no human being could endure without loss of health such constant speaking with such long and tedious journeys as Mr. Clark had undertaken."[15]

Olympia was astonished at such a statement. Surely the reporter had not looked very far. Lucy Stone and her husband had traveled for weeks out on the prairie with no ill effects. Susan B. Anthony and Elizabeth Cady Stanton were in Kansas at that very time, traveling and speaking every day, and neither one of them was suffering. She herself had been campaigning every day for over two months and had survived very well under the climate. Why should they excuse Mr. Clark for frailty when women easily outlasted him? It was just another case of politicians and newspapers ignoring the facts and painting their candidate in the most favorable colors, she decided.

The final two weeks before the election, a new campaigner came into the state. He was George Francis Train, a political dynamo with an eye on the presidency. He launched a vigorous campaign for woman suffrage. A colorful crusader, he drew large crowds wherever he went, but even his endeavor failed to get the vote for Kansas women. It either came too late or he was not able to convince enough voters of his convictions.

Olympia had hoped that this campaign was going to bring about major changes in society. She saw in every man a person who had the power to vote for or against a very simple proposition: that all persons had a right to a vote in their own government. Political differences, religious beliefs and education should all be forgotten in this one issue. It was imperative that all citizens of this great country have the ballot.

Liquor interests, however, fought the issue with newspaper advertisements, posters and speakers who went out across the state. The speakers warned the men that women wanted prohibition. If they got the vote, they claimed, women would close all the saloons.

Perhaps that campaign slogan was the most effective. Enfranchisement for women was defeated 19,857 to 9,070 votes.

Olympia was crushed and she asked herself over and over, why did men vote against a law that would give their wives, mothers and sisters a voice in their own government? Did they really consider women inferior beings? How could such an idea have originated, and how could it be changed? But she had asked these questions many times before and there was no answer.

Humiliation washed all of her hopes and dreams aside leaving behind anger mixed with pain. Could she have done more? How else might she have campaigned?

A letter from Susan B. Anthony reached her shortly before she left to return to Weymouth Landing. It was written only two days after the election, and brimmed with hope and high spirits.

Leavenworth, Nov. 7th, 1867

Dear Olympia,

Never was so grand a success—never was defeat so glorious a victory . . . But don't despair. We shall win. The day breaks. The eastern sky is red. Mr. Train consents to lecture for our treasury's benefit all the way down to Boston & back to Philadelphia . . . and my dear Olympia—if ever any money gets into my power to control you shall have evidence that I appreciate the Herculean work you have done here in Kansas the past four long months.

If only Geo. F. Train could have lighted the fires you had prepared all over the state—we should have carried it overwhelmingly. But depend upon it—there is a wise destiny in our delay—it is not defeat. So let us hope & work to the brighter day. God bless you & keep you safe & alive to see the glory of our work accomplished.

Affectionately yours,
Susan B. Anthony[16]

The letter from Miss Anthony helped her put her work in perspective. Her spirits lifted. She would have gone farther and done even more for those words of appreciation. Miss Anthony was her "pole star," her unquestioned leader, and she treasured her every word. When she finally

92

put the letter down, the realization came over her that all of the workers were as disappointed as she. They had all been deceived by the Republican party. Fifteen years later in 1882, Olympia still laid the blame for the Kansas defeat on the party's doorstep. She wrote,

> It is deemed in certain quarters, wicked heresy to complain of or criticize the Republican party . . . but if there is to be any truth in history we must set it down, to stand forever a lasting disgrace to the party that in 1867, in Kansas, its leaders . . . defeated the woman suffrage amendment.[17]

Such deep resentment was not one of Miss Anthony's traits, Olympia soon learned. The day after the election Miss Anthony was already planning her next strategy. Olympia admired her for not holding a grudge and for her ability to move on after defeat. The courage and determination of the other woman set her to thinking about her own discouragement and feelings of humiliation, and she resolved that she would learn to look ahead instead of behind. She would learn to make plans for the future as soon as each campaign was over. The Kansas campaign was her first major defeat and, although she never forgave the Republican party for its betrayal, she never again let defeat undermine her spirit.

Long after she returned to Weymouth Landing, she still received letters complimenting her on her campaign work in Kansas. She never forgot the experience. She had, after all, learned many lessons. She went forward alone, met and overcame numerous obstacles, faced danger and opposition, dealt with contempt, whetted her speaking skills, and learned how to accept failure and go on.

All of these experiences brought about changes in Olympia. She knew people usually resist new ideas, but she also learned that all of her logic could not move people as much as the emotional plea that the liquor interests had used. She also learned that men would jealously guard their power over women. Nevertheless, she nurtured the hope that men would realize their error and soon women would have the ballot in state after state. If only Kansas had led the way!

When she returned to Weymouth Landing, she found that her parishioners had been working on the church building while she was gone. They had cleaned out the basement, previously used as a meat market and remodeled it for reading and social rooms. They also installed a new organ and built a new pulpit. She settled back into her ministry, happy to be preaching and doing parish work again.

She scheduled a new lecture series similar to the previous series that had proven so popular among the townspeople. One of the lecturers was

William Lloyd Garrison, the noted abolitionist. He accepted the invitation, advising her that he was not going to speak "for the purpose of endorsing any peculiar denominational views." He also stipulated that all of the announcements preceding his visit make this clear to everyone. She assured him that it would be done. How amusing, she thought, that he did not want to be labeled a Universalist, that he should so fear a particular religious designation.

After his speech she talked to him about woman suffrage. "You had a perfect opportunity in your speech to bring up the subject of woman suffrage," she said, "but you said nothing about it."

"Oh, that has all been taken care of by the anti-slavery movement," he replied airily.

When she expressed astonishment at this statement, he assured her that women would soon be voting. There was no doubt in his mind about it, he said.

She took part in the ordination of another woman minister in nearby Hingham, Massachusetts, later that year. Olympia had encouraged the young woman, Pheobe Hanaford, to enter the ministry, and she was delighted to learn that she had a parish only a few miles away from her. They soon became good friends and worked together to help found the Massachusetts Woman Suffrage Association and took part together in many campaigns over the years.

A letter came from Susan B. Anthony only two months after the Kansas campaign. Olympia sensed that this was probably more than another expression of gratitude for her work. Might it be another invitation to dash away somewhere across the country on a new campaign? She found instead, that she was facing a momentous decision. Miss Anthony asked her to change her career, to give up the ministry and serve the woman suffrage movement as a lecturer. "Would any certain salary above that you now get induce you to go into the lecture field this year—to speaking your own highest thought in your own way, and to get subscribers to our paper? If so, what?" she asked.[18]

Olympia could give no answer. Her first impulse was to say no, but she decided that she needed time to think about it.

Two months later a letter came from Elizabeth Cady Stanton. Olympia knew that this letter too would ask her to devote herself to the cause. Mrs. Stanton's fine script flowed across the page, difficult to read but full of warmth. "We know of no one better suited to lecture. You could travel around the country, wherever you wished, and get subscribers for *The Revolution*. You would not have to work as hard as you did in Kansas, only lecture three times a week."[19]

Olympia put the letter aside. Did she want to spend her time and energy traveling, speaking and getting subscriptions for *The Revolution*, Miss Anthony's new woman suffrage newspaper? Surely it was a noble cause, but she needed time to rest and heal. She wanted only to preach and serve her parish in peace.

A few days later, March 12, 1868, another letter came from Miss Anthony. Olympia fingered the envelope for a few moments before opening it. It was, she knew, another plea to leave the ministry and work for suffrage. The words marched across the page promising travel, money, excitement.

Will you take the World *for your* Pastoral Charge *and choose your pasture from time to time—canvass for—or solicit subscribers to* The Revolution *at the close of lectures—by the way side and any & everywhere you shall choose—if you are* guaranteed one thousand dollars *per year* above expenses?

One thousand dollars! She was not getting nearly that much—only eight hundred dollars a year as pastor of the Weymouth Landing church, and she had served the church four years now. She grew troubled, uneasy at the thought that she was actually considering giving up her career. How hard she had worked to become a minister, and how she wished to set a precedent of continued preaching! She took up the letter and read on. "What say you? If you will engage in the work on any terms—please state them to me."[20]

Olympia had much to think about. For one thing, even though she worshipped Susan B. Anthony and deeply admired Elizabeth Cady Stanton, she realized that some basic differences existed between the three women's philosophies. Miss Anthony believed that everyone should be working for universal suffrage. She had once said to her, "Olympia, you have no right to say one word more for women than you do for the Negro."

Olympia, however, felt very differently about that. She told Miss Anthony about the insults she suffered when Charles Langston spoke during the Kansas campaign. Women should speak for themselves as the Negro has spoken for himself, she said. She also told Miss Anthony about her experiences with Frederick Douglass, well-known Negro reformer, at a meeting in New York City. Everyone should work for the Negro male to the exclusion of women, he had said. "There are no Ku Klux Klans seeking the lives of women. The voters are their fathers, their husbands and brothers."[21]

Olympia quickly pointed out to him that countless Negro women feared for their safety, even their lives, at the hands of men. They needed the protection of the ballot even more than the Negro male, she claimed, but Mr. Douglass disagreed with her. They could not reconcile their differences. Neither could she convince Miss Anthony that women must work for their own suffrage to the exclusion of the Negro male. After all, she pointed out, the Negro male would soon be enfranchised. Indeed, the Fourteenth Amendment to the Constitution was ratified a few months later on July 23, 1868. That amendment gave the ballot to the Negro male but specifically excluded women.

Olympia also recognized that there were other problems likely to develop among three such strong-willed individuals as Miss Anthony, Mrs. Stanton and herself. Each woman was certain that her opinions were the right ones, and it would be difficult to resolve their differences. Lucy Stone had already discovered such was the case, and she had broken away from the original group. Surely, Olympia thought, she would face the same problem as Mrs. Stone. The ministry afforded her the opportunity for her own development and well-being. She chose to stay with that work and do what she could for suffrage as her time permitted.

It was a wrenching decision, one that affected not only her own life but also her place in history. Had she accepted Susan B. Anthony's offer, she likely would have ranked in fame with Miss Anthony, Mrs. Stanton, and Mrs. Stone. Her name would have been linked with theirs in almost every decision made in the early woman suffrage movement. Olympia, however, could not compromise. It was probably her fatal flaw. She chose to go her own way, alone, if need be. It would be enough, she thought, and so it was, for a while.

Chapter 6

A Different Life

If her decision to remain in the ministry instead of campaign for woman's rights ever troubled Olympia Brown, she gave no indication of it. She tucked Susan B. Anthony's letter into her pocket and went before the board of trustees of her church. It was time, she told them, to give her a substantial raise in salary. Not only had she been their faithful minister for nearly four years, but she had just spent a rigorous four months on the Kansas plains, speaking for the noble cause of woman suffrage. The strength of her words settled on their ears like the hoofbeats of the prairie buffalo as she told them that she had just been offered another job at a thousand dollars a year.

The trustees glanced at each other in some surprise. They had not expected anything like this. Consternation lined their brows. Surely they could not let this devoted, energetic and capable leader slip through their fingers. It was not long before they agreed to the salary increase. Olympia left the meeting, victory flooding through her. Of course she had been right to stay in the ministry! She would set the precedent she had fixed upon as her goal, and she would work for woman suffrage as she could.

She decided to attend a meeting of the American Equal Rights Association at Cooper Institute, New York, in the spring of 1868. Since ratification of the Fourteenth Amendment to the Constitution giving Negro males the right to vote was progressing steadily, she planned to help devise strategies for future work toward the enfranchisement of women. "I am ready to help plan campaigns for woman suffrage now that the Negro vote is virtually assured," she said to the group. None of the leaders seemed to be particularly interested in her offer, but she was elected a vice president of the association. She now felt that she could exert influence in the decision-making processes.

The meeting dragged on as one man after another rose and addressed the group on the subject of work still to be done to enfranchise Negro males. Not once did one of them mention the issue of woman suffrage.

97

Olympia waited her turn to speak, seething with impatience that the leaders could so blatantly ignore woman suffrage. At last it was her turn to speak and she rose and made her way to the platform.

"I am here today to speak on equal rights for women," she announced. Her voice resounded in every corner of the room. Her years of practicing voice control and elocution bore fruit, and all of the members heard her every word. She spoke for nearly thirty minutes, her eyes fixed on the leaders. As she neared the end of her speech, she told about a hearing she recently attended before a committee of the Massachusetts legislature.

> *Mr. Dana said that Nature is against it [equal rights]. He says that it will take the romance out of life to grant women equal rights. Can you imagine such a thing? I say that if romance is subservience, we want to get back to nature and God. We all love liberty and desire to possess it. No one worthy of the name of man or woman is willing to surrender liberty and become subservient to another. Woman may be shut out of politics by law, but her influence will be felt there.*

She pointed out that the American Equal Rights Association was organized to work for equal rights for *all* people, not just the Negro male, and she made it clear that when she helped found it, the organizers agreed that they would work for woman suffrage as well as the Negro vote. She then made her final point.

> *It is no use to tell us to wait until something else is done. Now is the accepted time for the enfranchisement of women. . . We will push on, keeping in view the rights of our common nature until woman is the peer of man in every sphere of life.*[1]

Frederick Douglass shifted in his chair as she spoke. He crossed and recrosssed his legs, tapped his toes and clasped his fingers impatiently from time to time. His impatience with Olympia's speech was clear to everyone. At last it was his turn to speak. He stood up, walked to the platform and raised his hand for silence.

> *"I champion the right of the negro to vote," he said. "It is with us a matter of life and death, and therefore cannot be postponed. I have always championed woman's right to vote; but it will be seen that the present claim for the negro is one of the most urgent necessity. The assertion of the right of women to vote meets nothing but ridicule; there is no deep-seated malignity in the hearts of the people against her; but name the right of the negro to vote, all hell is turned loose and*

the Ku-Klux and Regulators hunt and slay the unoffending black man. The government of this country loves women. They are the sisters, mothers, wives and daughters of our rulers; but the negro is loathed." [2]

She stared at him as he spoke, and her anger rose as she listened to the words she had heard so many times before. They were empty arguments, and at last she could be quiet no longer. "Do you really believe that it is more important for two million Negro men to vote than it is for seventeen million women?" she cried in a loud voice.

Frederick Douglass paused for a moment, startled by her question. He shook his head, then ruffled his papers, but he was not to be stopped. "The negro male needs suffrage to protect his life and property, and to ensure him respect and education. He needs it . . . for his own elevation from the position of a drudge to that of an influential member of society." [3] He went on to remind the audience that Wendell Phillips, Horace Greeley and Theodore Tilton all spoke eloquently for woman's rights, but they backed the right of the Negro male to vote first.

Olympia was ready once again. "You say the negro male needs suffrage to protect his property and to gain education and respect for him. That is just as true for women, Mr. Douglass. They need suffrage for all of those reasons and more. They raise the next generation. How can they teach children to become responsible, conscientious citizens, if they are not educated and treated as influential citizens themselves?"

When the conference ended, Olympia decided that the debate was futile. Clearly, the American Equal Rights Association was not going to support women. It was time for women to organize their own suffrage association.

Immediately upon her return to Boston, Olympia rented a hall and advertised a woman suffrage meeting. Notices appeared in local newspapers, and posters were put up in the Boston area. On the day set for the meeting, so many people came that the hall overflowed and people had to gather outside on the walk and lawn. She was surprised at the overwhelming response to the idea of a woman suffrage organization. Why hadn't anyone organized such a meeting before?

There were many stirring speeches. It was the one thing expected at every public meeting, and people listened attentively to pro and con arguments. After the speeches came the business meeting. Here, the real work began. Committees were formed and people were assigned specific tasks. In this way, the New England Woman Suffrage Association was organized. The first convention was held in Boston in November of 1868, six months after its formation.

Olympia, feeling largely responsible for the success of this organization, was understandably nervous when she reached the door of the hall that first day of the convention. She stepped inside and could only stare in amazement at the crowd of people. They were everywhere. Many were sitting, waiting patiently for the meeting to begin. Distinguished men and women moved about, talking quietly, lending an air of eminence, of distinction to the gathering.

Again, speeches followed one after another in steady succession. William Lloyd Garrison and T. W. Higginson chided the leaders of the new association, assuring everyone that all was well and this convention was unnecessary. "In the progress of every great cause there are three periods," Mr. Garrison began. "First there is a period of indifference when no one cares, and there is no hostility; second, a period of opposition and ridicule, people have begun to notice and disapprove; third, the period of victory, opposition has been overcome, ridicule has been silenced and people are ready to receive the truth. In this cause we have passed through the first two periods and are now entering on the period of victory." He stepped down, confident that his words had convinced the audience that they did not need a special woman suffrage organization after all.

Mr. Higginson was not one to be outdone. He called forth a familiar metaphor. "The seed has all been sown. The work has been done. We have only to gather in the harvest."[4] The two men, certain that women were already assured of the ballot, exuded a patronizing air toward the leaders that immediately set Olympia at odds with them.

Frederick Douglass came forward and spoke, as always, about the disabilities of the Negro compared to women. Olympia waited for him to finish, her impatience manifesting itself in barely contained displeasure. The moment he finished and was turning from the podium, she rose quickly and hurried forward. Fixing her eyes on both Garrison and Higginson, she declared firmly, "Reformers are often deceived by a kind of mirage and suppose that victory is at hand when in reality, generations are yet to pass before it can be realized." Then, in turning and casting a glance toward the retreating figure of Mr. Douglass, she continued. "I believe most of these matters were well covered at the American Equal Rights conventions. However, this is a woman suffrage association convention, and as such, members will work toward the ballot for women to the exclusion of all other issues. Only those who are willing to work for that cause are invited to join."[5] She turned and marched back to her seat on the stage, the audience clapping their approval.

This association was one of the first woman suffrage organizations in the nation and it became one of the most successful.[6] Olympia worked within it as an officer and speaker for many years. She appeared regularly before New England state legislatures in eloquent appeals for the ballot for women.

A major shift was taking place in the struggle for woman's rights. In the beginning, women worked for property and custodial rights. With the passage of the Fourteenth Amendment giving voting privileges to Negro men but still excluding women, they began demanding voting privileges themselves. Their anger at being excluded from having a voice in their own government was understandable. There were many cries of outrage and frustration by many of the workers who had been concentrating on equal rights for women; now they changed their minds. The new goal became enfranchisement. Many reformers earnestly believed that equal rights for women would immediately follow enfranchisement once they had gained that privilege. Olympia, realizing that the heart of the struggle had changed, joined in putting her efforts into woman suffrage work from that time forward.

She still spoke of woman's rights, but her work was directed primarily at getting the ballot for women. Her letters and speeches were often laced with resentment that women were still denied the ballot, particularly after passage of the Fourteenth Amendment, and she did not hesitate to state her feelings. Consequently she soon learned that some people were criticizing her personally, calling her outspoken and thoughtless, even arrogant in some of her statements. Ironically, she was as quick to judge other reformers, particularly those who would not help with woman suffrage work, as she claimed many were to judge her.

She wrote a letter to Susan B. Anthony letting her thoughts spill out across the paper, forgetting that written thoughts could be far more volatile than the spoken word. Her letter was short and personal; she did not even expect a reply. She could hardly have expected the minor storm it brewed.

Weymouth, Jan. 3

Dear Miss Anthony,

I am delighted to learn that we are to have a paper. It is what we most need. When we have a paper and a party, we shall have weapons to fight with. For years I have ceased to hope anything from our best friends! I mean prominent liberal men like Phillips, Garrison, Tilton, and others, though Tilton is better than the rest. These men, being human, have the frailties peculiar to their race. They, of course, have no extra stock of self-sacrificing spirit on hand. They have exhausted their fund of heroism in behalf of the negro, and are just now reaping their reward of popularity in return for having been martyrs to an

101

unpopular idea. They are the last persons in the world to do anything
for us: we must look for our support to new men.

> *Yours, sincerely,*
> *Olympia Brown.*[7]

Miss Anthony agreed with Olympia whole heartedly. She was, in fact, so partial to the comments in the letter that she decided to publish it in her suffrage newspaper, an idea that would have shocked Olympia almost beyond words had she suspected such a thing. She knew only too well the reaction to such a step.

It was only a short time later that she received a letter from William Lloyd Garrison. Upon opening the envelope, her eyes fell on his handwritten copy of her letter to Miss Anthony. Surprise turned to dismay as she read it. Mr. Garrison had underlined the comments which he found decidedly objectionable. "You are most unjust," he wrote, after which he listed his latest speeches for the enfranchisement of women. Shock settled down over her. How could she rectify her words? She certainly had not phrased them in a manner likely to please Mr. Garrison, but, then, she had not expected him to see them. His final comment, "Your letter is untruthfull and defamatory," was most unsettling. She had worked with him many times, and he had lectured at her church. She could not afford his enmity for he was a valued reformer. She must apologize, in all fairness, she decided. One can only speculate on her thoughts concerning Miss Anthony as she penned the letter to Garrison.

> *...I know full well that at the present time no person in the world has power to aid us like yourself. I feel prepared to say that I had no right to ascribe motives... it was unjust and I am sorry I did so. I still believe women cannot expect those who have given thirty or forty years to the abolition of slavery to enter into the cause of woman's rights with the same zeal and earnestness as young workers. That was all I meant in my letter...* [8]

Mr. Garrison accepted her apology, and they continued to work together amicably for many years. Olympia, of course, reproached Miss Anthony for publishing her letter in *The Revolution* without permission, but Miss Anthony was a veteran when it came to smoothing ruffled feathers. She agreed with Olympia about the early reformers. "It was true not one of the *old leaders* in *anti-slavery* now puts *himself* or *herself* in the *front ranks* for women—it is a *fact*—neither you nor *I make the fact*—we simply state it," she said, passionately convinced that Olympia's letter was the reality of the matter.[9]

Although Miss Anthony accepted Olympia's decision to work for the cause only as her time permitted, she often urged Olympia to give more time to suffrage work, as did Elizabeth Cady Stanton. Her time could be put to much better use, they argued. Olympia, however, declined. She was busy and happy in her church work and could not be persuaded to give it up.

Universalist meetings and conventions occupied some of her time, too, along with the suffrage conventions. At first her entrance into this sacred male bastion caused more than a murmur of surprise. There were inward gasps, some shuffling of feet, and the swiveling of heads from side to side. She ignored the agitation her entrance occasioned, smiling at the sudden hushed silence in the room. These gentlemen soon learned to accept her presence, but not newspaper reporters. After listening to one of her speeches at a meeting in Boston, one reporter decided the activity warranted an article in his newspaper.

> *It seems odd to see women in the preaching business; but it is one of their "rights," no doubt, if they see fit to exercise it; yet we are sorry that any women are found imitating so poor a "lord-of-creation" example. Miss Brown is a woman of intelligence, but not so pleasing an orator nor as liberal in her sentiments as Miss Lizzie Doten, the Spiritualist."*

As might be expected, Olympia took strong exception to such statements. She carefully cut out the article, penciled along the margin the words, "I should hope not," and filed it away among her papers.[10] She did not discriminate among the positive or negative articles about her, often enjoying the reporters' whimsical and sometimes bizarre comments.

She was asked one time to read her essay, "Woman's Place in the Church," at a multi-denominational Ministerial Union meeting in Boston. The essay was a forceful statement for the rights of women in the church, a matter to which she had given much thought. "It is the church's duty to encourage women to become ministers. Women must have the freedom to act out their own roles in the church," she declared, as though bent on creating a new policy among all denominations. She continued reading for another fifteen minutes to a surprisingly receptive group. When she finished, the men voted to publish the essay in pamphlet form and distribute it among the area churches. It was an unexpected gesture considering the general attitude against women preachers, and a gesture that gave her much pleasure.[11]

Five years had passed since she first came to the Weymouth Landing

103

church. A restlessness was stirring in her, an urge to move on, to look for a larger church. Perhaps she needed new challenges, new experiences. Whatever the reasons were, when she read one day that a church in Bridgeport, Connecticut, was without a minister, she decided to apply for the position. The congregation there immediately invited her to come and preach a trial sermon.

Once arrived at the Bridgeport church, a very vocal group within the church demanded a hearing, protesting that they did not want a woman preacher. Olympia decided to meet with the protesters and see if they would respond to an appeal for justice. "I ask only that you be fair and listen to my sermon. Do not judge me until you have heard me," she said in her talk to them. She must have been remarkably persuasive in her arguments, because they agreed to hear her without further protests.

After her trial sermon, the congregation immediately voted to accept her as their minister and offered her fifteen hundred dollars a year. Such an inducement could hardly be ignored and she accepted their offer. If she had any misgivings about the small troublesome faction that had protested her presence so vigorously, she put them in the back of her mind, happy in the realization that she now had a larger church with a new future to think about.

Painful duties lay ahead for her. When she returned to Weymouth Landing, she would have to offer her resignation to a group of people with whom she had close, emotional ties. Many would urge her not to leave them, and it would be a difficult time for all. Her thoughts settled on a man who was on the board of trustees, a man who had been especially patient and understanding with her, and toward whom she felt a strong attraction. His name was John Henry Willis. She had felt for some time now that it might be best to go away and see if the affinity remained, but it would be particularly painful to leave him.

When she returned to Weymouth Landing, she offered her resignation to the congregation. Many of the people were so dismayed at the idea of her leaving that they refused to accept her resignation. She then reminded them that she had come to the church when it was having problems. "I do well with just such churches," she said. "Now you have a growing and healthy congregation. It is time to turn it over to another minister so that I can go on and continue my work elsewhere."

Although she tendered her resignation on July 8, 1869, the Parish Committee tried to delay her departure. They asked her to finish out the year at the Weymouth church, but Olympia refused. "I can only stay until the end of September," she said. "I have promised to begin serving the Bridgeport church by October first." Surely three months was sufficient time for them to find another pastor! Ultimately the congregation had to accept her resignation, although many of the parishioners hoped until the last that she would change her mind.

At a farewell testimonial dinner, the congregation presented her with a gift of one hundred twenty-five dollars, a sizeable sum at that time. She took the gift, seemingly overwhelmed for a few moments, then managed to thank them, her voice trembling with emotion. Would parting from every parish be this painful, she must have wondered? She then told them that she would use the money to purchase a set of Encyclopedia Britannica. She could think of nothing that she would value more. "Continue in your good work and keep the Sunday school growing," she encouraged them.[12]

Her move to Bridgeport was uneventful and she assumed her new duties in the month of October. New challenges were the very breath of Olympia's life. She reorganized the Sunday school and began visiting the parishioners. "Lone man, addicted to the use of wine," is jotted after one name in her calling book. "Offended at an informality in an afternoon visit. Would take no apology," causes one to wonder what happened to occasion such a response. Most of the entries were simple, such as "widow", or "young parents with children," but after the name of James Staples she wrote simply, "a bad man."[13] This is the only clue to her problems within the church at the beginning of her pastorate. Staples seemed to be the leader of a small group of members who vigorously opposed a woman preacher, none of whom would have anything to do with her. Agitating against her, at first only within the church, did not prove effective. It was only later, after several years had passed, that they spread their efforts out into the community with grievous results.

Olympia found that members of the Bridgeport church were quite different from those at Weymouth Landing. "They are apathetic and narrow-minded," she wrote to some of her friends. She was, however, aware that they had not had the cultural advantages of Boston, and she made a special effort to rouse their enthusiasm and set their sights on new goals. In spite of feeling that she was preaching the best sermons of her ministry, underneath it all ran a thread of suspicion that the people did not really understand her high ideals and aspirations. Coupled with that was the knowledge that a small minority simply would not listen to her. Here she began to absorb the very difficult lesson that some people were immutable. Somehow, she was inclined to believe that she held all the answers, that she could bring people around to her way of thinking. Certainly her campaign in Kansas had taught her something about people's reluctance to change, but she still held fast to the belief that she could eventually win over all of her parishioners.

Olympia found a warm friend in Phineas Taylor (P. T.) Barnum the great American showman and circus entrepreneur. He lived in Bridgeport and attended the Universalist church there. Often, when she came down from her pulpit and walked past his pew, he would compliment her on her sermon, something that she especially appreciated in view of the enmity of James Staples and those who supported his position. It was said of her that when the church was in need of additional money, she was not above asking that the rich be more generous in their contributions, and she would say, "Mr. Barnum, I mean you." According to the report, Mr. Barnum never failed to oblige her.

When Susan B. Anthony organized the National Woman Suffrage Association in the spring of 1869, Olympia supported her in every way that she could. She urged all women, both vocally and in her writings, to join the association and begin working to get a woman suffrage bill through Congress. Only a national organization with thousands of women as members could launch a successful drive to get the ballot for women nationwide, she declared. Less than six months later, a split among the leaders sent Lucy Stone and her followers off to organize the rival American Woman Suffrage Association.

Olympia immediately wrote a letter to Mrs. Stone and Henry Blackwell. That letter reveals some of the petty jealousies and political rivalries that erupted among the various leaders of the movement.

Bridgeport, Ct.
Nov. 8, 1869

Mr. Blackwell & Mrs. Stone.
Dear Friends,

Your kind letters are just received. I thank you for the kind spirit they manifest and for the friendly manner in which you have ever treated me. I should like to see you and talk all these woman's rights affairs over with you as I fear I shall not make myself understood in a letter; but I will express a few thoughts that now occur to me.

Mr. Blackwell says, "We want a society, too, completely representative of the friends of the cause, all over the country, not to be controlled by any individual, clique, newspaper, or locality; too impartial to be ever perverted into advocating or attacking side issues on which friends of the cause honestly differ."

Now this is precisely what I should like to see and if my going to Cleveland (to help form the new American Woman Suffrage Association) or five times as far as would bring about such an organization, I would go, let it cost me what it would; but I fear no such result will be attained at Cleveland. It seems to me, rather, that the states will fail to send delegates as, in fact, Mr. Blackwell seems to anticipate; and some will be kept away by a feeling that there is a division in the ranks of the advocacy of the cause. They don't wish to be engaged on either side, and finally, as the idea of calling such a convention started from the N. E. Suffrage Association, those persons will be there, and will control the convention and the association which is to be formed, unless your influence shall be sufficient to prevent. It will then, like the New England Suffrage Association, be controlled by a little clique of Boston people who wish to do things in their own way, and have matters all in their own hands.

There are a few things which I will speak of which, as they are strictly confidential, I shall rely upon you to make no mention of whatever. You say, "I think you would cooperate with it [the new organization) more heartily than you can with Mrs. Stanton's soc." Now, as you know, I did not approve of the course of action pursued by Mrs. Stanton and Miss Anthony in Kansas, nor of their misrepresentations of affairs there on their return. I still think, however, that they have the good of the cause at heart and deserve credit for working through long years when it was new and unpopular. Miss Anthony in particular has really given her life to it and has borne more odium than any other person connected with it. We cannot wonder that she should desire to be identified with it in its success. She certainly will be recognized as one of the principle persons instrumental in securing suffrage to women. Her name is too thoroughly identified with woman's rights to prevent it. However, I was not in New York when this association was formed, of which Mrs. Stanton is the Pres., and I have never joined it and do not now think I ever shall.

As to the new one to be formed at Cleveland, if it could be such as you indicate, of course I should join it and work heartily for it; but I suspect it will be governed by a clique of whom several are persons in whom I have not as much confidence as I have in Miss Anthony; besides that they are very recent converts to the cause and some, at least, of them I think have come into the cause for their own selfish purposes. . . As matters stand I think it better that I should not identify myself with either association, but work as occasion may offer on my own hook. Be assured I shall lose no opportunity which opens for me to serve the cause.

It is not against the cause that there are such women, nor that they should be found in our ranks. It is but human nature, and as the cause advances to success such women will be ready to identify themselves with it. For my own part I wish to work for principles, not individuals or cliques.

Truly your friend,
Olympia Brown[14]

Although she had a high regard for Miss Anthony, she refused to work under Elizabeth Cady Stanton's leadership—or anyone's leadership who could not put the goal of enfranchisement above personal ambitions. Olympia was an idealist. Her expectations of people were so high that she could not accept the reality of such human frailties as ego and pride. Nor could she recognize these weaknesses in herself. Her own ego was strong. She was so proud of her accomplishments that she clipped newspaper articles about herself and saved flyers advertising her many suffrage campaigns. Perhaps some of her resentment stemmed from jealousy, but personality clashes played a part, also. She was as stubborn and uncompromising as any of the leaders. When she could not make them see things her way, she would go and work alone, "on her own hook" as she would say over and over again.

Lucy Stone and her followers adhered to a policy quite different from that of Susan B. Anthony and her national organization. Leaders of the American Woman Suffrage Association believed that women must work within each state to get the vote, and that a great national movement was unnecessary. They believed this so ardently that they refused to do any work toward an amendment to the Constitution. By so limiting their work, these suffragists failed to realize that there would be some states that would probably not ever enact a woman suffrage law. A national amendment was surely the only way to bring about enfranchisement across the nation.

Most of the leaders of both organizations also failed to realize that they must rally the working woman and the homemaker to their cause. Instead, they focused their energies on wealthy and upper middle-class women, many of whom did not particularly care about either voting or equal rights and actually feared they might lose certain benefits if such an amendment was passed.

When Olympia first met the arguments presented by these privileged women, she was surprised by the strength of their opinions and their resistance to any change in their status. Although she tried to explain to them the important benefits they would gain, many could not see beyond their own narrow spheres. Nevertheless, she held fast to her hope that they would ultimately understand and join in the great movement to gain the right to vote and the right to participate in their own government.

Olympia's name is on the executive committee rosters of both woman suffrage organizations, whether she actually joined them or not. It is certainly an open question where her loyalty lay. "I am willing to work for principles, but not individuals or cliques," she often said. For Olympia, there was a very fine line between working for a particular leader or working under her leadership. She rejected any idea or particular work if she felt that it would only aid a specific person or group. When a leader bathed in the publicity of either cause, she nipped at her leadership qualities by voice and by pen. In such a situation, she usually left and went her own way.

Her uncompromising spirit cost her much in effective leadership. Her actions and statements were often contradictory, yet she worked unstintingly in any way that she could to gain the ballot. Although she had disagreements with the leaders, she would eventually reconcile her differences and rejoin them in new campaigns. Always, her first priority reemerged and she marched into new forays as though she had never caused the slightest ripple on the surface of the movement.

It was only a year after her move to Bridgeport that she entered another name in her church membership book: J. H. Willis. He sold his business in Weymouth Landing, invested in a local tea and food store in Bridgeport and became an active member of her church.[15]

Courting Olympia must surely have been a slow process, since she thrived on the degree of independence with which she steered her way through the snags and open waterways of her life. John Henry Willis, however, was a patient man. He was committed to equal rights and woman suffrage and she soon began to realize that he was also committed to her. He pursued her with a gentle persistence that she found increasingly difficult to resist as the months slipped past in a whirl of suffrage work, sermons and house calls, meetings and speeches. She circulated petitions, spoke before congressional committees and state legislatures, and campaigned wherever she felt that she could achieve some small gain. In between these activities, Mr. Willis paid his visits.

The issue of woman suffrage was settling into a stalemate. With no major advances, progress had come to a standstill. Neither Congress nor the state legislatures had made any effort to bring the issue to a vote. Many of the workers suffered in the doldrums, lethargic and depressed that all of their work was to little or no avail. Hannah Comstock, one noted suffragist, struck a chord in the hearts of reformers. "We cannot look to man for help; they are determined to keep us as we are if they can and I sometimes think our deliverance will come only through blood. What the end of this great social upheaving will be no human being can tell. Surely the reality and beginning of the storm are terrible."[16]

Susan B. Anthony decided to take a drastic step in the fall of 1872. She was going to vote! Either she would be successful and prove that women could vote, or she would gain much needed publicity for the cause. What did she have to lose? Probably none of the women could visualize the repercussion of her act, nor the opportunities it generated.

On election day, she and several other women walked to the local polling place and cast their ballots. Remarkably, their votes were accepted. The victory did not last long, however. On Thanksgiving day, Miss Anthony and her friends were arrested. The news made national headlines.

Olympia read the story in the newspaper and immediately wrote to Miss Anthony, extolling her for such a brave act. She was in high spirits, believing that when Miss Anthony went on trial, the court would find in her favor. When that happened, then women all over the nation would have the right to vote. It was, indeed, an exciting time and women everywhere watched the progress of the trial.

They had pinned their hopes on a falling star. The judge ruled that Miss Anthony was guilty of voting without having a lawful right to do so and fined her one hundred dollars. Miss Anthony refused to pay the fine and, in fact, never did so. Olympia, furious with the judge's decision, urged Miss Anthony to sue. "Women should join together and file a suit against the federal government," she declared. Unfortunately, it would have been a costly proceeding, particularly if it went all the way to the Supreme Court, and the women simply had no money for such a battle. The opportunity for gaining justice in the courts, and thus cutting short a long, bitter battle for enfranchisement, fell.

Meanwhile, Olympia was having trouble in her church. At the annual congregational meeting in 1873, the members of the church accepted a new resolution which called for the "united effort of all true Universalists." They agreed to "work together in the spirit of Christian charity mutually forbearing one another in love and that overlooking trifling differences of opinion we will each labour according to our ability to serve our common cause submitting in all cases of disagreement to the vote of the majority." Thirty-five members voted to hire her for another year, while eight voted "Nay."[17]

Olympia was not sure if the group of dissenters was swaying the minds of regular parishioners or if they were bringing in protesters whose sole purpose in joining the church was to oppose her. A deepening rift greeted her every effort at unity. One may wonder why she elected to stay in a pastorate where there was such discord and enmity, particularly when she had received an offer from another church.

The Gospel Banner, April 1873, reported that, "Rev. Olympia Brown has decided to stay in Bridgeport another year, even though a Pittsburgh church has offered her a larger salary."[18]

Clearly, she must have had good reason to make such a decision. The reason became clear when she announced that she and John Henry Willis were getting married.

Her own mother opposed the marriage at first. "It will interfere with your preaching and suffrage work," Lephia warned her. She did not want to see Olympia's education go to waste, and she feared that her daughter would soon be tied down to domestic chores and motherhood. Olympia disagreed.

"With a husband so entirely in sympathy with my work, marriage cannot interfere, but rather assist," she argued. She would not listen to advice from anyone. The couple married in Rhode Island at the home of relatives in April of 1873. Years later Olympia noted that her decision had been right. "I could not have married a better man. He shared in all my undertakings, and always stood for the right," she said.[19] It could not have been an easy life for Mr. Willis, to live with a crusading feminist and her strong-minded mother, but John Henry Willis was not an ordinary man.

Olympia kept her own name after marriage, and she was known as the Reverend Olympia Brown all of her life. The custom of a woman changing her name to her husband's upon marriage was so deeply ingrained in society that even some of her friends and associates erred in calling her Mrs. Willis instead of Reverend Brown. They rarely made the same mistake twice. She corrected those who made the mistake in such a way that it adhered sharp and clear in their memory as the day she apprised them that she wished to be known as Olympia Brown! A letter she wrote to a Brother Start is a particularly poignant example.

I received a letter from you inviting me, Olympia Brown, no one else, to speak anniversary week, May 30th. In Boston, at the conference of the churches I, Olympia Brown, no one else, accepted that invitation and expect to be on hand to meet the engagement.

I have, in my private capacity, made various changes since accepting your invitation. I have bought a new stove, joined a sewing society, moved into another house, joined a social club; but none of these things concern the audience to whom I am to speak or the committee who invited me. To intrude them would be forcing my private affairs upon the attention of the public. It would be obtruding my personality where the people ought to think only of the subject of which I am to speak, viz the welfare of the churches.

My marriage is an arrangement I have made in my individual capacity as a private person. It doesn't concern the audience and I don't wish it thrust upon them. I shall be much obliged to you if you will see to it that my name appears on the program and is announced when I am introduced to the audience as ever, Rev. Olympia Brown, neither more nor less.[20]

Her troubles with the misogynic faction in the Bridgeport church continued throughout the following year. The man who originally refused to have anything to do with a woman preacher agitated continually for a "change in the Pastorate." He pecked away at her ministry like a raucous crow, attacking from any and every direction whenever he felt like it. She began to fear that she was fighting a losing battle, even as she tried to bring about unity. Slowly, the flock began to scatter. A few members told her that they did not like the dissension among church members, and they left. One man left because the name of Abraham Lincoln was mentioned in a sermon. "I do not believe politics has any place in the church," he said. Another man left because he felt that too much time was given to the communion service. Several members became spiritualists, saying the church no longer had any place in their lives. There were some families who only attended while the children were going to Sunday school. They left the church when the children were grown.[21]

Olympia realized that, although each person had a different reason, James Staples was responsible for causing many of her parishioners to leave the church. A bitter agitator can unsettle a peaceful environment and influence even stable individuals, she learned. She worked hard on her sermons, and loyal parishioners supported her, but she felt a great uneasiness about the future of the church.

In spite of the problems, it was a time of great personal happiness for her and her husband. A note by a local wholesale grocer sheds some light on the warmth of their relationship. "I was just telling him [J. H. Willis] that your ministry has wrought a wonderful change in his countenance. Before his marriage he looked a selfish, dried in, misanthropic old bachelor. Now he smiles genially. There seems a warm, kindly, benevolent atmosphere around him . . . you have wrought such a change in him."[22]

Their happiness increased when they learned that they were going to have a child during the summer of 1874. On August 14, Olympia gave birth to a son at Elmira, New York, a place noted for its health care. They named the boy Henry Parker Willis, and he was affectionately known as Parker the rest of his life.

Lephia Brown came from her home in Michigan to help take care of her new grandchild. Although it was the custom at the time for the mother to come and help in the household for a while, Lephia was embroiled in a separation from Olympia's father.[23] Coming to help her daughter was an acceptable solution to her problems. She soon made herself a permanent niche with Olympia and John H. Willis, and she lived with them the rest of her life. By helping take care of the house and children, she relieved Olympia of the most pressing duties of family and child care. This was crucial to Olympia's career because she could spend more time on ministerial and suffrage work with her mother's domestic help.

James Staples enlarged his campaign against her over the next two years. He organized meetings in the town and invited ministers of neighboring churches to come and speak out against women preachers. At a special meeting in 1875, the dissenting group within the church requested that the "acting Trustees of said Society are not hereafter restrained from employing any *Gentlemen in good standing* as a *clergyman*."[24] Although she remained pastor of the church for another year, she realized that almost any man could be hired as minister of the church under the ruling made by the Court of Common Pleas. The key words in the ruling were, "Gentlemen in good standing," regardless of qualification. It was as bitter a blow as any that she had ever received, but there was no alternative for her except to take it in stride. She did have the loyalty of the board of trustees and faithful parishioners, but she lost the church. In March of 1876, the trustees announced that there was not enough money to hire a preacher due to an injunction put upon the church the year before by the dissenters, and the officers resigned in protest.

Olympia now began to give more of her time to woman suffrage work; she realized her ministerial career was floundering in the wake of sex discrimination. She may have run aground briefly in rough waters, but she would not quit. In time she would consider serving another church. Meanwhile, she had woman suffrage work to keep her busy.

She appeared before a Congressional committee in Washington, D.C., in January of 1876, and delivered a speech laced with barbs and reproaches; yet the speech was a moving appeal for suffrage. Women had been working for years for enfranchisement and still were no closer to getting the ballot. The futility of their struggle pained them deeply. Her speech before the Congressional committee echoed the sentiments of the "Founding Fathers," but she quickly pointed out that women were citizens, too.

I would not intrude upon your time and exhaust your patience by any further hearing upon this subject if it were not that men are continually saying to us that we do not want the ballot; that it is only a handful of women that have ever asked for it; and I think by our coming up from these different States . . . and giving our testimony . . . we shall convince you that it is not a few merely, but that it is a general demand from the women in all the different States of the Union . . . that we all desire the right of suffrage. Nor shall our mistakes and inability to advocate our cause in an effective manner be an argument against us, because it is not the province of voters to conduct meetings in Washington. It is rather their province to stay at home and quietly read the proceedings of members of congress, and if they find these proceedings correct, to vote to return them another year. So that our very mistakes shall argue for us and not against us.

In the ages past the right of citizenship meant the right to enjoy or possess or attain all those civil and political rights that are enjoyed by any other citizen. But here we have a class who can bear the burdens and punishments of citizens, but cannot enjoy their privileges and rights . . . I would add, "What can be more universal than the rights of woman?" extending further than the rights of man, because woman . . . by her influence and in her office as an educator makes the character of man; because women are to be found wherever men are to be found, as their mothers bringing them into the world, watching them, teaching them, guiding them into manhood. . .

I will not insult your common sense by bringing up the old arguments as to whether we have the right to vote. I believe every man of you knows we have that right—that our right to vote is based upon the same authority as yours. I believe every man understands that, according to the declaration and the constitution, women should be allowed to exercise the right of suffrage, and therefore it is not necessary for me to do more than bear my testimony from the State of Connecticut, and tell you that the women from the rank and file, the law-abiding women, desire the ballot; not only that they desire it, but they mean to have it. And to accomplish this result I need not remind you that they will work year in and year out, that they will besiege members of congress everywhere, and that they will come here year after year asking you to protect them in their rights and to see that justice is done in the republic. . . Our interests are still uncared for, and we do not wish to be thus sent from pillar to post to get our rights. We wish to take our stand as citizens of the United States, as we have been declared to be by the Supreme Court, and we wish to be protected in the rights of citizenship. . .[25]

The logic of her arguments settled over the heads of the committee members with the pungency of wood smoke. They nodded slightly from time to time and appeared to frown occasionally as though a sudden idea disturbed their state of tranquility. Was there no way to get the woman suffrage amendment out of the committee and onto the floor? They were out of touch with the reality of women's needs. They did not comprehend the enormous burden of discrimination and subjugation under which women worked. Olympia could see that the men were not moved by her appeal. They were, indeed, determined to keep women as they were.

She was expecting her second child in the fall and she curtailed her activities during the summer. Victorian society decreed that a pregnant woman should not appear in public. Although she often dismissed such

114

stodgy customs, her pregnancy is likely the reason she did not join Susan B. Anthony and four other suffragists in a rights march during the July 4 Centennial Celebration in Philadelphia. This was 1876, the one-hundredth anniversary of the Declaration of Independance. The Centennial Committee had refused to accept the women's "Declaration of Rights of the Women of the United States" document during the official ceremonies. Miss Anthony, however, effected a coup by marching directly to the platform with her delegation and handing the paper to the master of ceremonies. In the surprise and confusion wrought by this activity, he accepted it and it thus became part of the official ceremony. The women turned and marched back through the crowd, distributing copies as they went. They mounted another platform nearby and there they read aloud the Declaration publicly.[26] It was a bold and dramatic act, the kind Olympia herself delighted in engineering. Her name appears on the document along with those of a number of other suffragists.

In November, she gave birth to a daughter, Gwendolen Brown Willis. Olympia devoted herself to her family for the next year. In time, however, she grew restless once again. The call to the ministry sounded once more, and in 1878, when her daughter was fifteen months old, she began a search that was to take her nearly a thousand miles from New England.

The Asa Briggs Brown family, circa 1848, was photographed when Olympia (opposite page) was about 13 years old. In 1834, her mother, Lephia (opposite page above) and her father, Asa, came from Vermont to Schoolcraft, Michigan. Arthur (above right) is about 5 years old and sisters Oella (lower left) and Marcia, are about 11 and 9. *Photos from Marcia's granddaughter, Marcella Chalkley Holmes*

During her student years, the Amelia Bloomer costume gave Olympia and many other women who wore it greater freedom of movement. Olympia stopped wearing it after her graduation because of widespread public ridicule of the dress.

Impartial Suffrage
MEETINGS!

MISS OLYMPIA BROWN will address the people of Doniphan County at the following times and places, on the subject of Impartial Suffrage:

White Cloud,	Tuesday,	Oct. 29,	7 P. M.
Macy's School House,	Wednesday,	" 30,	10 A. M.
Conklin's "	"	" "	2 P. M.
Iowa Point,	"	" "	7 "
Martin's School House,	Thursday,	" 31,	10 A. M.
Rounsavell's "	"	" "	2 P. M.
Iola "	"	" "	7 "
Prairie Grove "	Friday,	Nov. 1,	10 A. M.
McNemee, "	"	" "	2 P. M.
Norwegian "	"	" "	7 "
McClellan, "	Saturday,	" 2,	10 A. M.
Columbus "	"	" "	2 P. M.
Burr Oak "	"	" "	7 "

Miss Brown will preach at Troy, on Sunday, November 3d, at 11 o'clock, A. M., and at Wathena, at 3 and 7, P. M.
Go and hear this gifted lady speak.

"Chief" Print, White Cloud.

"Go and hear this gifted lady speak," urges one of the many Kansas Impartial Suffrage posters. She toured Kansas from July to November, 1867, campaigning for the woman's vote. *Photo reproduction from the Schlesinger Library, Radcliffe College*

Olympia Brown, circa 1863, at the time of her graduation from the Theological School of St. Lawrence University and her ordination to the ministry by the Universalist denomination. *Photo from Schlesinger Library, Radcliffe College*

Susan B. Anthony wrote to Olympia Brown from Leavenworth, Kansas, just after the defeat of the Impartial Suffrage Amendment. "Dear Olympia, Never was so grand a success—never was defeat so glorious a victory . . . But don't despair. We shall win. The day breaks. The eastern sky is red. Mr. Train consents to lecture for our treasury's benefit all the way down to Boston & back to Philadelphia.

consents to lecture for our League's benefit—all the way down to Boston & back to Philadelphia—commencing the 20th—And my dear Olympia—if ever any money got into my power to control you shall have evidence that I appreciate the herculean work you have done here in Kansas the past four long months. If only Geo. F. Train could have lighted the fires you had prepared all over the State—we should have carried it overwhelmingly—But depend upon it—there is a wise destiny in our delay—it is not defeat—So let us hope & work to the brighter day—God bless you & keep you safe & alive to see the glory of our work accomplished. Affectionately yours—

Susan B. Anthony

"... and my dear Olympia—if ever any money gets into my power to control you shall have evidence that I appreciate the Herculean work you have done here in Kansas the past four long months. If only Geo. F. Train could have lighted the fires you had prepared all over the state—we should have carried it overwhelmingly. But depend upon it—there is a wise destiny in our delay—it is not defeat. So let us hope & work to the brighter day. God bless you & keep you safe & alive to see the glory of our work accomplished." *Photo reproductions from the Schlesinger Library, Radcliffe College*

Photo from the Racine County Historical Society and Museum, Inc.

Olympia Brown.

Photo from the Unitarian Universalist Church, Racine, Wisconsin

When Olympia Brown became its minister in 1878, the Church of the Good Shepherd had a shepherd's crook rather than the cross of traditional churches. A replica of that crook adorns the present church, built in 1895 at College Avenue and 7th Street, which replaced the old church at Main and Sixth Street that was razed to make way for a new hotel. Pictured above is the interior of the Main Street church. *Photos from the Unitarian Universalist Church, Racine*

The Racine Times-Call staff and office, photographed in 1896, with Olympia standing behind her daughter, Gwendolen Willis, and Angus Callender. After her husband, John Henry Willis, died in 1893, Olympia bought out his partners and for seven years managed the newspaper located on Fifth Street and Monument Square. Willis invested in the newspaper after moving to Racine where Olympia had become the minister of the town's Universalist church. *Photo from the Racine County Historical Society and Museum, Inc.*

Olympia at 82 helps lead the Racine Women's Suffrage Association, all wearing silk ribbons saying "Votes for Women," in a mile-long, rainy Loyalty Day parade viewed by thousands just 56 days after the United States entered World War I.

Olympia, circa 1905, wears her characteristic shawl and a touch of white at her throat.
Photos from the Schlesinger Library, Radcliffe College

Olympia is surrounded with beribboned baskets of flowers in her yard in 1920. She is pictured with an unidentified guest and her daughter, Gwendolyn, right. *Photo from Racine County Historical Society and Museum, Inc.*

A float promotes votes for women in the 1916 Fourth of July parade. Woman Suffrage Association of Racine's President, Jeannette Bull Reed, left, Olympia Brown's daughter, Gwendolen Willis, center, and Olympia's niece, Genevieve Chalkley, on the float, pose proudly before the parade. *Photo from The Journal Times, Racine*

Olympia Brown at age 90 in her garden overlooking Lake Michigan in 1925.
The Willis residence was at 941 Lake Avenue, Racine. *Photo from the Racine
County Historical Society and Museum, Inc.*

Chapter 7

A New Beginning

Olympia's heart suddenly picked up a beat when she read in January of 1878 that a Universalist church in Racine, Wisconsin, was without a minister. Racine, stretching along the shores of Lake Michigan, was close to Chicago where her sister Oella lived. It would be nice, she thought, to live near her sister again. They could visit each other often and raise their families together. Oella, who married while the family still lived in Yellow Springs, now had seven children.

Olympia sat down at once and wrote a letter to the Racine church. Would they be interested, she asked, in having her come and give a trial sermon? She was not acting in haste in making this decision. She and her husband had already decided to move away from Bridgeport since there was nothing to keep them in that city. Willis had sold his business and the idea of going west appealed to him.

When a reply came from Racine, she opened it with the eagerness of a long-anticipated invitation. Mr. Fish, the secretary of the church, had no invitation for her, however. The essence of his letter is contained in two brief sentences. "The Racine church is in a run-down and unfortunate condition. It is adrift, in debt, hopeless, and doubtful whether any pastor can again arouse them."[1]

These might have been discouraging words to some, but not to Olympia. This, she realized, was just the kind of church where she did her best work. Urging him to reconsider, she told him about her success with the Weymouth Landing church and assured him, "I am sent to just such churches. Let me come and see what I can do."[2]

Such spirit deserved consideration, Mr. Fish decided, and he sent a short note. "The parish is willing to hear you and you will be welcomed," he wrote. Olympia's reply, remarkably brief and business-like, masked her eagerness to make the journey.

Yours just received. I infer that there is no objection to a Sunday's service in Racine, therefore I shall be there one week from next

Sunday, February 24th. You will oblige me by giving the proper notice. I will preach morning, afternoon, or evening, or all three as the people may desire.

Yours for the good cause.
Olympia Brown.[3]

Perhaps she did not trust herself to say more. She was standing on the brink of a new life, and the flame beckoned very brightly.

Leaving her two children in the care of her husband and mother, she set out, "like one of old to find my own way," as she said later. If she felt the slightest guilt in setting out on her journey, it quickly dissipated as she traveled westward. One of her greatest joys in life was to travel. She delighted in seeing new country, meeting new people, having new adventures. Life was made for challenge, not quiet acceptance, she had learned a long time ago.

When she arrived in the bustling little port town of Racine, she was met at the train and taken to the Winship home instead of to a hotel which she had expected. Her heart warmed with the friendly concern of the parishioners. How different from the staid New Englanders who had left her to fend for herself so many times. Her hostess led her to a bedroom on the second floor where the windows faced out over Lake Michigan. Here she had her first view of the great lake stretching away to the east as far as her eyes could see. Slate-blue swells rolled in toward shore, breaking into white foam on the rocks and sand below. The majesty of the view, the restlessness of the water and the changing colors of the lake enthralled her. She could have watched it for hours.

Although a heavy rain was falling and continued to fall steadily during her entire stay, she began at once to make calls on the church members. She asked each family to come to the church and hear her preach on the following Sunday.

Getting about the city during the heavy rains was not easy. The unpaved streets became a sea of mud and there was hardly a sidewalk in the whole town. Some merchants had board walks, but few homes boasted such a convenience. John Willis must have wondered just what kind of a frontier town Racine was whenever Olympia wrote to kept him posted on her adventures.

"The mud is the deepest I have ever seen. Racine, situated on the banks of the winding Root River is dependent upon its bridges. These are now out of commission."[4]

She had to cross the river to visit the church members who lived on the other side, an act she was determined to accomplish. One day when she walked down to the river, a man stopped her. "You can't go across the river now. The only way over is by walking on a bridge of boats. Too dangerous for a woman." Those were all the words that she needed to hear.

"If it is the only way to get across the river, then that is the way I shall get across," she said, and stepped sprightly aboard the first boat rocking in the choppy water. Although the men tried to discourage her, she waved them away with a flip of her hand. "I can manage quite well," she said, and continued on across the makeshift bridge. She, who had crisscrossed the Kansas prairie eleven years before without a conveyance of her own, hotel accommodations or even an escort, could very well manage to walk across a temporary bridge of boats. She managed to visit every family in the church in spite of rain, mud and washed-out bridges.

The people of the parish were friendly and interested in the church's well-being. She could not understand Mr. Fish's discouraging remarks in his first letter to her until she had visited in the homes of a number of parishioners. It did not take her long to delve beneath the surface of the problems and discover that many members drifted away because of "impractical and disreputable" pastors. Her spirits rose as these words fell on her ears again and again. If that was the major problem with the church, then surely she could solve the dilemma. She would preach the best possible sermons and convince the parishioners that she was just the practical, sincere and dedicated pastor they needed.

As she traveled about the town, visiting and exploring the streets and neighborhoods, her mind skipped ahead. John Willis would find the business climate good. Everywhere she looked people were building new homes and opening new stores. Racine was a warm, open and friendly community, quite different from New England. She found she had forgotten that mid-western characteristic. "I believe this city will be a good place to live and raise a family," she wrote back to her husband in her most business-like way. In the back of her mind, however, the practical aspects of life in Racine gave way to the call of that great expanse of slate-blue water, the lake that seemed as restless as her own heart.

Mr. Fish suggested that she might stay and give sermons on two Sundays, thereby "giving everyone in the congregation an opportunity to hear you preach." Olympia agreed at once, and she set about preparing two warm, inspiring sermons. Although she missed her family, she had disciplined herself to a degree of loneliness, coupled with hard work that few people embrace.

The church was filled on both Sundays. Perhaps some people came just to hear a woman preach, she realized, but she didn't let such a thought bother her. After the second Sunday's service, the congregation met and quickly voted to call her as its minister. Delight streamed through her; she had a church once more. A whole new life was opening up before her. Packing her bags to begin her journey back to Bridgeport, she could not help casting a long, wistful look at the lake. Joy echoed in her heart like the song of a meadowlark on a spring morning as she realized that she would see the lake again soon.

When Olympia returned to Bridgeport, Willis prepared to travel to Racine to find a home for the family. When he got to Racine, it did not take him long to find a spacious, two-story house overlooking Lake Michigan, and he purchased it at once. He then returned to Bridgeport to help the family move. Olympia was caught by surprise. Her mind danced ahead. She could watch the sun rise over the lake in the morning, see the silver sheen give way to steel gray, then, as the sun rose higher, watch a shimmering dark blue spread like a stain over the water. She could see the great swells and white caps roll in when a storm blew in over the lake and listen to the waves crashing on shore. She could plant a garden in the long slope of yard that led down almost to the water's edge. It was a haven, a place where she could forget her cares for a few minutes while she stood and looked out over the lake's rippling surface, aware that underneath were the surging currents that gave the lake its life. Here she could focus her energies.

The house at 941 Lake Avenue was within easy walking distance of downtown where the Church of the Good Shepherd stood on Haymarket Square. In a few years, her children would go to nearby Winslow school. Surely life was sweet, she thought. She had been a long time reaching this standpoint. Now she would devote herself to her new church and her family. Perhaps she could even find the time for woman suffrage work sometime in the future.

Mr. Willis soon invested in a newspaper publishing and job-printing business. His newspaper, *The Racine Times-Call*, would later become part of *The Journal-Times*, the present Racine daily newspaper. He quickly became active and well-liked in the Racine community. He served as vestryman in the church, taught Sunday school and joined the music committee. He often helped Lephia take care of the two children whenever Olympia went to meetings around the state. She could not have asked for a better man; he supported her in everything that she did. He must have been remarkably patient and understanding to live in a household with two such ardent feminists as Olympia and her mother. Surely the air crackled like an electrical storm with woman suffrage and woman's rights issues, particularly when those issues suffered continued defeats.

Olympia plunged into her church work. She organized a Sunday school, young people's group, ladies' afternoon social club and evening social meetings. "Quite an accomplishment," she must have thought to herself as she watched the membership grow, "in a church that Mr. Fish called adrift, hopeless, and doubtful whether any pastor can again arouse." The evening social meetings were much like those that she had introduced at Weymouth Landing, and she began inviting the public to the lectures and musical programs. The church soon became well-known as an educational and social center in Racine under her capable hands, and it grew and prospered. Elizabeth Cady Stanton, Susan B. Anthony, Julia Ward Howe, Mary A. Livermore, Pheobe Hanaford, Mary Wright Sewall, Theodore Tilton, and many other friends from the east came to lecture.

After living in a tight circle of church work and family life for a year or so, the time came when she began to feel the invisible bonds of church and family care were anchoring her in a very small harbor. She felt that she must reach out beyond her immediate focus.

For a time, the district Universalist meetings and conventions had answered her need. When she was asked to take part in some of their plans and programs, she accepted with alacrity. Each new challenge opened up a new opportunity, and soon she, too, was giving speeches at the district conventions. She began taking issue with some of the speakers and challenging their opinions when she found them in conflict with her own. The first time that she openly differed with a lecturer in the district meetings was during a convention in LaCrosse, Wisconsin. The speaker was talking about the many advantages young men enjoyed while they were training as ministers at Lombard College in Illinois. His continued references to young men at last wore her patience thin.

"What about young women, Doctor?" she asked suddenly. "Can't they enjoy these same advantages?"

The idea was so new to the speaker and the group that it roared into the peace of their minds, leaving a cloud of thick thoughts behind it. Some of the people shifted in their chairs; a few coughed and busied themselves with their handkerchiefs. The speaker grasped both sides of the podium and gazed at her in astonishment. For a few moments he could not reply, then a frown deepened on his brow and he shook his head.

"As far as I know, no church has ever asked for a woman preacher." He looked out over the audience. Slowly the frown began to leave his face as he talked about the many problems he believed a woman would encounter while going to a theological school. Even if she managed to finish the course of study, he ended, she would probably not be able to find a church that would hire her.

Olympia said no more until he finished talking, not because she had nothing more to say, but because she felt that she should address the issue with him privately. As soon as he finished his speech, she made her way to the platform and introduced herself.[5]

I am Reverend Olympia Brown, minister of the Church of the Good Shepherd in Racine, Wisconsin. I graduated from theological school and was ordained nearly twenty years ago. The Racine church is my fourth pastorate and I know other women preachers who have their own churches. You are doing a grave wrong to women in discouraging them from going into the ministry. My own feeling is that men simply do not want women preachers and they deliberately create prejudice against them.

She told the speaker that new ideas or even new discoveries were usually rejected at first, but eventually people began to understand and accept them. Surely Universalist ministers should lead the way in encouraging women to enter the ministry. Although it might seem like a new and strange idea, it was perfectly logical, she said. Women were good ministers; it was a natural career for them. She, herself, had been encouraging women for years to go into the field, both personally and in articles published in journals and periodicals. It was a battle that she would not ever surrender, she finished. Then she turned abruptly and marched from the hall. She wanted her words to filter down into his conscience where they could root and grow. Besides, it was good strategy to have the last word and leave the opponent without a rejoinder.

Phoebe Hanaford was one of the first women Olympia had encouraged to become a minister. Olympia had even taken part in Hanaford's ordination in Massachusetts years before. Reverend Hanaford enjoyed success at first. Eventually she had accepted a pulpit in New Haven, Connecticut, not far from Bridgeport. The two women became close friends and often worked together on woman suffrage campaigns. However, Reverend Hanaford soon began to meet organized opposition among the men in her congregation. The pain of rejection echoed along the lines in one of her letters to Olympia.

"I have left my pastorate in New Haven," she wrote. "The men in the congregation opposed me and they asked for my resignation . . . I do not think that I will continue my work in the church because of the treatment accorded women ministers."

In referring to Olympia's troubles within the Bridgeport church a short time before her own, Reverend Hanaford wrote, "I was placed in an unfortunate position towards you by reason of the friendship . . . in the family of those opposed to you. I . . . grieved more than you knew over the treatment you received."[6]

For some women, the pain was too deep.

Olympia's first four years in Racine slipped quickly past. Besides her work in the church, she wrote numerous letters and articles, campaigned for woman suffrage, and devoted herself to her family. The church was growing and prosperous and all seemed to be going well. Then in the summer of 1882, it became clear that the church building needed major repairs. When the estimate for renovations came in at five thousand dollars, Olympia's spirits tumbled. Would the congregation even consider spending such an amount, she wondered? Visions of having to go and find another church entered her head, but she had roots in Racine by now and the thought of leaving was painful.

At this point, a wealthy church member, Jerome Increase (J. I.) Case the well-known manufacturer of farm machinery, came forward and announced that he would donate half the amount if members of the congregation would donate the other half. "That sum must be raised in ten days," he stipulated. He understood human nature very well. If he put a time limit on his generosity, people would be more likely to donate to the cause before they had second thoughts about it.

Olympia seized the challenge at once. It became a crusade for her and she and another church woman set out to visit every member of the congregation to try and get them to increase their pledges. "I spent ten of the hottest days I have ever experienced in my life, but we did it," she wrote.[7] They claimed Mr. Case's pledge, and work on the church began at once. She tasted a triumph doubly sweet. The church never seemed more unified and prosperous as the members gathered to support the repairs to the building, and she realized that they were supporting her as well.

Meanwhile, a steady trend toward conservative and conventional beliefs and behaviors was changing the suffrage movement. Militancy was no longer in fashion; even Susan B. Anthony recognized the change. Anthony was still an active campaigner, but she was growing older. By 1880 she was sixty. She announced that year from her home in Rochester, New York, that it was time for women to start writing a history of the woman suffrage movement from its inception more than thirty years before to the present, and she asked for help from the suffragists. "The only way we are going to get our experiences recorded is to do it ourselves, because men write the history books and they have not included any woman's rights history in them," she said. Men had not included much of anything else about women in their history books, either, and she was determined to see that their work and experiences in trying to get the ballot were published.

When she wrote to Olympia asking her for a written account of the 1867 Kansas campaign to be published in the book, Olympia agreed to write it for her.[8]

There was so much material on the woman suffrage movement to be put in the book that the three authors, Miss Anthony, Elizabeth Cady Stanton and Matilda Joslyn Gage, found they had to write a second volume just to cover the 1860s and begin the 1870s. None of them could have dreamed how many more volumes still would have to be written before women won the right to vote.

Olympia was feeling, by now, a growing urge to work for the woman suffrage movement again. She attended national conventions whenever she could, and she joined the Wisconsin Woman Suffrage Association. First organized in 1881, it had soon floundered from lack of support by state women. How is it, Olympia wondered, that they do not seem interested in their own organization? Is it lack of leadership, poor publicity or just apathy? Surely there were many women in the state who wanted to vote, but where were they?

After turning these thoughts over in her mind several times, she decided to act. Like an eagle after its quarry, she focused on the leaders. She would invite the board members to her home for a meeting, she decided. The plan worked well. Besides the election of new officers, they discussed activities for the coming year and made plans for a membership drive, state convention and the organization of branches in some of the larger towns. However, none of these things came to pass. She wrote letters, complained, and made suggestions. The following year, 1884, the Wisconsin Woman Suffrage Association elected her their president, a post she would hold for the next twenty-eight years.

Now she held the reins in her own hands. She immediately appointed committees, made plans to hold suffrage meetings around the state, organize branches, and hold an annual woman suffrage convention. She organized fund and membership drives, both crucial to a successful organization, and taught many women how to campaign.

After recruiting a nucleus of dynamic reformers in the Madison area, the members of the association went before the state legislature and urged the legislators to pass a woman suffrage amendment. In 1885, a limited woman suffrage bill did pass the legislature after much argument and compromising. Many people believed it was a full voting rights bill, although the language was ambiguous.

Every woman who is a citizen of this State of the age of twenty-one years and upward, except paupers, etc., who has resided within the State one year and in the election district where she offers to vote ten days next preceding any election pertaining to school matters, shall have the right to vote at such election.

There were those, however, who were not sure what the bill meant.

Did it mean that women could vote on school matters only, or could they vote for municipal and state offices as long as the election pertained to school matters, they asked? School officials were elected annually, so every election actually pertained to school matters. There were no separate ballots. All of them carried the names of every candidate running for office. Therefore, it seemed logical to believe that women could vote for school, municipal and state officials. State Senator Norman James told the suffragists, "That bill is all you want. Take it and work it for all it is worth. It is a woman suffrage bill."[9]

Voters ratified the bill in 1886, opening the door to a tumultuous campaign effort by suffragists to encourage women to get out and vote in the next election. Olympia asked Susan B. Anthony to come and help her organize a statewide canvass. It did not take long for Miss Anthony to assess the situation and still less to speak her mind. "Olympia, I have had years of experience organizing and campaigning, and I must tell you that Wisconsin women need a strong leader, one who can travel, campaign and organize." She paused a moment to let the words settle on Olympia's ears, then she said, "You should take over that job."

Olympia, brought suddenly face to face with a troublesome decision again, did not know what to do. True, she had faced it twenty years before and managed to choose the ministry without too much difficulty. Now it was a different time; she was a different woman. A wife and the mother of two children, she had been a minister for nearly twenty-four years. Surely she had set a precedent for women ministers by this time. There were other women preaching, other women in ministerial schools, she told herself.

She felt the strong, persistent pull of campaign work, almost like the call which first brought her into the ministry. A restlessness seized her and would not let go as she thought the matter over in the weeks that followed. At last she realized that her happiness lay in giving up the church and working for suffrage. Only then did she sit down and begin her letter of resignation.[10] "It is almost nine years since I first came to Racine," she began writing and, suddenly, the years fell away before her in a kaleidoscope of dreams, sermons, organization work, education and triumphs.

It was 1887. Olympia was fifty-two years old. What better time to start a new career, she asked herself? She was still in good health, yes, even attractive. Her eyes were bright, her smile quick. Her dark hair, though now beginning to gray, was neatly braided, wrapped around her head and pinned in the back. A spirit of energy crackled around her and she walked with her head high, a whisper of arrogance circling her. She usually dressed in black with a white lace collar at her throat or a fine white shawl over her shoulders.

Her decision made, she finished her letter of resignation and presented it to the board. At first, the congregation refused to accept it, but Olympia remained firm. She was going to devote her full energies to getting the ballot for women, she told them. There was much work to do, and she could not fill both jobs. "I will find a minister to fill my pulpit until you can find one yourselves," she said, but she would always stay with the church, she assured them in the face of their protests.

With that, she turned and set out across the state on a campaign trail that lasted through Wisconsin's worst winter months—January, February, and March. When April came, it was time to return home to cast her own ballot.

It was a momentous day when she and several co-workers gathered at her home to go to the polling place together. After more than twenty years of hard work, she was actually going to vote! She could scarcely believe it to be true. The anger and vengeance of all those men opposed to women casting a ballot flared up in her memory again, then sank into a mound of gray ashes. It was all over. Soon, women across the nation would be voting, too.

It was nine-thirty in the morning when the small group of women stood before the inspector. He looked up, startled. "We have come to vote," they said.

For a few moments he remained silent, then recovered himself and shook his head. "You can't vote," he said. "There aren't any ballots or separate ballot boxes for women. They didn't furnish us with any."

Olympia, after hesitating briefly to weigh the advantages of challenging him, suggested that the women return to her home. "We'll try again in the afternoon," she told them. She was confident that the inspector was making a mistake and would realize his error by the afternoon. When they returned later in the day, however, the inspector was ready for them.

"Women have to use separate ballot boxes," he said. "You can only vote for school officials and the state hasn't furnished us with those boxes, so you cannot vote."

The old outrage that had dogged reformers for more than thirty years suddenly sprang to life again in Olympia's breast, and new wounds opened. She stared at the inspector for several moments. Surely this man was over-stepping his authority. "I'll file a formal protest," she said. "You are doing a grave wrong. The legislature has granted us the right to vote." Nevertheless, she had to accept the inspector's refusal, and the women returned home without being able to cast a ballot.

Ironically, many women in the state actually did vote in the election, and their votes were accepted. When the officers of the Wisconsin Woman Suffrage Association learned of the refusal by some inspectors to

126

allow women to vote, they demanded that Olympia, as president, start a lawsuit against the inspectors. She hesitated at first, not knowing what their chances of winning such a lawsuit might be. Then she wrote to Susan B. Anthony for advice. Miss Anthony, who had been watching the situation in Wisconsin, replied at once.

> *I have your letters relative to bringing suits under the school suffrage law, and hasten to say to you that Mrs. Minor's and my own experience in both suing and being sued on the 14th amendment claim leads me to beseech you not to make a test case unless you know you will get the broadest decision upon it. If you get the narrow one restricting the present law simply to school district voting, there it will rest and no judge or inspector will transcend the limit of the decision. My judgment would be to say and do nothing about the law, but through the year keep up the educational work, showing that such and such cities allowed women to vote for mayor, common council, etc. and by the next election many others will let women vote; and so in a few years all will follow suit. Let what you have alone and try for more; for all your legislature has power to give. It will be vastly more likely to grant municipal suffrage than your supreme court will be to give a decision that the school law already allows women to vote for mayor, council, governor, etc.*[11]

It was the most logical advice of any that she heard, and she tried to explain it to the members of her executive board. After a long and stormy session, where their anger and frustration surfaced many times, she finally had to accede to their demands. She filed the lawsuit, demanding a judgment of five thousand dollars against the inspectors.

There was much at stake. A victory by Olympia could bring enfranchisement to Wisconsin women. Defeat would mean pain and humiliation. Reporters savored the case, their delight streaming through their stories with every word. They joked about women wanting to vote and attacked woman's rights with all the viciousness of small boys. They twitted Olympia for preferring her own name to that of her husband's and accused her of wanting to change her children's last name to Brown. Through it all she bore the brunt of their taunts. Reporters had not changed since her days of campaigning in Kansas, she decided. They were, for the most part, an untruthful and defamatory lot, twisting words, making assumptions and innuendos.

Olympia tasted victory when Racine Circuit Court Judge John B. Winslow ruled in her favor. The inspectors, however, decided to appeal the case to the State Supreme Court. Two months later that Court reversed

Judge Winslow's decision. Women could vote on school matters only, the justices decreed. This was the narrowest possible interpretation of the law and precisely what Susan B. Anthony had predicted would happen if women took the case to court. The ruling was doubly bitter because the legislature did not provide separate ballot boxes for them for another fifteen years.

The decision struck the reformers like a giant swell, tumbling over them and washing them up on an empty beach. Some were eager to take up the fight again, but others drifted away. It was useless to continue the work, they said.

Olympia, long disciplined to swallow defeat and take up a new battle position, turned her energies to establishing a state suffrage newspaper called *The Wisconsin Citizen*. Published once a month, it carried both state and national woman suffrage news, and it soon proved to be an effective tool for educating women about working for the ballot. *The Citizen*, as it was called by the suffragists, became a unifying force, too. It published letters and comments, and Olympia used it extensively to promulgate various activities, announce campaigns and conventions, and even counteract gossip. One such letter she wrote squelched rumors that had circulated ever since she attempted to vote in the 1887 election.

February 1888

Dear Sisters—

I have never struggled to force my ballot into the box, or to get it in by any illegitimate means. Last spring, I merely offered the slip of paper to the inspector and on his refusal to take it, went immediately away.

The women at the Circuit Court in Racine behaved with the utmost dignity and propriety. They kicked up no dust (as reported by the Herald), they did nothing but listen in silence.

The only interviews I had at Madison were with my attorneys who were paid for their time, and with the officers of the Wisconsin Woman Suffrage Association under whose direction I acted.

Now, dear timid friend, whoever you may be, let me entreat you, trust your own knowledge of the officers of the Association rather than newspaper sensationalism and idle or malicious gossip. Judge of us by our works.

Olympia Brown.[12]

A short while later another personal note appeared in *The Citizen*, which must have ended more speculation about her children and husband while she was campaigning around the state.

March 1888

I have heard, from my co-workers, that a number of women are worried that my children are being neglected. I would like everyone to know that my children are fine. They are being carefully watched over by their father and grandmother and a private tutor is training them in Greek and Latin.

The Wisconsin Citizen files are the repository of news items gleaned from national suffrage newspapers, local newspapers, notices of meetings, pleas for money, and informative articles by state reformers. Olympia read all with utmost care, pen poised to take issue with whatever struck her as incorrect or unfair.

Tactics and arguments used by reformers changed from the time women first began to demand equality as human beings. If one argument did not procure results or an improvement, they tried another. Just gaining educational and property rights took years, but by 1885 many women were admitted to colleges and universities. When mass immigration occurred in this country, particularly by the 1880's, women saw many of the immigrant men become citizens with the right to vote. This, they protested, was not fair. Women who had been born and educated in this country should have the right to vote before those who had come from overseas. As early as 1886, a man by the name of Major Hudson introduced such an argument during a speech in Topeka, Kansas. His words set the stage for verbal attacks on both immigrants and blacks.

We place the ballot in the hands of the foreigner who cannot read or speak the language, and who knows nothing of our government; we enfranchised a slave race, most of whom cannot read; and yet we deny to the women of America the ballot, which in their hands would be the strongest protection of this republic against the ignorance and vice of the great centers of population.[13]

Olympia first used the argument at a county fair in Rockford, Illinois, in 1888. It was just after her Wisconsin Supreme Court defeat. Her words may have seemed reprehensible, but how could they be so when college-educated women were not allowed to vote, when church leaders used ancient, patriarchal arguments to keep women from getting the ballot, when they cited passages from the Bible claiming that only men should have a voice in the government, and condemned women for wanting equal rights? Everywhere women turned, men were barring doors and shouting threats, alarmed that they might lose their power over half the human race. She told the fairgoers, "Four-fifths of the school teachers are women. We enfranchise the saloon and the poorhouse, the irresponsible classes. We disfranchise the home, the church, the school. We make the daughters of America subject to the serfs and slaves from the old world . . . We are the first people to try the experiment of enfranchising ignorance, drunkenness and all forms of vice, and subordinating intelligence, patriotism, religion."[14]

They were strong words, words of condemnation. Yet who can blame women for fighting against men who still refused to give women the right to a voice in their own government? It was an exceedingly difficult time for reformers. They were being slapped in the face by defeat again and again. Many of the older workers began to fear that men really were determined to keep them as they were. Could their freedom come about only through bloodshed, they asked themselves?

In 1889, the National and the American Woman Suffrage Associations, founded twenty years earlier, voted to merge. The decision was not unanimous and the barrage of words wounded many. The philosophies of the two were quite different. The National Woman Suffrage Association had always worked to gain woman suffrage through a Constitutional amendment, whereas the American Woman Suffrage Association espoused gaining suffrage through each state legislature. Olympia foresaw only conflict and frustration if the two associations merged. Each would pull in its favored direction in a power struggle that could destroy the organization, she argued.

Susan B. Anthony disagreed with her on the issue, however, and asked her to support the merger. Olympia refused. "No, I cannot. A merger will only weaken the National and its purpose which is, after all, to get a suffrage amendment to the Constitution. "

Miss Anthony countered, "Elizabeth Cady Stanton will be the president of the merged association. That is part of the agreement."

Olympia was unmoved. "It will make no difference. The American workers are determined to work only in the state legislatures. They do not believe in an annual convention in Washington, or our appearance before a Congressional committee every year. They will not work for a national amendment as we have done. The American association is controlled by a little clique of Boston people who want to do things in their own way, and have matters all in their own hands. I said that years ago, and it is still true."

Although she vehemently opposed the merger, it did take place. She held Miss Anthony personally responsible. "It will be a major setback for woman suffrage," she said, her disappointment verging on bitterness. Her true feelings emerged later when she wrote, "I used to say that Susan B. Anthony was my pole star until I learned to make no one my guide but to follow truth wherever it might lead and to do the duty of the hour at whatever cost."[15]

Miss Anthony, however, was undeterred by Olympia's alienation. She considered Olympia a friend and staunch worker and she announced publicly that she was placing the names of four pioneer workers permanently on the rolls of the new National American Woman Suffrage Association. "Now I intend to make Mrs. Minor, Olympia Brown, Phoebe Couzins and Matilda Joslyn Gage life members. I had thought of others, but these four are of longer standing, were identified with the old National, and have suffered odium and persecution because of adherence to it."[16]

An unmistakable reluctance shadowed the lines of Olympia's acceptance speech.

> *I am grateful to Susan B. Anthony for the honor conferred in making me a life member of the National Association. I shall go and vote in her meeting for I am willing to "pull" with anybody that is pulling for woman's suffrage; but that will not prevent me from joining any other society, should there ever be one, based on the broad demand for suffrage as a national right to be secured by a provision in the national constitution. The free ballot, free school and free church is what our government stands for.*[17]

She still had not forgiven Miss Anthony. For a long time afterward, as a matter of fact, she continued to use the name "National" instead of "National American" when she referred to the association. In her eyes, the two groups could not work together.

On February 1, 1890, a gala early birthday party for the venerable Susan B. Anthony was held in Washington, D.C. It was Anthony's seventieth birthday. Olympia, however, did not attend. Instead, she sent a letter to be read at the celebration. Her letter is brief and eloquent yet she expressed no affection for her old friend.

> *I think I express the feeling of most if not all of the workers in our cause when I say that the women of America owe more to Susan B. Anthony than to any other woman living. While Mrs. Stanton has been the standard bearer of liberty, announcing great principles, Miss Anthony has been the power which carried those principles on toward victory and impressed them upon the hearts of the people.*[18]

Perhaps it was a somewhat grudging tribute; Olympia did not easily forgive. She, herself, arrived in Washington a day later to attend the National American Woman Suffrage Association convention. Miss Anthony, however, took no note of the slight and immediately asked Olympia to accompany her on a campaign trip during the summer. Olympia, never one to refuse help when her services were needed, agreed to go.

Miss Anthony chose to discuss their differences at once. She assured Olympia that she was right in protesting the merger. "But the pressure the other leaders brought to bear upon me was overwhelming," she said, and, finally, she had to agree to the merger. "I simply could not fight them any longer." It did not take long for Olympia to let logic sweep away the remnants of vexation with her old friend. The cause, after all, was more important than individual differences of opinion.

Working with the single-minded and indomitable Anthony was much like working in a whirlwind. Both women thrived on hard work, travel and public speaking. It was late summer of 1890 that they campaigned across Wisconsin, Minnesota and South Dakota. Sometimes they campaigned alone, sometimes with other reformers. As they drove across the plains, traveling between fifteen and twenty miles to get from afternoon to evening meetings, visions of her Kansas campaign twenty years earlier sprang before Olympia's eyes. It was the driest summer on record. The sun scorched the plains day after day. Clouds of dust swirled up behind the horses' hooves as they followed narrow dirt roads or drove across fields where the grain dried on stems and the corn turned brittle on yellow stalks. They held handkerchiefs to their faces so they would not breathe in the dust, but it settled on their clothing in a fine, gray powder.

Russian, Scandinavian and Polish immigrants had homesteaded on the South Dakota land. They made their feelings about woman suffrage starkly clear. Whenever the suffragists rode into a village where they were to speak, they did not know if they would be welcomed or assailed. One contingent of Russians came to a meeting wearing huge yellow badges with large letters reading, "AGAINST WOMAN SUFFRAGE AND SUSAN B. ANTHONY."[19] They were noisy, rude, and single-minded in their opposition.

South Dakota had adopted as its motto, "Under God the People Rule." The suffragists, turning the motto to their advantage, printed on their banners, "Under God the People Rule. Women are People."[20]

Some of the immigrants complained to Henry Blackwell, who was also canvassing the state, that women suffragists were antagonizing them. That they themselves might be antagonizing the women did not seem to cross their minds. Most men, viewing the world solely from the male perspective, could not put themselves in a woman's place. Henry Blackwell, although a staunch suffrage worker, fell into that mold. He addressed a letter of protest to Susan B. Anthony. "The suffragists are upsetting the foreigners," he told her. "They are going to have to be more careful what they say to them and how they treat them." Miss Anthony, in her letter to Olympia, could not help underlining the irony.

Mr. Blackwell writes that each and all of us female missionaries must be very careful to speak of the foreigners only in the most respectful manner—it took him an hour to reconvert a Norwegian who had been repelled from voting by one of our women at Highmore having "abused" the foreigner . . . but he got him back into the fold again.[21]

Clearly, the suffragists resented the immigrants and their position against woman suffrage. Many continued to refer to them as foreigners even though they had become citizens of this country. Learning to laugh at such incongruities as Mr. Blackwell's stand against the women suffragists' arguments, to measure their daily defeats and triumphs against the trail they were slowly cutting through the tangle of ignorance and hostility, they tried to keep a sense of humor amid the heat and dust of the campaign. The day came, however, when the woman suffrage amendment went down in defeat. It was a stunning comment on the mood and prejudice of the immigrant voter.

Between 1887 and 1893, Olympia traveled and lectured more than at any other time of her life. She canvassed in Ohio, Illinois, Minnesota, Iowa, Wisconsin and South Dakota. She went to suffrage conventions and lectured in New York, Boston and Washington, D.C. Reporters were becoming kinder to her. One called her the "female Beecher of the rostrum." Another noted, ". . . her character warms and mellows and ripens with the years." Still another reported, ". . . she grows with the years . . . makes more and more eloquent speeches and is more and more lovable in character." It was a far different assessment than those usually accorded her, and she must often have wondered about the perversity of reporters.

Her mind was rapidly coming to the realization that women were making little headway towards getting the ballot. The National American Woman Suffrage Association—led by people with little vision, in her opinion, and having their own popularity at heart—would not be able to get an amendment out of committee and before Congress, particularly since they were working more closely within the states than at the national level. It was just as she had said. Women needed a new association, one that would work once more toward an amendment to the Constitution. In 1892, a meeting took place in Chicago wherein she spearheaded the organization of the Federal Suffrage Association. Its goal was to work through Congress to pass a law allowing women to vote for members of the House of Representatives. Women hoped thereby to gain a voice in Congress. In this way they believed that they could win a woman suffrage amendment to the Constitution much sooner than otherwise.

No sooner did that news appear than a deluge of letters descended on Olympia. How could she take such an outrageous step, they asked? Didn't she have faith in the great National American Woman Suffrage Association and its gallant leaders? Why was she trying to split the strength of the group now that they were forging ahead with new drives in every state and the nation's capitol?

Some of the letters were vicious; the workers attacked her personally. A few declared that she would only bring disgrace and hatred down on her head by trying to form another suffrage organization. Olympia, always ready to cross swords, averred that they were all trying to reach the same goal. "There is always room for more workers and more organizations," she retorted. Surely they could all pull together. Their hostility surprised her, but she ignored their words.

The first annual meeting of the Federal Suffrage Association in Chicago was almost like a reunion with her former co-workers. Her heart leaped when her eyes focused on Frederick Douglass and the famed singer John Hutchinson who had campaigned with her in Kansas twenty-seven years before. They all stood together on the stage for the last time, acutely aware of their own mortality. Many of the pioneer reformers had already died. The early leaders, distressed that young women failed to step forward to lead the fight, feared that suffrage work was once more bogging down, and they were right. No charismatic leader, so essential for the progress of great social movements, appeared to direct the cause.

Olympia struggled with indifference among Wisconsin workers, too. Every issue of *The Wisconsin Citizen* carried an urgent appeal for funds. "Those who cannot work for the cause should at least help out financially . . . wherever I go in the state I see rich farms and well-dressed people traveling everywhere. There is sufficient money. It is just that people are no longer interested in this struggle, not even women," she declared, but all of the rhetoric at her fingertips could not give the cause momentum.[22]

The next decade found Olympia struggling with personal tragedies that greatly affected her life and work. How she coped with losses and exigencies and still held on to her dream is a tribute to the vision that had taken root in her psyche so many years before when she was growing up on the little Michigan farm.

Chapter 8

On Her Own

It was January 5, 1893. Olympia Brown's family and friends had gathered to help her celebrate her fifty-eighth birthday. The birthday party was a complete surprise to her. She was astonished at the number of friends who came to call and at the old friends and acquaintances who wrote, sending messages of love and good wishes. Some of the letters were from college friends who reminisced about their experiences long ago; some from co-workers whom she first met when she began suffrage work in 1866. Overwhelmed with the surprise of the party and the many friends who had come to help her celebrate, she sat that evening in the quiet of the house and read over the letters and notes. It had been one of the best times of her life. She had not realized how much these people meant to her or how much they had influenced her life. What a fitting climax the party was to a joyous holiday season when both of her children were home from the University of Chicago and all seemed to be going well.

Olympia, busy in her world of reform work, had given little thought to changes in the family. Most changes came gradually, as when the two children went away to school. She was totally unprepared therefore, when shortly after the birthday party, her mother suffered a nervous breakdown. Lephia Brown, that beloved, independent, forceful and energetic mainstay who had stood by her for so many years, suddenly sick? She struggled to grasp the reality of such a thing. Her mother was scarcely ever sick. Indeed, she gave the impression that she would live forever. How could this be, she asked herself? She cancelled her speaking engagements and set about reorganizing her life. Her first duty now was to take care of her mother until she recovered her health. The thought that Lephia might never recover did not enter her mind.

As if this blow was not enough, John Henry Willis suffered a stroke a short time later. She nursed both patients in her home, as most people did at the turn of the century, all the while feeling her world slipping from beneath her feet. Mr. Willis, however, died on March 1, scarcely two months after her memorable birthday party. Grief overwhelmed her and she moved in a world suddenly gray with shock and loneliness. For the first time in twenty years, she felt that she was standing alone again.

Endless sorrow has fallen upon my heart. He was one of the truest and best men that ever lived, firm in his religious convictions, loyal to every right principle, strictly honest and upright in his life. ... much more may be said of his absolute sincerity of character, such as I have never seen in any other person, his lack of pretension, his appreciation and recognition of talent outside the lines of his particular work which we see in so few.[1]

In the days that followed, numerous tributes to John Henry Willis poured in with the words of consolation to Olympia. Slowly groping her way back to reality, she sent Parker and Gwendolen back to their classes at the University, then began to learn the intricacies of managing her husband's publishing and printing business. She considered selling the business, but a deep recession held the country in its grip. Such a move, she saw, was almost impossible at the time. Perhaps she should just rely on her husband's partners to operate the company in a trustworthy manner. It did not take long to learn that such an idea was a poor business decision. She would have to buy out the partners and operate the business herself, and that was what she did. Perhaps that was the only good decision for her to make because it is likely that no one else could have operated the business to her entire satisfaction.

Olympia had always believed that newspapers should report the news as factually as possible and that editors should educate the people. Certainly newspapers should not be the tools of politicians or special interest groups. With this philosophy as her basis for publishing news, she tried to be fair and impartial. It was, she quickly learned, a complex and difficult task. As a woman long accustomed to voicing her opinions whenever and however she pleased, she now felt herself fenced in with restrictions. There were issues which she yearned to assail and could not, if she was to be fair.

Ironically, she quickly recognized that women should have wooed the press long before. Journalists had the power to mold public opinion but women failed to take advantage of their power. They had for so long been the objects of journalistic ridicule that they did not actively enlist the support of reporters or editors. Few newspapers, she knew, promulgated woman suffrage, nor did they try to educate the public on the issue. Most were quick to condemn it. It was a mistake that cost women many years of work, some were beginning to recognize, but how to rectify their error?

Not long after her husband's death, she heard that a church in the town of Mukwonago, not far from Racine, needed a part-time preacher. She decided to help out. Almost every weekend Olympia traveled there to deliver a sermon, socialize with other Universalists, and drink of the shared faith that had sustained her for so long a time. Later, she served the Neenah and Columbus, Wisconsin, churches as guest minister from time to time.[2] This work seemed to restore her sense of direction as well as provide a great deal of comfort to her.

Caring for her mother and working at the newspaper office left her little time to devote to a floundering woman suffrage movement. The national movement suffered the doldrums, too, partly because some of their greatest leaders were gone. William Lloyd Garrison had died in 1879, Lucretia Mott in 1880, Lucy Stone in 1893, and Frederick Douglass in 1895. Where were the young leaders, she asked, and why didn't they step forward and take over the reins of the movement? The officers of the National American Woman Suffrage Association, set in their ways and limited in their perspective and ambition, seemed to feel that getting a national woman suffrage bill before Congress was beyond their ability or even their vision.

Her two former co-workers, Elizabeth Cady Stanton and Susan B. Anthony, were approaching the limits of their endurance. Mrs. Stanton, ready to retire from public life, wanted to devote her remaining years to writing. Susan B. Anthony, loathe to give up her life work, still kept her fingers on the pulse of the National American association. In 1899, when the Wisconsin Woman Suffrage Association could not afford to pay its National dues, she made a personal contribution to their treasury for that amount. Her letter to Olympia is moving in its sincerity.

My dear Olympia, the reason I do this is because I cannot bear to have the national records of 1900 go down to history without your name standing at the head of the Wisconsin Suffrage society. I enclose a copy of my letter to Mrs. Upton, which I am sending also to Mrs. (Carrie Chapman) Catt and Mrs. Foster Avery to pass around because I want all the members of the Business Committee to know exactly how I feel and what I say to you and of you.

Your affectionate and lifelong friend,
Susan B. Anthony.[3]

Miss Anthony's affection for her old friend and co-worker was as constant as ever. The letter served notice on the officers and members that they were to respect Olympia Brown in spite of their own personal feelings about her, particularly after she had helped found the Federal Suffrage

137

Association. Bitterness and recrimination died slowly among some of the leaders.

Many changes were occurring in Olympia's immediate family as the years passed. Upon graduating from the University of Chicago, her son, Parker, announced that he wanted a doctorate in the field of economics. Olympia had hoped that he would take over the publication of the newspaper in Racine, but Parker adamantly refused. Recognizing her own strong will in her son's character, she knew that he would not change his mind. Gwendolen graduated from the University a short time after her brother and soon decided that she wanted her doctorate so that she could teach Latin and Greek. Olympia accepted what she could not change, and her children continued with their education.

Her mother was an invalid for seven years. Olympia bore the major burden of Lephia's care, and why shouldn't she, she asked? She had benefited greatly from her mother's unstinting care of the two children for nearly twenty years. Now she would repay her in some measure by providing her with the best possible care.

If Olympia's two sisters and brother had lived close to Racine, it is likely that they would have shared in their mother's care. Two of them, however, lived in the far west and one in Kansas. Although Oella had raised her family in Chicago, she had moved to Everett, Washington, and was teaching school there. Marcia was raising a family in Kansas while Arthur, the youngest, lived in Salt Lake City, Utah. He had given up his law practice in Michigan and moved west for his health. He ultimately became a United States senator. Olympia encouraged them to visit whenever they could, and sometimes the house rang with their memories and laughter. For the most part, however, she and her two children had to provide most of Lephia's support and companionship.

Lephia was a cheerful and optimistic patient in spite of being virtually helpless. She spent her days reading, writing letters and poems, and sewing by hand.

When the business climate finally improved, Olympia once again offered the publishing and printing company for sale. She soon received an offer from a buyer that met her specific requirements. He was honest and had no political connections. Although she sold the business at a financial loss, she felt a great burden was suddenly lifted from her shoulders. Her husband would have been pleased. She had at last put the newspaper into trustworthy and efficient hands. Ironically, on the very day that the property was transferred, Lephia Brown died.

Olympia was now alone in the house to which she had brought her mother twenty-two years ago. She was, in fact, altogether alone for the first time in twenty-seven years. She thought back over those years and marveled at how swiftly they had flown past. Her Bridgeport pastorate, marriage, birth of her two children, Racine pastorate, her work for suffrage—how busy she had been! Then came the first loss in her family, the death of her father in 1887. She had not been close to Asa Brown, but she had felt the sudden sense of loss one feels when a parent dies. He was buried in Kalamazoo, Michigan, where he had lived since the family moved from Yellow Springs, Ohio. Whatever his faults may have been, he had provided a happy and secure childhood home for them, she remembered. Now her mother, her lifetime confidante, was gone, too. Her own children, grown and leading lives of their own, no longer needed her. She had only herself to think about. Not since her earliest days in Bridgeport had she been so free! "All those long years when I needed a little time alone, and now I have endless days to myself. I can read, write letters and articles, travel, campaign again!"

Slowly, she began to taste the freedom that comes when the last ties of family duties are cut. She turned to woman suffrage work again. Although she had done some work while caring for her mother, directing fund and membership drives and helping organize the annual convention, she had not been free to travel and take an active part in campaigns. Now she could do so.

An article about her son appeared in *The Wisconsin Citizen* in 1901. It was an excerpt from the *Nation*, a noted magazine of that time, detailing an honor accorded the young professor. Olympia, proud of her son's accomplishment, had submitted the report to the editors.

HONOR TO RACINE YOUTH

The Nation, probably the highest critical publication in the country, in its issue of April 4, pays a very high tribute to the genius and learning of a former Racine boy, Professor Henry Parker Willis, now of Washington and Lee University. Nearly five columns of its very valuable space are devoted to a review of Prof. Willis' late work, "A History of the Latin Monetary Union." The many friends of this brilliant young man were pleased to hear of the success of his work and will be interested in knowing what the Nation has to say of it. Following is the introductory to the long review of the Nation:

"Prof. Willis has laid all students of monetary science under lasting obligation by this remarkable work. We hold it to be remarkable for its insight and grasp on economic principles but still more for its laborious sifting of all the documentary and extemporaneous evidence available in the several countries forming the Latin Union. Much of this material will be new to French and Italian as well as English and American readers. No such history of the Latin Monetary

Union has hitherto been produced in any language, nor, it seems to us, will any future one be needed." [4]

In the fall of that year, Parker changed careers. He gave up his professorship and accepted a position as writer with *The New York Evening Post* in New York City. One of his first acts was to write and ask Olympia to come and help him establish a temporary home there. Perhaps he was also assuring himself and Gwendolen that their mother did not have to spend a long, lonely winter alone in the Racine home on the lake. She accepted the invitation at once, delighted to spend the winter in New York.

She arrived in the bustling metropolis and looked about. It had been thirty-five years since she first visited New York to attend a woman's rights convention. How the city had changed in that time! Now crowds of people were rushing about everywhere, streaming into buildings through one door, spilling out onto the sidewalks through another. Why the great hurry, she wondered? Whatever the answer, she would learn to cope with it. There was much to see and learn, many places to go, and old friends to visit. "I'll find my way around the city, somehow," she resolved, and find her way around, she did.

She attended meetings and lectures, visited settlement houses and diet kitchens, found a church of her choice, went sightseeing, and visited old friends, all the while observing the people of New York. She particularly enjoyed watching the children playing on the city's sidewalks and in the parks. "What an astonishing array of playground equipment and activities the city provides for them," she reported back to her *Citizen* readers. New York children were fortunate. They had countless opportunities to develop their talents and skills, she noted.

From the letters and articles she wrote for *The Wisconsin Citizen*, it seems clear that all of the services that the various organizations provided for people amazed her. Women in need with no place to live or no job to support themselves could obtain shelter and job training in the settlement houses. If they had children, the settlement houses provided child care, too. Diet kitchens furnished food for the sick, the poor and the elderly. The opportunity to learn about the social services New York offered its residents opened the door to many exciting hours, and her reports provided interesting reading for *The Citizen* readers. She attended meetings and lectures all around the city, traveling by streetcar from one end of New York to the other. She was not to be confined to one borough and likely caused her son some worry as she carried out her daily plans. Olympia was too adventurous at heart to limit her excursions. Besides, she was gaining an education in big city living.

The minister of the church she attended was too young for her tastes, she decided, and expressed herself in a letter to *The Citizen*. "Perhaps it is not possible for a young man to be possessed by a great controlling idea; such power comes only by experience; it is through the baptism of sorrow, that we rise to the highest mount of vision. It is a mistake to insist upon very young ministers."[5]

Having dispensed with this matter, she did not refer to it again in her journalistic adventures.

Elizabeth Cady Stanton lived in New York City as did the Reverend Phoebe Hanaford. Olympia was soon visiting both women often. They reminisced about old times but they also talked about the future. Olympia had helped Mrs. Stanton write *The Woman's Bible*, published in 1898, a non-sexist version of the King James Bible.[6] Such a startling idea was heresy. Most of Mrs. Stanton's friends avoided the matter as they would avoid a nest of hornets. One poke, they feared, and a swarm of painful questions and realizations might descend on their hapless heads. "The Bible was written by men for men, and it relegates women to subservience," Mrs. Stanton claimed. It was responsible for woman's state of abasement. She tried to explain her position in more detail in one of her articles. Marriage, she wrote, was the crux of the woman problem. Most women entered into marriage in a subservient status and never expected to gain equal footing with their husbands. The marriage ceremony stressed the subjugation of women, and that was the fault of the church. This was a position that she had taken early in her adult life and she wrote extensively on the subject to the very end of her life. Olympia shared the same feelings, although how she rectified that position with her theology she did not explain.

She also visited Antoinette Brown Blackwell who was living in nearby New Jersey. She could not forget the woman who had been her inspiration as a young girl. They had shared many dreams and now shared many memories. Both were optimistic enough to believe that they would still someday be able to cast a ballot.

The Wisconsin Citizen came promptly every month in the mail. Many of Olympia's letters and articles were published along with news items garnered from state newspapers. Not all of the articles dealt with suffrage work. Sometimes an enterprising reporter, with tongue-in-cheek humor, would cast out a line of comments certain to arouse mixed reactions. One such article appeared in *The Citizen* while she was in New York.

Olympia Brown Willis, a Racine lady, peculiar in dress and manner, holding advanced views on suffrage, temperance and religion, has been for years the subject of much bantering and twitting at the hands of Wisconsin editors who felt sure the good old way was the path in which women should walk. She is what a conservative would style a "crowing hen." It appears, however, that while many sons of her conservative critics are holding responsible positions as off-bearers in sawmills and digging holes in Mother Earth for the extension of illuminating facilities, the offspring of this eccentric lady has quietly slipped into the post of chief economic writer for the New York Evening Post. It may be that the lady has not spent the years reading the jibes of our unpromoted smart Alecs of the press. The chances are that she was devoting those years to unfolding her boy's mind and introducing him to large questions. Those mothers who have ideas which possibly preoccupy them to the point of neglecting conventionalities should be snubbed with caution. They breed original and forceful children.[7]

Olympia did not bother to reply to such comments, but one of her staunch co-workers wrote to defend her manner of dress.

Mrs. Brown wears a bonnet, a gown of orthodox length, jacket or shawl of regulation order. She has not affected bloomers, short skirts or any other fad of that sort; in fact she is very apt to be gowned in that essentially feminine style of dress which has a train. To be sure she is not possessed of an overweening fondness for clothes, and as minister's salaries are small, and sending children to college costs money, she may not always have been able to follow the latest fashion if she desired it. No man would be called singular in dress and manner who kept as near the conventional as does Rev. Olympia Brown.[8]

Olympia was not concerned with what other people thought about her dress. That was a private matter with her. It struck her as humorous that the first eleven words of the article could trigger such a response from one of her co-workers. The article, after all, dealt with the honor accorded her son and was highly complimentary of her, although written in a whimsical manner.

Before winter drew to a close, Parker transferred to Washington, D.C., and Olympia moved with him. She was as delighted with Washington as she had been with New York City. Few duties and obligations taxed her and she was free to go about the city as she wished. Like one visiting an old familiar habitat, she began at once to attend suffrage meetings, lectures and conventions. Her letter went out to Wisconsin workers, weighty with news and advice.

You must keep the question of suffrage distinct from any other

*topics . . . You must not get involved with temperance or the employ-
ment of women outside the home, or anything else that will divert
attention away from suffrage. When you invite a man to dinner, you
do not invite all of his poor relations, and when you entertain a subject
of discussion you do not . . . consider all the distantly related subjects
that may be suggested. Let the subject be . . . advocated on its own
merits, and half the difficulties . . . will disappear.*[9]

In another article for *The Citizen*, reminiscing about a journey home
after a suffrage meeting in LaCrosse, Wisconsin, Olympia displayed a
poetic trait that she seldom envinced.

*We get anxious as it nears train time; away go the horses uphill,
downhill, a turn to the right, a turn to the left, five turns in all; we catch
glimpses of lovely by streets with quiet homes, the shades are down,
all is still in the early morning; the dying vines still cling to deserted
porches, the flowers in the yard droop, "Heavily hangs the Tiger Lily,
over the grave in the earth so chilly."*
*We push on, here we see a little group of trees clad in gorgeous
autumn robes, down yonder in the distance a little glade, how we
would like to wander there, and far away stretch the rolling prairies.
On we go, the horses give a plunge; down hill to the right, one more
turn to the left and we round up at the station, where the train stands
smoking, snorting, panting. We get on board, take our seats and in a
twinkling off we go. Platteville is behind us, a day's ride before us.
We look out of the window at the panorama of autumn forest and
foliage, at the mist rising from the marshes, at the sun sending its early
beams across the sky. On we go all day. What a time to think!*[10]

Olympia returned to Racine every spring. The house on the lake must
be opened, her garden must be started, and there was suffrage work to
organize. Even though the movement seemed to be stymied, women must
keep up the work, she said. One day soon new momentum would carry the
cause forward to success, and they must be ready.

Her son announced his plans to marry a young southern woman.
Olympia, privately dismayed that anyone in her family would be marrying
into a former slave-owning household, made no move to oppose the match,
however. Perhaps she recalled her own wedding and how her mother and
friends had opposed it; yet she had married John Willis anyway. Her son
knew his own mind. Nothing she could say would change it. She had
learned to accept the inevitable where her family was concerned.

The marriage ended her winters in Washington and she adjusted once more to living alone in the house on the lake. Her daughter, after receiving her doctorate the following year, accepted a teaching position at Downer College in Milwaukee. Olympia was pleased. Not only would Gwendolen be close to home, she would be able to work for the cause. How hard it was to let her children go and live their own lives!

The years brought more changes to her circle of family and friends. Elizabeth Cady Stanton died in 1902. Olympia's brother, Arthur, died suddenly in 1906, as did Susan B. Anthony. When her sister Marcia died in 1910, she had a particularly difficult time accepting her death. They had been very close. Now, only she and Oella were left of the family, and Oella was living on the west coast. They would not see each other often.

She fought loneliness in the only way she knew how, and that was by work. She began to travel and lecture. Circulars went out over the state advertising her availability as a lecturer on education, labor reform, politics and woman suffrage.[11]

Her monthly report went out regularly to *The Citizen*. She had lost none of her sting as she took women to task for using the woman suffrage organization as a vehicle for their social life. "They are not ready to fight for suffrage. They can't see beyond receptions with beautiful gowns and flowers . . . and the celebration of birthdays . . . And, of course, there are those who don't want suffrage unless it's achieved by their favorite methods."[12]

President Theodore Roosevelt soon became a target for her pen. She could not bear to have women relegated to the position of breeders and housewives, and his speeches were laced with such comments. A man's prime duty was to work, he said, and a woman's was to bear children and be a housewife. He called upon the women of the country to have large families and he urged farmers to raise a "large crop of children."

"Might not the same result be secured by reducing the death rate?" she wrote. "Surely each man should be the one to determine how many children he can support in good health with the money he earns. It is far better to bring up one child to noble manhood . . . [or] to an honorable and cultured womanhood."13

When he began promulgating the idea that the economy might improve if women workers were excluded from the factories, Olympia countered, "What then should those women do who have to support themselves or their families?" When he tried to smooth over criticism with the sweet oil of his rhetoric claiming that he represented all of the people of the nation, Olympia retorted, "That is not true. Over half of the citizens of the United States are denied the ballot. He can hardly represent the women of this nation."

In 1908 Olympia detected a new grass roots interest in woman suffrage. Perhaps the long drought of inactivity was over, she thought. She and several co-workers began visiting college campuses around Wisconsin. They organized a suffrage league on every campus and they visited and found many young women interested and excited about voting rights. She often told the students about her experiences in trying to find a college that would admit a woman in 1856. They were astonished to learn that women could not attend a university anywhere in the United States in the 1850's, and that she had been the only woman enrolled at the St. Lawrence Theological School. The young women became more aware of their own limitations and the restrictions that hemmed them in on every side. As they listened to her stories, they began to see themselves in a new light.

Publicity about a dynamic new suffrage movement in England called the Pankhurst movement was appearing in newspapers across the nation. People read with growing interest about Emmeline Pankhurst and her militant activities. The suffragettes, as they were called in England, staged protest marches and sit-ins in the legislative halls. Some went even further, breaking windows and taking part in other acts of destructive violence. Many women were arrested, jailed and treated harshly. When the women prisoners went on a hunger strike, demanding more humane treatment, they were force-fed by jail personnel. It was an inhuman measure, both painful and humiliating. Newspapers carried pictures and stories of the cruel treatment. Loud protests began to sound across Europe and America, adding to the protests already rumbling in England. Interest in woman suffrage began to flare up once again, first in isolated areas, then, catching hold, it spread across Europe and America. Dedicated reformers in this country sensed that changes were coming, and they began to marshal their energies for a new fight to win the ballot. Olympia felt the winds of change, and she resolved anew to be a part of the new wave of commitment.

Chapter 9

On the Move

The year 1910 began on a positive note for Olympia. In the spring she attended her fifty-year class reunion at Antioch College in Yellow Springs, Ohio. Riding now in comfort on a fast train, she found her mind drifting back to her trip fifty years ago. She remembered bouncing along in a dusty stagecoach along a trail cut through heavy woods. Hills rolled away on either side. Sometimes they passed a clearing where a house and barn stood, lonely, rugged, defiant. Sometimes they left the woods behind and crossed rolling prairie. Here there were more farms, but always they were small, usually with rough-hewn buildings and fences.

Now she looked out at the large, well-tilled fields, neat houses and barns, fat cattle and horses. What changes had come about, she marveled. There were more to come, however. She saw a few automobiles on the roads, and she had even read that some men had invented a machine for flying. There was conjecture that in another fifty years people would travel everywhere by airplane. What a strange and fanciful dream, she thought, but perhaps it, too, would prove practical.

There had been twenty-eight graduates in Olympia's class. Eleven were still living in 1910 and five of them came to the reunion. They shared many warm memories and reflected back over their lives. Olympia came to realize how very busy she had been as she compared experiences with her old classmates. "However," she told them, "I have much more to do. Even after women get the ballot, we must start working toward an equal rights amendment. That may take a long time."

Her words must have been unsettling to her former classmates who were now in their seventies and retired. For Olympia, there was no such word as retirement.

Back in Wisconsin, her summer passed swiftly as she divided her time between her garden and suffrage work. She soon began detecting a strong undercurrent of dissent among the younger women in the Wisconsin Woman Suffrage Association. Some were not happy with her leadership. "Nothing is being done," they complained. "We need a new president."

She was not overly concerned at first, but she and some of her faithful co-workers went to Madison to urge State Senator David G. James, an ardent suffragist himself, to present a woman suffrage bill at the next meeting of the legislature. He agreed to do so. Still, the younger women agitated for a change in leadership, suggesting that Olympia resign as president in the spring of 1911.

"You would be given the title 'Honorary President,'" the leader of the agitators assured her. "You will receive special honors and you will have no work to do."

Olympia was shaken by the suggestion. To lose the honor of the office was distressing, but to have no work to do was worse. "I have never sought honor. I wish only to work for suffrage. I expect to work for suffrage as long as I live. I will gladly work in any position in the association, or as an individual outside of the association if need be."

She reminded them that the Wisconsin Woman Suffrage Association had secured the enactment of the most comprehensive school suffrage law in the United States when she was its president then she added, "The proper time to change officers is in September, not April."[1]

This was not quite the response the younger women had anticipated. Eager to have matters in their own hands, they promptly left the association and formed their own organization, which they named the Political Equality League. Olympia was not particularly disturbed by this chain of events, either. She believed there was always room for other groups who wished to work for the cause in their own way, but people should not join an existing association and expect to change it according to their own desires. She had condemned many who did not want to work for suffrage unless it was achieved by their favorite methods, yet she did not want anyone else to come into the association and institute new policies. She had, after all, walked along the same path for so many years that she failed to see that she was contradicting some of her own statements. She also had a bevy of staunch supporters who did not want her to step down.

During the winter she compiled a history of the woman suffrage movement in Wisconsin which was published in *The Milwaukee Free Press* and *The Wisconsin Citizen* in the spring along with pictures of the pioneer workers.[2] It came at a time when interest in the ballot for women was begining to stir once more. She was also writing a book at this time, *Acquaintances, Old and New, Among Reformers*.[3] The book was a sketch rather than a detailed account of the lives and contributions of some of the early suffragists. It was published in 1911. She dedicated all of the proceeds to the state suffrage association.

In 1912 a woman suffrage bill was passed by the legislature. It had to go before the voters of Wisconsin for ratification. Logically, suffragists from both organizations would have to work together to help assure its ratification. Some of the young dissidents were not interested in unity, however. Still angry with the older women, particularly Olympia, they referred to them as a "bunch of doddering old ladies," a term that ruffled many feathers.

"They would not be so free with their tongues if they had suffered some of the bitter experiences we have endured," Olympia retorted. It took all of the skill and patience of Ada James, one of the young women workers, to restore harmony.[4] Even then antagonism surfaced from time to time as the women set out to campaign across the state.

This time, they started work at the grass roots level. It was a dramatic shift in strategy. Instead of appealing only to the upper classes, they addressed working women, housewives and farm women. They campaigned across the state, trying to speak in every city and village. Scarcely a settlement anywhere did not have a speaker visit and talk about the issue. In spite of their enthusiasm and many long, hard hours of work, the referendum failed by more than 91,000 votes. Olympia was stunned when she learned that more votes were cast against the ballot for women than for any of the other three referenda measures. It was starkly clear that men did not want women to vote.

In discussing the campaign later, after their anger had cooled, Olympia joined those who believed it was the political strategy that defeated them. The woman suffrage amendment had been submitted to the voters on a pink ballot; the other three amendments were on white ballots. Those opposed to the vote for women could easily register their opposition.

That same year, the story was different in Kansas. There Olympia had campaigned during the summer months, traveling over much of the same countryside that she had covered during her 1867 campaign. A new generation peopled the Sunflower state, and they granted suffrage to women that fall. It was a bittersweet victory, too late for her sister Marcia and many of the reformers she had known. Still, it was a grand victory, she said.

Three days after their Wisconsin defeat at the polls, the young women in the Political Equality League offered to merge with the Wisconsin Woman Suffrage Association members. "Women can work together much more effectively if they belong to the same association," they said but they had a stipulation. "If we are to merge, the presidents of the two organizations must resign and will not be eligible for the presidency of the new association."

Olympia did not hesitate. She resigned in spite of the protests of her loyal friends and supporters. "I am seventy-seven years old, too old to waste time on political infighting," she said.

149

When the new organization retained the old historic name of Wisconsin Woman Suffrage Association and she was named Honorary President, she was pleased. However much she expected to work alone, she remained as active in the group as she always had. She attended board meetings so regularly that one board member noted, "I believe Olympia Brown feels slighted because she does not receive notices of our meetings." It made little difference to Olympia what they thought about her as long as she managed to find out when and where the meetings were to be held.[5] The officers, however, soon had to pass a resolution that "an honorary member is not a voting member." She could not be silenced. Old habits die slowly. How difficult it was to give up a position she had held for twenty-eight years and to sit silently on the sidelines.

Her life took a sudden dramatic turn in 1913 when she received an invitation from Alice Paul and Lucy Burns to join a new party, the Congressional Union. They were experienced suffragists, having worked in England with the Pankhurst woman suffrage movement. They were now in Washington, D.C., working under the auspices of the National American Woman Suffrage Association. The sole purpose of the Congressional Union was to get the Susan B. Anthony amendment through Congress.[6] That amendment stated simply, "The right of citizens of the United States to vote shall not be denied or abridged by the United States or by any state on account of sex." It was precisely what Olympia had hoped for and worked toward for so many years. It was also the same proposal that she had made to the leaders of the National Association years before, and what had they done? They not only ridiculed the idea, but they immediately rejected it. Their lack of vision and inability to set goals had been an abiding frustration for Olympia at every turn. Alice Paul and Lucy Burns were different. They were activists, she realized, just what the movement needed. She joined the organization at once.

She usually spent the holidays and the greater part of the winter in New York City with her son and his growing family. Her letters to *The Wisconsin Citizen* readers flowed steadily throughout the winter months, brimming with advice. When spring came, she returned to Racine. Her announcement in *The Citizen* is almost royal in tone.

> *I have returned from my winter's sojourn in the east and am now in readiness to do what I can for our cause in Wisconsin. Shall be glad to fill any appointments to speak on Woman's Suffrage. Have had some opportunities of observing methods pursued in other states and think I can bring you a message of hope and encouragement, although all hope and real encouragement in any work implies effort and ambition and in this cause effort is just now very much needed. . .*

150

*Those wishing a lecture or visit, should address me at 941 Lake Ave.
There will be no charge except the necessary traveling expenses.*[7]

In the summer of 1914, Olympia gave a series of lectures on the history, goals and future plans of the woman suffrage movement. This was in conjunction with a suffrage school that the state association held in Madison. She covered the entire period from the Woman's Rights meeting in Seneca Falls, New York, in 1848, to the last defeat of the suffrage amendment in Wisconsin. Her last lecture was "History in the Making," in which she held out her own high hope that the time was now right for that final advance.[8] Many who enrolled in her series of lectures gathered afterwards to ask questions and listen to some of her stories. They tumbled from her memory, adventures, travels, reminiscences about Susan B. Anthony and Elizabeth Cady Stanton, and the young women absorbed them, facinated with the history of the long struggle and the people who had fought it.

The suffrage school was a success. Hundreds of people attended, men as well as women, and Olympia wished that they could hold more such schools. It was costly, however, and the board members felt the association should spend its money in other ways.

Olympia read one day that *The Wisconsin Citizen* was going to be reduced to a mere bulletin to save money. "I cannot let such a thing happen!" she declared, and immediately wrote to the executive board protesting that such a step would drastically reduce news content. She also wrote to Alice Paul. "Would it be possible to send sample copies of *The Suffragist* (the Congressional Union newspaper) to *The Citizen* subscribers?" she asked. "Perhaps many of the Wisconsin women would be willing to subscribe to it if their own paper is to be reduced to a bulletin."

There were immediate protests from Wisconsin workers, many of whom resented the forming of the Congressional Union in the first place. One woman expressed herself succinctly to the president stating that there really was not going to be a change in *The Citizen*. "It has always been a bulletin," she said. "Now I see very little difference between the old and new 'Citizen' except that Olympia Brown doesn't contribute to it. It never did cover the field at large." She ended her letter, "Olympia is evidently seeking other harvest fields."[9]

There were other instances of misunderstandings between Olympia and the younger women. A number of them viewed her with suspicion, even antagonism, particularly after she joined the Congressional Union. They began to accuse her of changing her interests and being disloyal to the old association. Few really understood her. She was of an earlier time, untrained in Victorian traditions of lady-like behavior, speech and manners. She had no patience with society's efforts to constrain women's speech, particularly when they were trying to gain enfranchisement, and she must have felt even more impatient as she grew older and realized her time was growing short. She had always thrived on action and she chafed at the dull routines of organization meetings which many of the women seemed to enjoy. After all, she wanted to get things done. No doubt her unexpected flashes of intense individualism upset many of the more conventional workers.

In the fall of 1914, her daughter left Downer College in Milwaukee to teach Greek and Latin at Bryn Mawr in Baltimore, Maryland. That move markedly changed both of their lives because Gwendolen asked her mother to come and live there with her during the winter months. Olympia accepted, the opportunity of living so close to Washington, D.C., and its political activities enticing her away from her home on the lake and the antipathy of the Wisconsin workers. She would be able to go to Congressional committee hearings, speak again on the Susan B. Anthony amendment, perhaps join the Maryland Suffrage Association, and take part in Congressional Union activities, working closely with Alice Paul and Lucy Burns. Her life once more took on a new vitality.

She spoke that year before the Congressional Committee hearings on woman suffrage, lacing her talk with subtle humor. "Further argument on the right of women to vote would be an insult to your intelligence. The claims . . . have been presented . . . again and again."

She told them that she knew how busy they were; she had read it many times. "I have read the long list of bills, pork barrel and all which it is said must be put through at this session. . . . I am also mindful of President Wilson's statement that human rights are preeminent above all other claims."[10] Gently needling them, she asked, "Does that not mean the rights of women?"

Finally getting the amendment out of the committee and presented before Congress took several months of combined effort. The bill had lain dormant in the committee for *twenty-seven years!* The first vote ever on woman suffrage in the House of Representatives stood at 174 in favor and 204 against the amendment. Olympia was deeply disappointed and she said, "We have much work yet to do," but Alice Paul was optimistic.

"We have come a long way," she said, "and we can change that margin by the next vote."

The *Baltimore Sun* published an article about Olympia's speech on the woman suffrage amendment. They included extensive biographical information and described her in a noteworthy paragraph.

Mrs. Brown is a dainty grandmotherly woman, who looks much

152

as if she had stepped out of an old-time picture—soft of voice and gentle of manner, but with an unfaltering and unswerving faith of the right of women to a voice in the government of their nation, their states and their cities. And she has been through many a hard-fought campaign with Miss Anthony in a number of states in behalf of her faith.[11]

In August of 1915, she embarked on a trip to the west coast. "It has been a rule of my life to go only where duty called me," she said to the press before she left. "That is why I have never been west of the Rockies before. But now I have broken it—for this is a trip of pleasure—pure pleasure."[12]

The trip soon gave evidence of being a minor campaign for woman suffrage. A Washington state newspaper account of her visit reported that she went as "one of the distinguished speakers at the recent convention of the National Council of Women Voters." She was invited to a reception for Col. William Jennings Bryan, renowned orator, and his wife. The guests "lingered to meet the little bent old lady with the youthful eyes and the beautiful speaking voice." They appeared to be even more interested in her than in Bryan, a reporter noted.[13]

Another newspaper article was even more complimentary.

Reverend in personality as well as title . . . one feels the strong purposes that have governed her life and made her a power in the lives of others . . . the clear depths of her bright blue eyes, the strong, sure cadences of her remarkable voice, the direct, clean-cut questions she asks, the concise arguments she puts forth, suggest the woman of affairs, a woman capable of building up and directing a church, a movement or a business.[14]

The reporter, noting that she had a "frail, delicate body," also described her as a "live wire, bright, witty, direct, effective" when she was on the platform.

As soon as she returned to Racine from her highly-touted western trip, she stirred up a nest of controversy. Her remarks may have seemed innocent to her, but they were taken personally by the Wisconsin leaders. "I am looking forward to the next session of Congress with very great anxiety and hope for success there depends upon the Congressional Union," she wrote to the president of the Wisconsin Woman Suffrage Association.[15] It was not the kind of remark that would endear her to the state women; her faith did lie in Alice Paul's party. They were already actively campaigning against the reelection of President Wilson. It was part of their political strategy to campaign against any elected official who did not support woman suffrage. Meanwhile, the leaders of the National American Woman Suffrage Association and their state affiliates joined together in denouncing the Union's militant tactics. They were conservative women, for the most part, and did not believe that ladies should be picketing or campaigning in public. There was something very improper, if not actually disgraceful, about such an activity, they claimed.

Olympia demurred. "There is no other way to gain the ballot. Women have been proper for years, and their rhetoric has gained them nothing. Now is the time for action."

She continued to provoke the state leaders. When they invited her to a state suffrage meeting that year, she replied by post card, simple and direct.

> *I do not think I shall be needed at Tower Hill. I never go where I am of no use.*
>
> *Olympia Brown.*[16]

Another time the president of the state association, Mrs. Youmans, wrote and asked her if she had a copy of the pink ballot used in the 1912 referendum. The defeat was still a bitter memory for Olympia.

> *I have no copy of the pink ballot and I do not know where they are, unless they are preserved in the archives of the State at Madison. It was a mean device to prevent us from getting a fair vote.*

In the same letter after recalling an earlier unfair attack on her dear friend, Emma Smith DeVoe, she brought up that subject.

> *I shall never cease to regret that Mrs. DeVoe could not have carried on the campaign as we had planned. It is amusing now to see the National, after discrediting Mrs. DeVoe here in 1912 and practically driving her from our state, appealing to Mrs. DeVoe for help. They sent a woman all the way to Cheyenne to seek ... Mrs. DeVoe!!— the same woman whose "methods" could not be tolerated in 1912.*[17]

When Dr. Anna Howard Shaw stepped down as president of the National American Woman Suffrage Association, Olympia was nettled by a request for a donation towards a gift for her. Some of the leaders felt that a retiring president should be given a gift of appreciation for her work. Olympia felt that it was a critical time in suffrage work and money was needed to carry on the campaign, not to be used for useless gifts.

Cora M. Stearns
27 E. 38th Street
New York City

Dear Madam:

Your appeal for a contribution to a fund for Miss Shaw received some days ago. I heard this annuity publicly announced at the recent convention in Washington, and supposed the money was already assured; since such is not the case, I will frankly tell you my opinion.

We are engaged in carrying forward the greatest reform that has ever been undertaken in behalf of freedom. We have only made a beginning; there is yet much to be done. All the money that can be raised should be applied to the accomplishment of the object for which we have all worked for so long. Besides, I do not approve of making such gifts of money to individual workers. It introduces commercialism into the advocacy of a cause which should be sacred, and which calls for self-consecration and self sacrifice; it suggests to the younger women the possibility of pecuniary reward, instead of placing before them the great ideal.

Again, such gifts are unjust. The work that has been accomplished is the result of the combined efforts of thousands of women in the different states, some of whom have given their all to the cause, and some have sacrificed their lives. Hundreds of women have worked longer than Miss Shaw and sacrificed more. The mere fact that an individual has occupied the position of president for a time does not justify us in singling her out as the recipient of large financial reward.

You speak of this as a 'national tribute.' This would surely be a misnomer. Not only because our doctrine of liberty has not been accepted in many parts of the nation, but also because even among the members of our own society and among our very best friends, there is a great diversity of opinion in regard to Miss Shaw's character and methods and a great variety of estimates in regard to the value of her work. Indeed, the ladies you mention as approving of this annuity seem, with a very few exceptions, to be confined to the Eastern coast and not one from the Pacific states. Surely this cannot be regarded as a 'national tribute.'

You mention as a reason for this contribution 'that those closest to her know that she has contributed of her capital.' The inference is

*that she is in need. This cannot be the case. Miss Shaw is strong, she
has a splendid gift of oratory, and she is most thoroughly advertised.
She can command, at any time, a fine salary by her own independent
effort; and, if she wishes to work for the cause, she has ample
opportunity to do so, as other women do. Under these circumstances,
I do not feel justified in making any such pledge as you request.*

*Yours truly,
Olympia Brown.[18]*

Perhaps the idea of giving a gift of appreciation to a person who
contributed her own capital touched a tender spot with Olympia. It had
been rumored that she, herself, had given most of her small fortune to
suffrage work,[19] but she did not ever make such a claim, and certainly
would not expect a gift of appreciation for her contributions. The fact that
Miss Shaw's leadership was considered weak and ineffective by many,
also seemed reason enough for Olympia not to contribute to a gift.

This same year, 1916, her very close friend and co-worker Clara
Bewick Colby died suddenly. Mrs. Colby was nationally known, both for
her campaigns for suffrage and as editor of *The Woman's Tribune* for
twenty-five years. The *Tribune* was the official paper of the National
American Woman Suffrage Association.

Olympia, stunned and deeply grieved that one with so much talent and
so much to give should die before the work was finished, began writing a
biographical sketch of Mrs. Colby's life and work. It was a tribute to a
remarkable woman whose true contributions to history, Olympia wrote,
"will never be fully known or appreciated."[20]   The book, published in
1917, was titled *Democratic Ideals—A Sketch of Clara Bewick Colby.*

The Congressional Union now changed its name to the Woman's
Party and became independent of the National American Woman Suffrage
Association. Alice Paul and her followers led a vigorous campaign against
President Woodrow Wilson in the 1916 election. It was so effective that
he very nearly lost the election. Although Wilson spoke frequently on
democracy, justice and human rights, he did not believe that women
should have the ballot and did in fact, oppose woman suffrage. His only
concession to suffragists was his often repeated advice, "If you want to
vote, you will have to ask your state legislatures for the ballot, not
Congress."

Only two months after his reelection, suffragists had organized a
protest march in Washington, D.C. Hundreds of women poured into the
Capitol. Dressed in heavy coats and shawls against the winter weather,
they formed a line and began picketing the White House on January 10,

1917. Hundreds marched every day from ten in the morning until five-thirty in the afternoon. Walking back and forth in front of the White House gates in stately procession, each woman carried a huge purple, white and gold banner or a sign with one of Wilson's remarks painted on it.

Olympia marched with the protesters although she had just celebrated her eighty-second birthday. She could not be kept away. She chose a sign which read, "We cannot any longer delay justice in the United States."[21] It was most appropriate, she decided. Could anyone miss the irony?

Her daughter often did not know where she was or when she would return home. Olympia felt that getting the attention of the president focused on the issue of justice was more important than anything else. They must convince him that women were determined to win the ballot. "All we ask is that he go before Congress and direct them to pass the Anthony amendment," she said.

President Wilson, however, displayed no change of heart from his original stand. He did begin to profess a certain uneasiness about the pickets. Every day he found them marching back and forth in front of the gates and every day, when he drove out, he had to pass among them. At first he smiled and nodded as he rode past in his car. At length, however, he began to look the other way. The pickets were beginning to embarrass him. Finally, he decided that the embarrassment was becoming intolerable; the marchers must be removed. Accordingly, he issued the order, "Arrest the women and put them in jail."

It was a dramatic step on his part. The women, after all, were only demonstrating peacefully for their rights under the Constitution; they were not actually breaking any laws. Some of the women who were arrested were kept in the jail at the Capitol, but when that became crowded, they were sent to a workhouse in Virginia. There, many of them were shocked to find themselves mingling with convicted women criminals and being treated in the same manner as they were. Many of them suffered personal abuse. In protest, some of the suffragists went on a hunger strike. It did no good. The jail personnel began to force-feed them as the English jailers had done to the suffragettes in England a few years before.

It was but a short time before newspapers picked up the story and began publishing the details with pictures showing the brutal treatment accorded the suffragists in the workhouse.

Women across the nation were horrified by the stories; the furor that erupted was unlike anything anyone had seen before. Women by the thousands simply packed their bags and descended on the Capitol. They immediatly joined the other pickets marching in front of the White House, swelling their ranks daily.

The excitement and publicity drew mobs of men to the area. Gather-

157

ing to watch the women march, they stood along the sidewalk, hooting and jeering. It was only a matter of time before one grew bold enough to attack a picket, pushing her down in the street. When the police did nothing, other men began to do the same. After pushing several of the women down, the men seized their banners and signs and destroyed them. The police, who had come to arrest the pickets, did not lift a hand to defend the women in any way. The brutality did not deter the women for still they marched and still more women joined them.   They were fighting now, not just for enfranchisement, but for their emancipation, their dignity, their very identity. Olympia, determined to do all that she could, marched regularly with them.

Through January and February they marched. The snow gave way to chilling rain but they would not give up. The Woman's Party organized a massive demonstration for March 4, 1917, and a thousand women answered. It was a cold, raw day, but they were ready and determined.

Olympia was ready to march, no matter what the weather. It seemed that nothing could keep her away, not even her family. Gilson Gardner, noted correspondent for *The Boston Transcript*, wrote a compelling description of the events of that day.

> *The weather gave this affair its character. Had there been fifteen hundred women carrying banners on a fair day, the sight would have been a pretty one. But to see a thousand women—young women, middle-aged and old women—and there were women in the line who had passed their three-score and ten—marching in a rain that almost froze as it fell; to see them standing and marching and holding their heavy banners, momentarily growing heavier—holding them against a wind that was half gale—hour after hour, until their gloves were wet, their clothes soaked through; to see them later with hands sticky from the varnish from the banner poles—bare hands, for the gloves had by this time been pulled off, and the hands were blue with cold—to see these women keep their lines and go through their program fully, losing only those who fainted or fell from exhaustion, was a sight to impress even the dulled and jaded senses of one who has seen much.*[22]

Inez Haynes Irwin also described the scene in one of her books, *The Story of the Woman's Party.*

> *People passing by, thrilled by the gallantry of the marchers, joined the procession. And as Gilson Gardner says, it was not because it was a pretty sight, or because these women were all young. Anna Norris Kendall of Wisconsin, seventy-two years old, and the Rev.*

Olympia Brown, eighty-two years old, one of the pioneer suffragists of the country, both took part . . . Of course, though, when one considers that the Rev. Olympia Brown took part in that rain-drenched and wind-driven picket deputation of a thousand women on March 4, and that Mary Nolan and Lavinia Dock both served their terms in prison, one must admit that they were as young in spirit as the youngest picket there.[23]

The picketing gained publicity for the suffrage movement but it also gained notoriety for it. Even more important, a vast wave of sympathy for the women swept the nation. "Why did Wilson have the marchers arrested?" people asked. "Why is he letting jail personnel brutalize them?" and then, "Why doesn't he do something about it?"

Newspaper reporters assumed that the National American Woman Suffrage Association had organized the demonstrations. Those leaders were shocked to find themselves blamed for, in their words, the "disgusting and reprehensible action" of the pickets. Carrie Chapman Catt, president, and Anna Howard Shaw, honorary president, immediately condemned the marchers publicly. They then prepared and mailed 250 letters claiming that their organization was not responsible for the picketing. "It is the Woman's Party who is instigating the protest marches," they insisted, "Our organization has nothing whatsoever to do with such demonstrations."[24]

Olympia, thoroughly disgusted with the National American leaders, accused them of lacking courage. "They are afraid to march and protest their second-class citizenship, and they are more interested in the honor of being president than in the success of the movement," she charged.

Such remarks did not endear her to either the leaders of the National American or their supporters, but Olympia believed that they should be setting an example for their membership. "Women should be working together, not opposing each other. It only weakens the movement. Women must be free to work in whatever way they chose."

In an article that she wrote about Susan B. Anthony, Olympia stated that Miss Anthony would have been marching with the women had she been alive. Had she not dared to go to the polls and vote in 1872? Had she not braved arrest and been put in jail for voting? Had she not marched and distributed copies of the Declaration of Rights of the Women of the United States at the Centennial Celebration in Philadelphia in 1876?

We ask, not what Miss Anthony did, but what she would do were she here today. Still it is interesting to know her opinion, and it is reassuring to find that in most things she was entirely in accord with the spirit and purpose of the present workers. If some of our methods were unheard of in her day, we may be sure that she would approve them now, were she here, and the criticisms which we meet in our time are mild when compared with those which Miss Anthony endured.[25]

She was concerned with the cause, not with what other people thought of her. She had the courage to do what she felt was right. More women need that kind of courage today," Olympia added.

When she returned to Wisconsin later that spring, she found herself virtually ostracized from the state suffrage association. Unwilling to sit back and accept their attitude toward her because of her picketing, she went before the board to explain her activities in Washington, D.C.

The ballot is founded on the Declaration of Independence and based on democracy. The pickets are not hurting the cause of suffrage. They are not criticizing the president as so many people seem to believe, but are merely quoting him ... The women who have been arrested and sentenced to the workhouse are highly intelligent and prominent women ... those who took part in the hunger strike are from prominent families. When the newspapers reported that they were being physically force-fed and confined to cells without ventilation ... people demanded Congress start an investigation. President Wilson knew about the workhouse conditions but refused to do anything about them. We believe it is inconsistent to carry on a war in the interests of democracy abroad when we have no democracy at home.[26]

She deliberately chose strong words to speak to these conservative women. The United States had now entered World War I and the nation's sympathies were swept up in the great cause of "making the world safe for democracy."

Olympia stepped directly into that controversy as she spoke to the board members.

We cannot say that the United States is a democracy as long as women cannot vote. We are being asked to give up our suffrage work until the war is over. Women were asked to do this same thing during the Civil War. They were told that as soon as the war was over and the Negro enfranchised, they would be given the ballot. But that did not happen. Instead, they were ridiculed for wanting to vote and we still do not have the ballot. We are being asked to do the same thing in 1917. We cannot afford to let the subject go by this time. If we do, women will have to begin the fight all over again. So much work and so much money has gone into the effort that it must be carried through.[27]

She was talking, of course, to women much younger than herself, women who had neither personal recollection of the Civil War nor of women's struggle to get property rights and education privileges. They knew nothing of the pain and ridicule women had suffered for more than fifty years. Most of them had only been involved in suffrage work for the past ten years. Olympia remembered, though, all of the pain, the broken promises. She began to see that they were not even listening to her words as she talked. They had simply closed their minds to what she was saying.

"It is highly improper for ladies to march and protest," several said to her. "Ladies should not be marching in the streets carrying signs."

"Ladies will never get the vote if they don't demand it," Olympia retorted. "Women have been dignified for over sixty years and we still do not have the vote. Is it because we are too dignified to fight for the ballot? Is being proper more important than being able to vote?"

Olympia campaigned as she could that summer and fall, speaking, writing, marching. Still Congress did not pass the amendment. When she returned to Racine again after her winter of work in the Capitol, she offered to campaign in Wisconsin. The president of the association, Mrs. Youmans, pointedly declined her offer.

July 27, 1918

Dear Mrs. Brown:

I dislike to enlarge upon differences but you must realize that your recent attitude of sympathy for the Woman's Party makes it difficult for us to assume your complete sympathy with the present methods and the aims of the Wisconsin Woman's Suffrage Association. While both organizations are working for the success of the federal amendment, their methods of work are different. The attitude of the Woman's Party toward the government during the war we find particularly objectionable.[28]

Olympia was furious. Pulling out pen and paper, she sent back an immediate reply.

My dear Mrs. Youmans,

Yours of the 27th just received. I cannot see why you doubt my sympathy with the Wis. Woman's Suffrage Society. I was one of those who organized the society near 35 years ago. I have worked with it and for it in some capacity ever since. I am working for the enfranchisement of women and I hope my interest is genuine and broad enough to enable me to sympathize with any individual or organization which is sincerely aiming to accomplish the same object. I sympathize with any honest effort to secure the right of women to vote. I belong to the National Woman's Party but I have never attempted to introduce it into this state.

I have for many years been president of the Federal Suffrage Association and I believe the method they propose would have secured the vote for women long ago had it been adopted as I wished by the National; as it was not adopted by them and as our state is auxiliary to them I have never tried to introduce it here, believing that our forces should be united and we should all pull together. I was in no way responsible for the division that occurred in our ranks in 1912. Not only that but in order that the people might join hands I resigned the presidency of the Wis. W. S. A. contrary to the wishes of all the members in attendance at the annual meeting and have never sought to thrust myself into the enterprise of the society or to interpose my own idea or personal opinions.

It seems to me too late to charge me with a want of sympathy with the work or aims of the society.[29]

In spite of her disagreement with the state suffrage leaders, she campaigned in Wisconsin during the summer, returning to Baltimore in the fall. Progress, she felt was very slow.

On November 11, 1918, World War I came to an end. The nation joined in a great victory celebration. Suffragists lost no time in turning to Congress for immediate action on the Anthony amendment. Congress, however, seemed to have more important matters at stake. The women then turned to President Wilson, urging him to direct Congress to pass the suffrage amendment. Wilson did nothing. More than anyone else in a leadership position, he symbolized men's resistance to granting women the ballot. He had, it was said, more important things on his mind than placating a handful of noisy demanding women. As head of the greatest democracy on earth, he had been asked to take part in the Paris peace talks, he said, and was sailing for France in December.

Olympia's response to this news was immediate and direct. In a speech she made before the National Advisory Council of the Woman's Party she said, "The thing that distresses me is the embarrassment accruing . . . our position as the survivor of world democracy when we cannot even boast that we have . . . democracy in our own country."[30]

The members of the Woman's Party felt the same way. In one mighty voice, they vowed to light a fire in Lafayette Park on the day that Wilson was officially received by France and publicly burn all of his speeches and books on liberty, freedom and democracy. The drama of that afternoon traveled across the nation to Europe. Subsequently, it proved to be an accute embarrassment to President Wilson during his visit in France and reportedly hampered his effectiveness there.

> *It was late afternoon when the four hundred women proceeded solemnly in single file from headquarters, past the White House, along the edge of the quiet and beautiful Lafayette Park, to the foot of Lafayette's statue. A slight mist added beauty to the pageant. The purple, white and gold banners, so brilliant in sunshine, became soft pastel sails. Half the procession carried lighted torches; the other half, banners. The crowd gathered silently, somewhat awestruck by the scene. Massed about that statue, we felt a strange strength and solidarity, we felt again that we were part of the universal struggle for liberty.*
>
> *The torch was applied to the pine-wood logs in the Grecian urn at the edge of the broad base of the statue. As the flames began to mount, Vida Milholland stepped forward and without accompaniment sang again from that spot of beauty, in her own challenging way, the Woman's Marseillaise. Even the small boys in the crowd, always the most difficult to please, cheered and clapped and cried for more.*

There was a short speech, telling the crowd why the women were burning Wilson's words.

> *The few hoots and jeers which followed all ceased, when a tiny and aged woman stepped from her place to the urn in the brilliant torch light. The crowd recognized a veteran. It was the most dramatic moment in the ceremony. Reverend Olympia Brown of Wisconsin, one of the first ordained women ministers in the country, then in her eighty-fourth year, gallant pioneer, friend and colleague of Susan B.*

*Anthony, said, as she threw into the flames the speech made by the
President on his arrival in France: "America has fought for France
and the common cause of liberty. I have fought for liberty for seventy
years, and I protest against the President's leaving our country with
this old fight here unwon."*

*The crowd burst into applause and continued to cheer as she was
assisted from the plinth of the statue, too frail to dismount by herself.[31]*

The moving spectacle seemed to have no effect on the lawmakers.
The Senate voted to defeat the amendment once again.

Women were stunned. They reacted with angry speeches. The
Woman's Party threatened to launch a political campaign against every
senator who voted against the measure. Deputations of women began
attending Congress every time the amendment was on the agenda.
Meanwhile, Olympia continued to carry on a verbal campaign of her own.
"The United States is an aristocracy of sex. It is the meanest aristocracy
on the face of the earth. Women have no recourse but to appeal by means
of reason and argument to the moral sense of men who still believe
themselves to be superior to women," she declared.[32]

President Wilson had considerable time to think over his position on
women and the ballot during the return trip to America. He began to see
at last that it was time for him to support woman suffrage in Congress. It
was almost too late when he finally urged the legislators to pass the
measure. Many women never forgave him for his reluctance to go to
Congress and ask it to give the ballot to women. Certainly Olympia did not.

The weeks dragged on and winter edged into spring before the House
of Representatives passed the bill by vote of 304 to 89. Women cheered
and their hopes rose along with their voices. It was two weeks later that
the Senate capped their hopes by passing the amendment. The vote was
56 to 25.[33]

Olympia reminded women that the amendment still had to be ratified
by two-thirds of the states, and she cautioned them not to celebrate before
they were assured of victory. The women, however, were weary of the
struggle. They laid down their banners and began to plan celebrations
around the country, confident that the ratification would not take long.

They were right.

But ratification was not fast or easy. Suffragists spent the next year
working with the state legislatures to get the amendment ratified in thirty-
six states. It was not until August 25, 1920 that the final state ratified the
Ninteenth Amendment and women could at last vote.

Suffragists also spent those last months attending final conventions
and preparing to disband the various woman suffrage organizations. Ida

Husted Harper was finishing the last volume of the *History of Woman Suffrage*, the project that Elizabeth Cady Stanton and Susan B. Anthony had begun in 1880. It had now reached six volumes.

Some of the members of the National American association decided to begin a drive for a gift for Carrie Chapman Catt in appreciation of her work as president of the organization. They planned to give her a $2,700 brooch as a gift. Others began a drive for money for a $5,000 fund for Alice Stone Blackwell so that she could write a biography of her mother, Lucy Stone. There were other requests for money for other projects, too, and Olympia soon became distressed and angry at the continual stream of letters asking for money. When there was a real need in the world, all of the gifts seemed frivolous by comparison. She wrote a letter to Mrs. Youmans expressing her indignation. Such a waste of needed funds seemed foolish if not reprehensible.

> *I am every day receiving requests for money for the Armenians who are starving; for the fatherless children of France; for poor women in our great cities. In view of these things and the high cost of living which makes it difficult for people to meet their bills, it seems to me that costly presents to wealthy women is, to say the least, very ill advised. Mrs. Catt is very wealthy and Miss Blackwell . . . is abundantly able to write her mother's life.*[34]

She adamantly refused to donate money to most such petitions. She felt the real tribute belonged to the workers not the leaders. She also felt that the vital part played by Alice Paul and the Woman's Party in achieving enfranchisement should be recognized. Unfortunately, Carrie Chapman Catt herself had taken offense at being associated in any way with the Woman's Party, and she hastened to make it clear that she did not approve of their methods.

Olympia began at once to attend the final suffrage conventions around the country. In January of 1920, a grand pioneer celebration in Chicago drew throngs of women. Olympia, a keynote speaker, lost no time in telling women that winning the ballot was only the beginning of their fight. She urged them to join in a concerted effort to get an equal rights amendment through Congress for, she said, the ballot did not give them equal rights. It only gave them the right to vote.

In February, the National American Woman Suffrage Association held a final convention in Chicago. Surprisingly, in spite of her often contentious disposition toward their attitudes and methods, the leaders asked Olympia to be their guest of honor. She did not hesitate to accept in spite of her long practice of trying to avoid publicity, and she basked in special attention all that week. Three other pioneer reformers were invited but were unable to attend. Emily Howland, Reverend Antoinette Brown Blackwell and Charlotte Pierce received congratulatory letters. Charlotte Pierce had the added honor of being the sole survivor of the 1848 Seneca Falls Convention, the historic meeting held seventy-two years before that marked the true beginning of women's fight for the ballot.[35]

Olympia also attended a Pioneer Suffrage Luncheon during the convention which brought together many of the early reformers. Their moods were mixed. Although they rejoiced in the passage of the amendment, many were saddened to realize that this was the last of the "love feasts" which they had shared together so many times. Many of them realized that they would not ever see each other again.

Olympia had been asked to give a speech and she prepared one aptly titled, "What the Modern Woman Owes to the Pioneers." She wanted every woman to know the cost of the ballot, the years of work done before many of them were even born and the names and contributions of the very first reformers. Reporters were surprised at the strength of her delivery, and most of all her elocution. They had not expected to hear such a dynamic voice from the tiny, eighty-five year old woman. "Her excellent voice was not equalled among any of the younger women," several reporters wrote in unmistakable admiration.

At a special evening program during the festivities, she shared the spotlight with five other women, each prominent in a specific field. Olympia was chosen for theology; in education, Professor Maria L. Sanford; in medicine, Dr. Julia Holmes Smith; in law, Miss Florence Allen; in journalism, Miss Ethel M. Colson; and in politics, Miss Mary Garrett Hay.[36]

Altogether, it was a heady experience for her, certainly far different from the treatment previously accorded her. Many of the National American leaders chose to ignore her contributions because of her close association with Alice Paul. Olympia had stepped on many toes and said frightfully distressing things. What does one do with such a person?

Ida Husted Harper, in finishing her final volume of the *History of Woman Suffrage*, wrote to Mrs. Youmans for information on the story of the suffrage work in Wisconsin. "Due credit must be given to Olympia Brown," she wrote. It is interesting to note that even Mrs. Harper had some reservations about Olympia's work with Alice Paul and the Woman's Party. She was also acutely aware of the dissension between Olympia and Mrs. Youmans, and she felt that the younger woman might want to ignore Olympia's early work. "She . . . has been, of course, on the watch tower in Wisconsin from the beginning and is entitled to full credit for all of the work that she has done . . . whatever Mrs. Brown did in Washington has no connection with it. I want her to have credit for the *State* work she has done and *not* for anything else," Harper wrote.[37]

Mrs. Harper, determined to deal only with the facts of Olympia's work in Wisconsin, did not intend to bring any emotional issues into the story, particularly in regard to her marching and picketing in the nation's Capitol. In a letter to Olympia, she explained some of her problems in writing the final chapters of the movement.

"There is everywhere the disposition to ignore the old workers and what they accomplished but it is not going to be done in this History if I can prevent it."

She noted with some dismay that younger women were taking the credit for the vote, ignoring the seventy-two years of work that had gone into the effort, and then she made a comment that warmed Olympia's heart. "Carrie Chapman Catt has been making extravagant statements to the effect that if it had not been for Alice Stone Blackwell that women would not have their suffrage today. It seems that her mother (Lucy Stone) at least might have had a little credit." [38]

And so the great cause came to an end. On November 2, 1920, millions of women went to the polls and cast their first ballot ever.

Olympia Brown was among the first to vote on that morning. One can only speculate on her thoughts as she cast her first ballot. Surely the spirits of Susan B. Anthony and Elizabeth Cady Stanton must have been with her. She may have felt a moment of sorrow for the entire vanguard of equal rights workers who had not lived to see the culmination of the dream. Of that original group of women, only she and Antoinette Brown Blackwell, the very person who had inspired her to reach out and become all that she could become when she was but a young girl, survived to cast their first vote. It is altogether fitting that both cast their first ballots that year—in a presidential election.

Postscript

There are many facets of Olympia Brown's life which will be forever unknown, but with the help of those who knew and remember her, a few interesting details about her private life can be added to the story.

She dearly loved her family and unabashedly played favorites with her grandchildren. Her little granddaughter Katharine Willis became "Queenie," and she taught her to read long before the little girl started school. Education was a driving force during all of Olympia Brown's life, and she stressed its role in the lives of her four little grandchildren at every opportunity.

She spent much of her time from early spring until late fall working in her garden at her Racine home. Even in her eighties when she lived in Baltimore with her daughter, she prepared early every spring to return to Wisconsin. Opening up the home in which she had lived since 1878 gave her great joy. She held fast to the dream all winter, planning her garden and summer of work. Every vegetable and every flower had to be planted at a specific time, or they would not produce abundantly, she insisted. No one could convince her to deviate from her schedule.

Perhaps the garden enabled her to work off some of her frustration, or perhaps it reminded her of simpler days when she had helped her mother tend the large garden at the Michigan farm. Whatever the reasons, it was work that she loved. The garden, extending all the way down the steep bank of the backyard almost to the edge of Lake Michigan, became a profusion of flowers and vegetables.

One summer when little six-year-old Katharine was visiting from New York City, Olympia took her by the hand and led her out into the garden. "Let's dig some potatoes and beets for supper," she said. Katharine, open-mouthed, watched her grandmother turn over a spadeful of dirt, reach down, and pluck out potatoes. "It was the first time I realized that food came from the ground," Katharine said, smiling at the memory.[1]

Olympia loved to cook, too. Many of her recipes came from New England, "the home of my ancestors," she claimed with a touch of pride. Lamb stew and baked codfish with cream were favorites. So, too, were baked beans prepared in a particular way. "A special piece of pork has to be put on top of the beans when they are ready to bake. You have to take the meat out every time you stir the beans, and you have to use a fork, never a spoon, to stir them," were her specific instructions. She always made her New England baked beans when her son and family came to visit.

Strawberry shortcake was her favorite dessert, made with biscuit dough. "Leave the strawberries whole. Don't mash or even cut them up," she ordered. "Keep the shortcake warm, and don't use whipped cream. That takes away from the strawberry taste."[2]

In her later years she seemed to treasure her time in the kitchen almost as much as the time she spent in her garden. Yet she always had time and energy for her suffrage work.

In the spring of 1916 when she marched in a huge suffrage parade in Chicago, she managed to make her way to the Kansas contingent of marchers. Her niece Genevieve Chalkley was marching with them. The daughter of her youngest sister Marcia, Genevieve Chalkley was active in woman suffrage work. Olympia urged her to come to Racine with her little daughter Marcella for a visit, and Mrs. Chalkley agreed. Many years later that little girl recalled the visit. "When my mother and I arrived, we started walking up the sidewalk toward the house. Great-aunt Olympia was so excited that she picked up her skirts and skipped down the sidewalk toward us. Eighty-one years old and she skipped like a school girl!" Marcella. Holmes exclaimed. "It was remarkable."[3]

Marcella had other memories, too. She remembered waking up in the morning to the sound of Olympia's voice in the garden below. Every morning, weather permitting, Olympia would go out into the back yard. There she stood, facing out over Lake Michigan, reciting her elocution lessons. Her great voice rolled out across the garden down to the waters below and beyond. "They toiled and moiled and boiled the boy and found no joy," she boomed. The words and voice struck terror into all the little children in the neighborhood. "She was not like anybody else I ever knew," Marcella recalled with a wistful shake of her head.[4]

Olympia loved fine clothes, but most of her life she had not been able to afford them, nor did she believe a minister should indulge herself in fancy dresses. They were impractical, too, for one who traveled as much as she did during her lifetime. However, she was feminine and felt that even the plainest garment must have a little lace at the collar or that she should wear a fine light shawl over her shoulders to brighten a dark outfit. Her favorite color was dark plum red, a family tradition, she said, but she did not feel that she could wear such a bright color. Her clothing was always modest and dark.

She was very set in her ways, but one had to be to get things done. Gwendolen Willis wrote of her mother

She was not popular. She was indomitable and uncompromising, traits that do not lend themselves well to politics and leadership. She cared little for society, paid no deference to wealth, represented an unfashionable church, promoted a cause regarded as certain to be unsuccessful. She was troublesome because she asked people to do things, to work, contribute money, go to meetings, think, and declare themselves openly as favoring a principle or public measure.[5]

Nevertheless, Olympia did enjoy some close friendships with other women, particularly Isabella Beecher Hooker, Clara Bewick Colby, and Emma Smith DeVoe. Her friendship with Susan B. Anthony had been close at first; Olympia virtually worshipped Miss Anthony at the beginning of their friendship. However, the 1889 merger of the National and American Woman Suffrage Associations changed that. Olympia never reconciled herself to the merger and she held Miss Anthony accountable for allowing it to happen. Ida Husted Harper in a letter to Olympia once wrote on a somewhat chiding note,

Miss Anthony retained her friendship for you *to a much greater degree than you did for her. I have often heard her say that she did not blame you a particle for opposing so strongly the union of the two associations, and that she never would have permitted it if all of the leaders of both of them had not brought so much pressure to bear on her and insisted that it would be of such an immense benefit to the suffrage movement.*[6]

There was little room for bitterness in Olympia's heart after women finally had the ballot. She did not like to look back; she was used to looking ahead. There were new organizations to join, new goals to set. She often wished that she could still preach, but at eighty-five, there was little opportunity for that. She received an invitation to be guest minister at her church in Racine on September 12, 1920. It was her last sermon. She entitled it, "The Opening Doors."* It was nearly thirty-three years since she had resigned as the pastor of that church, but she assured her audience that she had been a faithful church member ever since. "That is a long time, and many things have happened, but the grandest thing has been the lifting up of the gates and the opening of the doors to the women of America, giving liberty to twenty-seven million women."

She spoke of other reforms, too, noting that, "The world can never be made safe for democracy by fighting." She believed in demilitarization and disarmament and thought that diplomacy was the only tool that would bring lasting peace. Greed was a factor in causing war, she said. "The

* Appendix page 195

people of all the nations are children of God and must all share the wealth of the world.'[7]   Although she could not tell how to bring about such a revolution without bloodshed, she had great faith in the League of Nations and believed those leaders would solve the world's problems.

She sometimes wondered if she had made the right decision in leaving the ministry to work for woman suffrage. It was a futile question, she knew, but she was clearly troubled by her decision to give up the ministry. She would doubtless have been just as troubled had she stayed in the ministry and only worked for woman suffrage when she had the time. Since she had set a precedent by being the first woman ordained by a denomination in this country and the first to practice her profession for nearly a quarter century, she believed that soon there would be more women than men ministers. It was a profession particularly suited to women, she often said, and she was very disappointed to learn that there were only about sixty women preaching in Universalist churches around the nation in 1925.

If Olympia Brown had been able to separate herself completely from the ministry and devote herself to suffrage work, she might very well have become a leader of national renown. She spent considerable energy and time preparing sermons for some of her part-time parishes and writing articles for religious publications while she was working for woman suffrage. A woman torn by two vital concerns, she could not call forth her full devotion to her chosen cause.

Immediately after the Nineteenth Amendment was passed by Congress in 1919, many of the woman suffrage workers began to give credit for its passage to individual leaders. It had been a united effort by many individuals and organizations; no single person could have brought the necessary pressure to bear on Congress to induce those men to grant women the ballot. Olympia believed wholeheartedly that if it had not been for Alice Paul and the Woman's Party with their protest marches, women would not have had suffrage for many years, perhaps even another generation. They had visibly and vehemently protested their plight of second-class citizenship, focusing the attention of the nation and the world on a democracy that denied half its citizens the right to vote, much as it still denies them equal rights. Little credit is given in the book, *History of Woman Suffrage, Vol. 5*, to that final seven-year drive by the members of the Woman's Party who aided, some at the risk of their health and lives, in obtaining the ballot. Judge Walter Clark of the North Carolina Supreme Court, however, paid a tribute to women in a letter to Alice Paul. He wrote of the Woman's Party, "The feat of getting twenty-six special sessions called up to date is one that no other power on the planet could have accomplished. It will remain a marvel in political history, that with the odds against you, you have won . . . your enfranchisement."[8]

It did not seem a marvel to women, however. They knew what a long, hard struggle it had been, and how difficult it is to achieve justice. There were those who believed that they had won the battle and held victory in their hands. Many, however, realized that they had only won the ballot and that the fight for equal rights had not even begun yet. Olympia knew, and she privately grieved for the millions of women who would have to sacrifice so much in continuing the effort to gain equality as human beings.

She was an activist at heart, and her last six years were spent agitating for peace and military reform. She joined the Women's International League for Peace and Freedom, the League of Nations, and became a charter member of the American Civil Liberties Union. She also belonged to the organization which had changed its name from the National American Woman Suffrage Association to The League of Women Voters. Along with the change in name, its purpose moved from political action to education.

There were many things that needed to be done for women and the fledgling equal rights movement, but Olympia believed the danger of militarism was more important than any other. Women should protest compulsory military service and the expenditure of millions of dollars for "munitions of war," she said. If young men had to serve in the armed forces, the possibility of getting into another war was much greater than if there were no compulsory service. She was a staunch advocate of all peace efforts.

Olympia was honored in the early 1920's by the Racine Business and Professional Women, and she was listed as one of twenty-six great citizens of Wisconsin by the Wisconsin Women's Progressive Association. The League of Women Voters included her name on a memorial plaque in their Washington office as one of fifteen women most active in obtaining ratification of suffrage in Wisconsin.[9] Pleased with these tributes to her life-time of devotion to the cause of women's rights, she would have been even more pleased could she have known what honors lay in the future.

Her remaining years were happy and relatively trouble free. She continued to divide her time between Racine in the summer and Baltimore in the winter. She spent the holidays visiting her son and his family in New York City, but the better part of her winters were spent in Baltimore with her daughter. Her family and friends urged her to write her autobiography, and Olympia attempted to gather material for the work. She was not, however, interested in the past. That was over and done, she said. Her whole lifetime had been spent looking to the future, working for change. It was a difficult and frustrating task to try and change that pattern of thinking. She gave it up at last, impatient with all of the detail work, and her daughter had to complete the autobiography.

In 1926 when Olympia was ninety-one, her daughter took a sabbatical from teaching and suggested that they go to Europe for several months and tour the continent. Olympia, delighted at the idea of seeing some of the many places and things that she had only read about in books, could hardly wait. What a fitting climax to her life, she thought! They traveled by steamship, taking the southern route so that they could enjoy the warm weather on the Italian Riviera. There they spent several weeks visiting historic places and enjoying the scenery. They went shopping in Paris where Olympia found many things to delight the feminine side of her nature. In particular, she bought a dark purple silk hat fringed with pansies and a shawl of black, cobweb sheer Chantilly lace. She never did buy a dress of her favorite color, plum red, but she was pleased with both purchases and all of the wonderful sights that she had seen on her trip.

Her death came suddenly that fall after a brief illness at her daughter's home in Baltimore. Henry Parker Willis and Gwendolen Willis already knew that their mother had chosen to be buried in the family plot at Racine, Wisconsin, beside her husband and near her mother. So strong were the family ties that when her son died in 1937, he was buried there, too, as was Gwendolen after her death in 1969.

Tributes to Olympia Brown's memory poured in from all over the United States. Perhaps the most succinct and moving of all was the editorial in *The Baltimore Sun.*

> *Olympia Brown carried throughout her long and active life the dauntless courage and the mental freshness of the frontier environment whence she came.*
>
> *Queen Victoria had not been called to the throne of England when this pioneer American suffragist was born in a Michigan log cabin. Andrew Jackson was still President of the United States. Perhaps that helps to explain why there was so little of Victorian stodginess, so much of Jacksonian virility in the character of Mrs. Willis, to use the married name by which, in accordance with her principles, she was seldom known.*
>
> *It was a compliment to Baltimore when, at the age of 80, this interesting and charming lady decided to make her home here. At such an age no newcomer would be expected to write a name in current issues. But the Rev. Olympia Brown, though well past her allotted span, could not remain inactive. Perhaps no phase of her life better exemplified her vitality and intellectual independence than the mental discomfort she succeeded in arousing, between her eightieth and ninetieth birthdays, among conservatively-minded Baltimoreans.[10]*

174

Governor John J. Blaine of Wisconsin sent a telegram to the family in tribute to Olympia Brown.

> *Death was not necessary to fix the high value of your mother's service. In the history of Wisconsin and the nation Rev. Olympia Brown's name will stand on time's unfading scroll as a humanitarian and as a leader in the suffrage movement with the courage of her sister worker Susan B. Anthony. She carried on the fight to break the legal shackles which fettered women when the days were dark and when opposition was bitter. She won because she never compromised with wrong. She brought triumph and victory for women seeking the light and equality before the law by a dauntless courage, a fine sense of public justice and an appeal for righteousness that was answered. Wisconsin joins the requiem the nation is paying in just tribute to her name and her remarkable leadership.[11]*

Frances R. Greene, a former state suffragist who had worked closely with Olympia Brown, gave the eulogy.

> *Indomitable spirit . . . the very elements seemed to fear her open countenance and clarion voice . . . To know her was to feel the inspiration of a determined will to overcome obstacles in the path of human progress . . . Day after day and year after year found her unflinching in her efforts to uplift humanity and hew a new path to human liberty . . . whatsoever in any manner contributed to human advancement and happiness obtained from her the deepest interest . . . by an inscrutable providence her talents were safely guarded for the far-reaching work that was hers to perform for a suffering and needy world.[12]*

The finest tribute to Olympia Brown, she said, would be for every woman to go out and vote in the next election.

One of the first honors bestowed on her after her death was a tablet erected in the Memorial Universalist Church in Washington, D.C. It incorporates a portrait relief of her and designates her as the first woman in the United States to receive ordination by a recognized denomination. Her favorite quotation, "He who works in harmony with justice is immortal," is etched into the tablet.[13]

The American Association of University Women in Racine instituted an International Studies Grant in her name in 1950. In 1962, the Unitarian-Universalist Church of Racine and Kenosha, her former parish, dedicated a hall to her memory. An Olympia Brown Scholarship Fund was established by the New York State American University Women in 1963 to encourage young women seeking a career in religion. Also in 1963, St. Lawrence Theological School of Canton, New York, celebrated the 100th anniversary of Olympia Brown's graduation from the University. A bronze tablet was erected in Atwood Hall bearing an inscription honoring her as the first woman in the country to achieve full ministerial standing.

Perhaps the tribute that Olympia would have valued the most was the naming of an elementary school in her honor. In 1975, after the Racine Unified School District had purchased several of the former Dominican College buildings edging the Lake Michigan shore north of the city, school board members began a search for a suitable name for the school. It was to house elementary school children whose building had burned down a short time before.

A committee, spearheaded by Marcia Alexander, Jane Beaugrand and Margaret Wernecke, all of Racine, gathered material about Olympia Brown's life. They presented a brief chronological summary highlighting her experiences to the School Naming Committee. Included was an excerpt from her autobiography describing her field work. The letter accompanying the material is eloquent in its appeal to name the new school for Olympia Brown. Committee members pointed out that she had lived in Racine forty-eight years.

> *But to date, there is no landmark, no tangible evidence anywhere in Racine that one of America's most notable women lived and worked here during many of the years of her remarkable achievements in the struggle for women's rights.*
>
> *The City of Racine has been generous in formally recognizing the contributions of many of her good citizens. Surely the time has come to honor the work of one whose lasting achievements are exceeded by none.*[14]

After carefully reviewing the record of Olympia Brown's achievements, the school board voted unanimously to name the school for her.

The children attending that school today are the beneficiaries of her lifetime zeal for education, and the women of America are the beneficiaries of her unremitting determination to gain the ballot and to teach women to view themselves as human beings in their own right, not as "appendages to men," as she had phrased it so many times.[15]

Other honors will doubtless follow as her story becomes known. She is one of thirteen subjects in a 40-foot mural located in a multi-purpose room of the Unitarian Community Church of Santa Monica, California. The artist, Ann Thiermann, created the thirteen persons surrounded by religious symbols and banners expressing humanistic and social concerns. The title of the mural is "Four Hundred Years of Living Unitarian Universalist History." [16]

Today Olympia Brown would be in the vanguard of those women working for equal rights. She would work until she had reached her goal or until death claimed her. An indomitable and uncompromising reformer who has been completely overlooked by historians, this woman's many achievements are documented in this biography. Her place in history among noted leaders of woman's rights is now clear. She will be an inspiration to many.

Footnotes*

Chapter 1
[1] Bruce Catton, *Michigan* (New York: W.W.Norton and Co., Inc., 1976), pp. 77-78.

[2] Based on information given to the author by Marcella Holmes, granddaughter of Olympia Brown's sister, Marcia Brown Howland, in June of 1978.

[3] Original copies of *The Family Museum* are among the Olympia Brown papers, Schlesinger Library, Radcliffe College, Cambridge, Mass.

Chapter 2
[1] Arthur C. Cole, *A Hundred Years of Mount Holyoke College* (New Haven: Yale University Press, 1940), p. 36.

[2] Ibid, pp. 78-9.

[3] Ibid, p. 40.

[4] Ibid, pp. 81 and 139.

[5] Ibid, pp. 132-3.

[6] Ibid, p. 353.

[7] The letter is among the Olympia Brown papers, Schlesinger Library, Radcliffe College, Cambridge, Massachusetts.

[8] *Educating for Democracy, A Symposium* (Yellow Springs: The Antioch Press, 1937), pp. 116 and 117.

Chapter 3
[1] Essays are among her papers at the Schlesinger Library, Radcliffe College, Cambridge, Massachusetts.

[2] Letter written by Lucretia Effinger to Jessie Hutchinson, dated January 3, 1893. Schlesinger Library, Radcliffe College, Cambridge, Massachusetts.

[3] *Olympia Brown*, autobiography, unpublished. Brown papers.

[4] *National Encyclopedia of American Biography*, Vol. 29, p. 129.

[5] Brown, Autobiography, p 15.

[6] Brown papers.

[7] Quote by her granddaughter, Katharine Willis Hooton, June 1978.

[8] Brown papers. Autobiography.

[9] E. R. Hanson, *Our Woman Workers* (Chicago: The Star and Covenant Office, 1882), p. 430. There were twenty-eight students in the class.

[10] Autobiography, p.18

Chapter 4
[1] Olympia Brown, autobiography, unpublished, p. 19. Also Olympia Brown,

Acquaintances, Old and New, Among Reformers (Milwaukee: S.E. Tate Printing Co., 1911) p. 29. Olympia Brown papers. Schlesinger Library, Radcliffe College, Cambridge, Massachusetts.

[2] Ibid, p. 30.

[3] Olympia Brown papers.

[4] Brown, *Acquaintances,* etc., p. 30-31.

[5] Brown, *Acquaintances,* etc., p. 44.

[6] Brown papers. The letter from Antoinette Brown Blackwell (Mrs. Samuel Blackwell) is dated February 28 but refers to no specific year. Events mentioned in the letter lead the author to believe that it was written in 1864.

[7] Brown, *Acquaintances,* etc., pp. 47, 48.

[8] Brown papers.

[9] Taken from the records of the First Universalist Church of Weymouth Landing, submitted by Donald Towne Marshall, interim minister of the Unitarian Universalist Church of Weymouth, South Weymouth, Massachusetts, March 15, 1979.

[10] Brown papers.

[11] Elizabeth Cady Stanton, Susan B. Anthony, Matilda Joslyn Gage, *History of Woman Suffrage, Volume 3* (New York: Arno & The New York Times, 1969), p. 301.

[12] Brown, *Acquaintances,* etc., pp. 50-51.

[13] Brown papers.

Chapter 5

[1] Information is taken from letters written to Olympia Brown by Lucy Stone and Henry Blackwell. They are among her papers in the Schlesinger Library at Radcliffe College, Cambridge, Massachusetts. They are dated May 30, 1867.

[2] Brown papers.

[3] The speech and the Master of Arts Degree are among her papers.

[4] Olympia Brown, *Acquaintances, Old and New, Among Reformers* (Milwaukee: S.E. Tate Printing Co., 1911), p. 56.

[5] Ibid

[6] Letter from H. Blackwell dated June 12, 1867. Brown papers.

[7] Brown, *Acquaintances,* p. 59.

[8] Ibid, p. 60.

[9] Ibid, pp. 65-68. Although it appears in *Acquaintances,* the entire quote was originally taken from *The Kansas State Journal.*

[10] Brown papers. Essay, "Reminiscent Story of Kansas Campaign, 1867," pp. 44-45.

[11] Brown papers. *The Kansas State Journal,* Lawrence, Kansas, August 15, 1867.

[12] Brown papers. *The Border Sentinel,* Mound City, Kansas, August 16, 1867.

[13] Brown papers. *The Humbolt Union,* August 18, 1867.

[14] Olympia Brown's essay, "Reminiscent Story of Kansas Campaign, 1867," pp. 52-57, Brown Papers.

[15] Brown, Acquaintances, pp. 72-73.

[16] Brown papers.

[17] Elizabeth Cady Stanton, Susan B. Anthony, Matilda Joslyn Gage, *History of Woman Suffrage, Vol. 2* (New York: Arno & the New York Times, 1969), p. 260.

[18] Brown Papers.

[19] Ibid.

[20] Ibid.

[21] Brown *Acquaintances*, pp. 75-76.

Chapter 6

[1] Elizabeth Cady Stanton, Susan B. Anthony, Matilda Joslyn Gage, *History of Woman Suffrage, Vol. 2* (New York: Arno & The New York Times, 1969), p. 310.

[2] Ibid, p. 311.

[3] Ibid.

[4] Olympia Brown, *Acquaintances, Old and New, Among Reformers* (Milwaukee: S. E. Tate Printing Co., 1911), pp. 78-9. Olympia Brown papers, Schlesinger Library, Radcliffe College, Cambridge, Massachusetts.

[5] Brown papers.

[6] Caroline Severance became chairman of the committee to arrange for the convention. Olympia Brown, Julia Ward Howe, Lucy Stone, T. W. Higginson, and William Lloyd Garrison were on the committee. This information was obtained from Olympia Brown's lectures, "History of Woman Suffrage," June 18-24, 1914. It is among her papers.

[7] Ibid. Brown Papers.

[8] Ibid.

[9] Ibid.

[10] Ibid. Summer 1868.

[11] Ibid. May 10, 1869.

[12] Taken from the records of the First Universalist Church of Weymouth Landing, Massachusetts. Submitted by Donald Towne Marshall, interim minister of the Unitarian Universalist Church of Weymouth, South Weymouth, Mass., in a letter dated March 15, 1979. Brown papers. "Miss Brown responded in a trembling manner, accepting the present and thanking the friends for their expression of feeling, urging the Society to constant action and the Sunday school to maintain its excellent standard."

[13] The "Calling List" is a notebook in the possession of the Unitarian Universalist Church, Racine, Wisconsin.

[14] Brown papers.

[15] Edward T. James, ed., *Notable American Women 1607-1950* (Cambridge: Harvard University Press), p. 257.

[16] Brown papers.

[17] Per record book of meetings of the First Universalist Society of Bridgeport, Connecticut. Submitted by Jane Ciarcia in a letter dated February 24, 1979.

Brown papers.

[18] Brown papers.

[19] Olyrnpia Brown, *Autobiography*, unpublished, p. 26. Brown papers.

[20] Brown papers.

[21] Olympia Brown's "Calling List." Unitarian Universalist Church, Racine, Wisconsin.

[22] Brown papers.

[23] Information given by Katharine Willis Hooton, June 1978. Mrs. Hooton is Olympia Brown's granddaughter.

[24] Jane Ciarcia, letter dated February 24, 1979. Brown papers.

[25] Stanton, Anthony & Gage, *History of Woman Suffrage, Vol. 3* (New York: Arno & The New York Times, 1969), pp. 95-97.

[26] Ibid, pp. 30-31. The names of the five women were Susan B. Anthony, Matilda Joslyn Gage, Sara Andrews Spencer, Lillie Devereux Blake and Phoebe W. Cousins. Copy of Declaration is in appendix.

Chapter 7

[1] Olympia Brown, *Autobiography*, unpublished, p. 27. Brown papers, Schlesinger Library, Radcliffe College, Cambridge, Mass.

[2] Ibid.

[3] Brown papers.

[4] Brown, *Autobiography*, p. 28.

[5] Ibid, pp. 29 & 30.

[6] Brown papers.

[7] The original pledge signed by Jerome Increase (J. I.) Case and all of the contributing parishioners is in the Unitarian-Universalist Church in Racine, Wisconsin.

[8] Elizabeth Cady Stanton, Susan B. Anthony, Matilda Joslyn Gage, *History of Woman Suffrage, Volume 2* (New York: Arno & The New York Times, 1969), pp. 259-261.

[9] Brown, *Autobiography*, pp. 44.

[10] Brown papers. Her letter of resignation is dated Dec. 27, 1886.

[11] Brown papers.

[12] Wisconsin Woman Suffrage Association papers, State Historical Society, Madison, Wisconsin.

[13] Ida Husted Harper, *History of Woman Suffrage, Volume 4* (New York: Arno & The New York Times, 1969), p. 418.

[14] Brown papers. "Woman's Suffrage," address by Rev. O. Brown delivered at Rockford Fair, August 29, 1888. Report taken from the *Rockford Star*.

[15] Brown, *Autobiography*, p. 43.

[16] Ida Husted Harper, *Life and Work of Susan B. Anthony, volume 2* (New York: Arno Press, 1969), p. 659.

[17] *The Wisconsin Citizen*, February 1890, State Historical Society, Madison, Wisconsin.

[18] Harper, *Life and Work of Susan B. Anthony, Volume 2*, p. 670.

[19] Harper, *History, Volume 4*.

[20] Ibid, p. 554.

[21] Brown papers. Letter from S.B. Anthony dated September 2, 1890.

[22] *The Wisconsin Citizen*

Chapter 8

[1] Olympia Brown, *Autobiography*, unpublished, p. 47. Brown papers, Schlesinger Library, Radcliffe College, Cambridge, Mass.

[2] Ibid, p. 29.

[3] Brown papers, letter from Susan B. Anthony, circa 1900.

[4] *The Wisconsin Citizen*, State Historical Society, Madison, Wisconsin, May 1901.

[5] Ibid, issue of February 1902. The article was written by Olympia Brown.

[6] Elizabeth Cady Stanton, *The Woman's Bible* (New York: European Publishing Company, 1909). Olympia Brown was a member of the revising committee.

[7] *The Wisconsin Citizen*, issue of September 1901, "The Mothers of Sons," p. 1.

[8] Ibid.

[9] *The Wisconsin Citizen*, issue of February 1902.

[10] Ibid, issue of April 1902.

[11] Brown papers. See Appendix.

[12] *The Wisconsin Citizen*, issue of March 1902, p. 3.

[13] *The Wisconsin Citizen*, issue of May 1907.

Chapter 9

[1] *The Wisconsin Citizen*, State Historical Society, Madison, Wisconsin, April 1911, p. 2.

[2] Ibid, issue of July-August, 1911.

[3] Olympia Brown, *Acquaintances, Old and New, Among Reformers* (Milwaukee: S. E. Tate Printing Co., 1911), preface.

[4] *Wisconsin Magazine of History*, Vol. 64, No. 2, Winter 1980-81, p. 109.

[5] Brown papers, Schlesinger Library, Radcliffe College, Cambridge, MA. Her files contain many copies of inquiries to the president of the W.W.S.A. as to where and when the board meetings were to be held.

[6] The Congressional Union sprang from a committee of seven National American Woman Suffrage Association workers. The workers were appointed to do congressional work and to concentrate their efforts on the Susan B. Anthony amendment.

[7] *The Wisconsin Citizen*, April 1914.

[8] Olympia Brown's lectures are extant among her papers.

[9] Wisconsin Woman Suffrage Association papers, State Historical Society, Madison, Wisconsin. Letter of Lutie Stearns to Mrs. Youmans, August 15, 1914.

[10] Brown papers. Speech published in *The Suffragist*, Dec. 28, 1914.

[11] Brown papers. Quoted from *The Wisconsin Citizen*, February 1915.

Olympia Brown was the chief speaker at a meeting of the Just Government League of Baltimore, held in honor of the memory of Susan B. Anthony.

[12] Brown papers.

[13] Ibid.

[14] Ibid.

[15] Ibid.

[16] Wisconsin Woman Suffrage Association papers.

[17] Ibid.

[18] Brown papers.

[19] *The Sunday Sentinel*, April 16, 1922 (Milwaukee, Wisconsin). Headline: Pioneer Suffrage Leader Wins Place in Badger Hall of Fame. Brown papers.

[20] Olympia Brown, *Democratic Ideals — Sketch of Clara Bewick Colby*, published by the Federal Suffrage Association, 1917.

[21] *The Suffragist*, Sept. 1920, page 198. Brown papers.

[22] *The Boston Transcript*, March, 1917, as quoted in Inez Hayes Irwin, *The Story of the Woman's Party* (New York: Harcourt, Brace and Company, 1921), p. 204.

[23] Inez Hayes Irwin, *The Story of the Woman's Party* (New York: Harcourt, Brace and Company, 1921), p. 204, 313.

[24] Ida Husted Harper, *History of Woman Suffrage, Vol. 5* (New York: Arno Press, 1969), pp. 529-30.

[25] *The Suffragist,* March 31, 1917, "Miss Anthony and the Suffrage Movement," p. 5, Brown papers.

[26] *The Suffragist*, August 11, 1917, Brown papers.

[27] Ibid.

[28] Wisconsin Woman Suffrage Association papers, State Historical Society, Madison, Wisconsin.

[29] Ibid.

[30] *The Suffragist,* December 21, 1918. Speech at a conference of the National Advisory Council of the Woman's Party, Brown papers.

[31] Doris Stevens, *Jailed for Freedom* (New York: Liveright Publishing Corporation, 1920), pp. 302, 303. The story also appears in *The Story of the Woman's Party* by Inez H. Irwin, p. 388.

[32] *The Suffragist*, March 1, 1919, Wisconsin Woman Suffrage Association papers.

[33] The dates were May 21, 1919 and June 4, 1919.

[34] Wisconsin Woman Suffrage Association papers, letter to Mrs. Youmans dated August 20, 1919.

[35] Harper, p. 610.

[36] Ibid, pp. 615-617

[37] Wisconsin Woman Suffrage Association papers, letter of Ida Husted Harper to Mrs. Youmans, February 2, 1920.

[38] Brown papers, letter dated 1920.

Postscript

[1] Reflections of Katharine Willis Hooton as told to the author during an interview in June, 1978.

[2] Ibid.

[3] Reflections of Marcella Chalkley Holmes as told during an interview with the author in June 1978.

[4] Ibid.

[5] Gwendolen Willis, "Life and Work of Olympia Brown," paper presented Nov. 4, 1959 at "Highlights of Racine County," sponsored by Racine County Historical Society, p. 9. Racine Public Library.

[6] Brown papers. Mrs. Harper's letter of Dec. 28, 1917.

[7] The complete sermon, "The Opening Doors," is in the appendix.

[8] *The Suffragist,* Sept. 1920, p. 214. Brown papers.

[9] *Famous Wisconsin women,* Vol. 3 (Madison: Women's Auxiliary State Historical Society of Wis., 1973), p. 16.

[10] Issue of October 25, 1926. Brown papers.

[11] Brown papers.

[12] Ibid. Mrs. Greene was a past secretary of the Racine branch of the Wisconsin Woman Suffrage Association.

[13] The tablet was given by he son and daughter, Henry Parker Willis and Gwendolen Brown Willis.

[14] Brown papers and in the Unitarian-Universalist Church of Racine.

[15] The buildings house over five hundred elementary children as well as having facilities for special educational needs.

[16] UU World, March 1, 1981, page 8.

* The bulk of Olympia Brown's papers are at the Arthur and Elizabeth Schlesinger Library on the History of Women in America, Radcliffe College, Cambridge, Massachusetts. Copies of Olympia Brown's unpublished Autobiography; *Acquaintances, Old and New, Among Reformers* and *Democratic Ideals* are also at the Unitarian Universalist Church in Racine, the Racine Public Library and the University of Wisconsin-Parkside library, Kenosha, Wisconsin.

DECLARATION OF RIGHTS

OF THE

WOMEN OF THE UNITED STATES

BY THE

NATIONAL WOMAN SUFFRAGE ASSOCIATION,

JULY 4th, 1876

While the Nation is buoyant with patriotism, and all hearts are attuned to praise, it is with sorrow we come to strike the one discordant note, on this hundredth anniversary of our country's birth. When subjects of Kings, Emperors, and Czars, from the Old World, join in our National Jubilee, shall the women of the Republic refuse to lay their hands with benedictions on the nation's head? Surveying America's Exposition, surpassing in magnificence those of London, Paris, and Vienna, shall we not rejoice at the success of the youngest rival among the nations of the earth? May not our hearts, in unison with all, swell with pride at our great achievements as a people; our free speech, free press, free schools, free church, and the rapid progress we have made in material wealth, trade, commerce and the inventive arts? And we do rejoice, in the success thus far, of our experiment of self-government. Our faith is firm and unwavering in the broad principles of human rights, proclaimed in 1776, not only as abstract truths, but as the corner stones of a republic. Yet, we cannot forget, even in this glad hour, that while all men of every race, and clime, and condition, have been invested with the full rights of citizenship, under our hospitable flag, all women still suffer the degradation of disfranchisement.

The history of our country the past hundred years, has been a series of assumptions and usurpations of power over woman, in direct opposition to the principles of just government, acknowledged by the United States at its foundation which are:

First.   The natural rights of each individual.

Second.   The exact equality of these rights.

Third.   That these rights, when not delegated by the individual, are retained by the individual.

Fourth.   That no person can exercise the rights of others without delegated authority.

Fifth.   That the non-use of these rights does not destroy them.

And for the violation of these fundamental principles of our Government, we arraign our rulers on this 4th day of July, 1876,—and these are our

ARTICLES OF IMPEACHMENT.

BILLS OF ATTAINDER have been passed by the introduction of the word "male" into all the State constitutions, denying to woman the right of suffrage, and thereby making sex a crime—an exercise of power clearly forbidden in Article 1st, Sections 9th and 10th of the United States Constitution.

THE WRIT OF HABEAS CORPUS, the only protection against *lettres de cachet,* and all forms of unjust imprisonment, which the Constitution declares "shall not be suspended, except when in cases of rebellion or invasion, the public safety demands it," is held inoperative in every State in the Union, in case of a married woman against her husband,—the marital rights of the husband being in all cases primary, and the rights of the wife secondary.

THE RIGHT OF TRIAL BY A JURY OF ONE'S PEERS was so jealously guarded that States refused to ratify the original Constitution, until it was guaranteed by the 6th Amendment. And yet the women of this nation have never been allowed a jury of their peers—being tried in all cases by men, native and foreign, educated and ignorant, virtuous and vicious. Young girls have been arraigned in our courts for the crime of infanticide; tried, convicted, hung—victims, perchance, of judge, jurors, advocates—while no woman's voice could be heard in their defence. And not only are women denied a jury of their peers, but in some cases, jury trial altogether. During the war, a woman was tried and hung by military law, in defiance of the 5th Amendment, which specifically declares: "no person shall be held to answer for a capital or otherwise infamous crime, unless on a presentment or indictment of a grand jury, except in cases * * * * * of persons in actual service in time of war." During the last Presidential campaign, a woman, arrested for voting, was denied the protection of a jury, tried, convicted and sentenced to a fine and costs of prosecution, by the absolute power of a judge of the Supreme Court of the United States.

TAXATION WITHOUT REPRESENTATION, the immediate cause of the rebellion of the Colonies against Great Britain, is one of the grievous wrongs the women of this country have suffered during the century. Deploring war, with all the demoralization that follows in its train, we have been taxed to support standing armies, with their waste of life and wealth. Believing in temperance, we have been taxed to support the vice, crime, and pauperism of the Liquor Traffic. While we suffer its wrongs and abuses infinitely more than man, we have no power to protect our sons against this giant evil. During the Temperance Crusade, mothers were arrested, fined, imprisoned, for even praying and singing in the streets, while men blockade the sidewalks with impunity, even on Sunday, with their military parades and political processions. Believing in honesty, we are taxed to support a dangerous army of civilians, buying and selling the offices of government and sacrificing the best interests of the people. And, moreover, we are taxed to support the very legislators, and judges, who make laws, and render decisions adverse to woman. And for refusing to pay such unjust taxation, the houses, lands, bonds, and stock of women, have been seized and sold within the present year, thus proving Lord Coke's assertion, "that the very act of taxing a man's property without his consent, is, in effect, disfranchising him of every civil right."

UNEQUAL CODES FOR MEN AND WOMEN. Held by law a perpetual minor, deemed incapable of self-protection, even in the industries of the world, woman is denied equality of rights. The fact of sex, not the quantity or quality of work, in most cases, decides the pay and position; and because of this injustice thousands of fatherless girls are compelled to choose between a life of shame and starvation.

Laws catering to man's vices have created two codes of morals in which penalties are graded according to the political status of the offender. Under such laws, women are fined and imprisoned if found alone in the streets, or in public places of resort, at certain hours. Under the pretence of regulating public morals, police officers seizing the occupants of disreputable houses, march the women in platoons to prison, while the men, partners in their guilt, go free.

While making a show of virtue in forbidding the importation of Chinese women on the Pacific coast for immoral purposes, our rulers, in many states, and even under the shadow of the National Capitol, are now proposing to legalize the sale of American womanhood for the same vile purposes.

SPECIAL LEGISLATION FOR WOMAN has placed us in a most anomalous position. Women invested with the rights of citizens in one section—voters, jurors, office-holders—crossing an imaginary line, are subjects in the next. In some states, a married woman may hold property and transact business in her own name; in others, her earnings belong to her husband. In some states, a woman may testify against her husband, sue and be sued in the courts; in others, she has no redress in case of damage to person, property, or character. In case of divorce, on account of adultery in the husband, the innocent wife is held to possess no right to children, or property, unless by special decree of the court. But in no state of the Union has the wife the right to her own person, or to any part of the joint earnings of the co-partnership, during the life of her husband. In some States women may enter the law schools and practice in the courts; in others they are forbidden. In some universities, girls enjoy equal educational advantages with boys, while many of the proudest institutions in the land deny them admittance, though the sons of China, Japan and Africa are welcomed there.

But the privileges already granted in the several states are by no means secure. The right of suffrage once exercised by women in certain States and Territories, has been denied by subsequent legislation. A bill is now pending in Congress to disfranchise the women of Utah, thus interfering to deprive United States citizens of the same rights, which the Supreme Court has declared the National Government powerless to protect anywhere. Laws passed after years of untiring effort, guaranteeing married women certain rights of property, and mothers the custody of their children, have been repealed in States where we supposed all was safe. Thus have our most sacred rights been made the football of legislative caprice, proving that a power which grants, as a privilege, what by nature is a right, may withhold the same as a penalty, when deeming it necessary for its own perpetuation.

REPRESENTATION FOR WOMAN has had no place in the nation's thought. Since the incorporation of the thirteen original states, twenty four have been admitted to the Union, not one of which has recognized woman's right of self-government. On this birthday of our national liberties, July 4th, 1876, Colorado, like all her elder sisters, comes into the Union, with the invidious word "male" in her Constitution.

UNIVERSAL MANHOOD SUFFRAGE, by establishing an aristocracy of sex, imposes upon the women of this nation a more absolute and cruel despotism than monarchy; in that, woman finds a political master in her father, husband, brother, son. The aristocracies of the old world are based upon birth, wealth, refinement, education, nobility, brave deeds of chivalry; in this nation, on sex alone; exalting brute force above moral power, vice above virtue, ignorance above education, and the son above the mother who bore him.

THE JUDICIARY OF THE NATION has proved itself but the echo of the party in power, by upholding and enforcing laws that are opposed to the spirit and letter of the Constitution. When the slave power was dominant, the Supreme Court decided that a black man was not a citizen, because he had not the right to vote; and when the Constitution was so amended as to make all persons citizens, the same high tribunal decided that a woman, though a citizen, had not the right to vote. Such vacillating interpretations of constitutional law unsettle our faith in judicial authority, and undermine the liberties of the whole people.

THESE ARTICLES OF IMPEACHMENT AGAINST OUR RULERS we now submit to the impartial judgment of the people.

To all these wrongs and oppressions woman has not submitted in silence and resignation. From the beginning of the century, when Abigail Adams, the wife of one President and the mother of another, said, "we will not hold ourselves bound to obey laws in which we have no voice or representation," until now, woman's discontent has been steadily increasing, culminating nearly thirty years ago in a simultaneous movement among the women of the nation, demanding the right of suffrage. In making our just demands, a higher motive than the pride of sex inspires us; we feel that national safety and stability depend on the complete recognition of the broad principles of our government. Woman's degraded, helpless position is the weak point in our institutions to-day; a disturbing force everywhere, severing family ties, filling our asylums with the deaf, the dumb, the blind, our prisons with criminals, our cities with drunkenness and prostitution, our homes with disease and death.

It was the boast of the founders of the republic, that the rights for which they contended, were the rights of human nature. If these rights are ignored in the case of one half the people, the nation is surely preparing for its own downfall. Governments try themselves. The recognition of a governing and a governed class is incompatible with the first principles of freedom. Woman has not been a heedless spectator of the events of this century, nor a dull listener to the grand arguments for the equal rights of humanity. From the earliest history of our country, woman has shown equal devotion with man to the cause of freedom, and has stood firmly by his side in its defence. Together, they have made this country what it is. Woman's wealth, thought and labor have cemented the stones of every monument man has reared to liberty.

And now, at the close of a hundred years, as the hour hand of the great clock that marks the centuries points to 1876, we declare our faith in the principles of self-government; our full equality with man in natural rights; that woman was made first for her own happiness, with the absolute right to herself—to all the opportunities and advantages life affords, for her complete development; and we deny that dogma of the centuries, incorporated in the codes of all nations—that woman was made for man—her best interests, in all cases, to be sacrificed to his will.

We ask of our rulers, at this hour, no special favors, no special privileges, no special legislation. We ask justice, we ask equality, we ask that all the civil and political rights that belong to citizens of the United States, be guaranteed to us and our daughters forever.

LUCRETIA MOTT,	SUSAN B. ANTHONY,
ELLEN C. SARGENT,	ELIZABETH CADY STANTON,
MATILDA JOSLYN GAGE,	VIRGINIA L. MINOR,
PAULINA WRIGHT DAVIS,	CLEMENCE S. LOZIER,
SARA ANDREWS SPENCER,	ERNESTINE L. ROSE,
OLYMPIA BROWN,	LILLIE DEVEREUX BLAKE,
CLARINDA I. H. NICHOLS,	MATHILDE FRANCESKE ANNEKE,
PHEBE W. COUZINS,	MARY ANN McCLINTOCK,
MATHILDE F. WENDT,	JANE GRAHAM JONES,
AMY POST,	ADELAIDE THOMSON,
A. JANE DUNNIWAY,	SARAH PUGH,
LAURA DE FORCE GORDON,	BELVA A. LOCKWOOD,

N. B. This Declaration is engrossed in the Centennial Books of the National Woman Suffrage Association. Friends wishing to sign it are invited to call; those at a distance will please send their signatures on a slip of thin paper, to be pasted in the book. Address NATIONAL WOMAN SUFFRAGE PARLORS, No. 1431 CHESTNUT STREET, PHILADELPHIA, PA.

N. B.— And with your name for the Declaration of Rights, please do not fail to send a Contribution, a Dollar, or at least enough to equal the cost of the paper, the printing and posting of the documents you so gladly receive from us.

Address

SUSAN B. ANTHONY

National Woman Suffrage Parlors,
1431 Chestnut Street, Philadelphia, Pa.

The Opening Doors

Text: "Lift up your heads O ye gates and
be ye lifted up ye everlasting doors."—Psalm 24, Verse 7.

A Sermon Preached in the Universalist Church, Racine, Wis. by Rev. Olympia Brown, September 12, 1920

It is now nearly thirty-three years since I resigned my pastorate in this church. That is a long time and many things have happened, but the grandest thing has been the lifting up of the gates and the opening of the doors to the women of America, giving liberty to twenty-seven million women, thus opening to them a new and larger life and a higher ideal. The future opens before them, fraught with great possibilities of noble achievement. It is worth a lifetime to behold the victory. Then there have been other changes, Racine has grown larger and richer and the population has changed; many have come and some have gone. The everlasting doors have opened to some of our dearest and they have been permitted to behold the mysteries that lie beyond. We see them no more. We miss their ready co-operation and sympathy and love, but we know that wherever they are, they are in God's universe and they are safe and all is well with them. We have had our struggles and our triumphs, our labors and our victories, our sorrows and our joys and some of us are growing old, but I would say in the words of Browning,

> Grow old along with me!
> The best is yet to be,
> The last of life, for which the first was made;
> Our times are in His hand
> Who saith "A whole I planned,
> Youth shows but half/ trust God, see all
> Nor be afraid."

Meantime new proofs of the truths which we advocate have been accumulating, sustaining the faith in which we have lived, for which we have worked, and which has bound us together as a church. New and wonderful evidences of the truth of Universalism have come to us. We formerly were glad to be able to point to texts of Scripture as proof of our doctrines, showing to the people the impossibility of an endless hell, telling them of the one God "who will have all men to be saved and to come to the knowledge of the truth" and assuring them that "As in Adam all die even so in Christ shall all be made alive."

We relied on the promises of revelation and we still cherish these grand old texts. They are dear to our hearts and they will ever remain in our memories a precious possession.

But now they are fortified and confirmed by the promises that come to us from nature "new every morning and fresh every evening." Today we are not dependent upon any text or the letter of any book. It is the spirit that giveth life and the spirit speaks to our souls with every breath that blows. Science has been unravelling the mysteries of the universe and has brought to light new examples of the Divine power and purpose. Burbank and Edison and Madame Curie have lifted up the everlasting doors and revealed the Father's countenance, all radiant with love. Madame Curie, by working long in the laboratory has unlocked the rocks and released radium, a substance fraught with incalculable benefit to humanity. Creative chemistry has been at work and by its reactions and combinations has brought to light new powers in the earth and in the air for the use of men. We have not half measured or understood the capabilities of this planet. William Henry Perkins, a young boy of thirteen, became so much interested in chemistry that he voluntarily gave up his dinner and his noon hour to attend lectures on the subject. He went on with his researches until he had made discoveries invaluable to the manufacturer, among them that of aniline dyes, and other things which have added wealth to the people. Thus earth and air are filled with proofs of Divine love, goodness and power. The mountains and the hills have spoken and the rocks and the soils have added their testimony. "The dynamic symmetries revealed in nature such as the form of the fern leaf; the nautilus; and those vegetable products in which the regular pentagon occurred or where we find a geometrical arrangement of leaves about a stalk;" all show the skillful handiwork of the Divine, and all these wonderful scientific discoveries and revelations are proofs of God's unfailing love. The Opening Doors lead to no dark dungeons, open upon no burning lake, give no evidence of everlasting punishment. But all gladden us with assurances of Divine Goodness and indicate the final triumph of the good.

> "A charmed life old goodness hath.
> The tares may perish
> But the grain is not for death."

Not only by the researches of science are we shown the glories of creation, but the scenes of beauty which daily greet our eyes, the song of birds, fragrance of flowers, the moonlight shining on the waves all tell the same story of divine love. "The heavens declare the glory of God and the firmament showeth His handiwork." I have here a poem written by my mother in extreme old age in which the contemplation of the natural world seems to have lifted her above the weaknesses and pains of old age and enabled her to rise, in the entire confidence, into an atmosphere of Divine Love.

MORNING HYMN

From shades of night the morning woke;
Nature her hymn of praise began,
From all her keys the chorus broke,
Through all her chords the echoes ran.
    "Praise God," the roaring billow cried,
    The thunder's awful bass replied.
In dulcet tones of music sweet
Each lowly flower its fragrance lent;
Birds sang, the morning light to greet,
And every bough in homage bent.
        The sun arose in majesty;
        Nature in worship bent the knee.
Roll on, sweet harmonies of love!
Through all earth's blooming valleys, roll;
Above the world, the stars above,
Soars upward my enraptured soul.
        Borne on devotion's wing of fire,
        To Nature's God my thoughts aspire.

But more significant than even the voices of the natural world is the evidence of Divine life which we see in man himself. When a great heroic deed is done humanity is lifted up and ennobled and we have the assurance that there is a spirit in man and the Lord God giveth him understanding. Oh, what grand acts of self sacrifice and high courage, what heroism, have we seen in innumerable instances during the last few sorrowful years, all showing that there is a soul in man partaking of the Divine life. A thousand instances of depravity are forgotten in our admiration of one great heroic action by which human nature is lifted to a higher level, by which we know that man has a soul which is immortal and which enables him to utilize and make his own the wonderful resources with which the earth with all its glories is fitted up for his uses.

When the other day I saw crowds of women of all conditions coming into the polling booth all filled with great enthusiasm, forgetting old prejudices, old associations and former interests, only seeking to know how to serve the state, ready to leave their usual amusements and associations and give themselves to new subjects of study, not to serve any particular party, but only to learn how to help the world I said, they are grander than I thought. They have "meat to eat that the world knows not of," there is a Divine Life in them which this new experience is revealing.

The greatness of men, the grand capabilities of women attest the worth of the human being fashioned in the image of God.

It is true that the ignorance of men and the awful mistakes they make, the wrongs they do and the sins they commit, bringing with them, even here, terrible punishment and embittering life might cause us to doubt were it not that we see that there is a pardoning power in the spiritual world as there is healing in nature.

The riven rock soon covers itself with moss and becomes a thing of beauty. The tree deformed and disfigured puts out new twigs and branches and covers itself with verdure and so the warped and travel-stained, sorrow stricken souls of men shall at last put on the garments of Holiness. Men shall find remedies for their weakness, enlightenment for their ignorance and so rise out of their degradation and their sin.

One of our noted political prisoners said the other day in an interview: "I have never been more hopeful and more confident of the future than I am to-day. Nor have I ever had so great faith in the moral order of the universe as I have to-day."

"There is a kinship of misery that generates the true sweetness of human nature, the very milk of human kindness." Thus the sins of men and their sorrows come at last to confirm the great truths revealed in the natural world.

And so Science; the beauties of nature and the grand possibilities of humanity furnish overwhelming proofs of the final victory of the good and the ultimate purification of every human soul.

And this is Universalism: the grandest system of religious truth that has ever been revealed to man. The doctrine for which the world waits.

A short time ago a correspondent of the "Nation" wrote to the editor begging him to publish something hopeful. He said he was so tired of being discouraged he longed for something hopeful. And he spoke for thousands who in this time of uncertainty and chaos and confusion are longing for a ray of light, something to relieve the discouragements of the hour.

Mothers all over this land who have heard the solemn tidings that their sons have been slaughtered on the battlefield; wives who have been robbed of everything: companionship, support, all the joys of life; multitudes whom the terrible pictures of suffering, and torture have filled with horror, he spoke for all of these.

ALL NEED MORE HOPE, ETERNAL HOPE!

Hope! When I mourn, with sympathizing mind,
The wrongs of fate, the woes of human kind,
Thy blissful omens bid my spirit see
The boundless fields of rapture yet to be;
I watch the wheels of Nature's mazy plan,
And learn the future by the past of man.

He spoke for the whole world that is longing for hope, and Universalism is the answer to that cry. For this the world waits.

Oh! Lift up your heads, O ye gates, even lift them up ye everlasting doors, that the King of Glory may come in. The Lord mighty in love, rich in tender mercies, abundant in pardoning power. He comes to bring consolation to the sorrowful, inspiration to the toiler, hope for the sinner. He comes to bless the world and to help humanity to rise out of its selfishness and ignorance.

We talk of reforms. We have hoped to make the world safe for democracy; to establish a league of peace; but the very first necessity in reform work is the recognition of Divine capabilities in man. The foundation of democracy is the realization that every human being is a child of God, entitled to the opportunities of life, worthy of respect, and requiring an atmosphere of justice and liberty for his development.

We can never make the world safe for democracy by fighting. Rather by showing the power of Justice done to each humble individual shall we be able to create a firm basis for the state. We can establish a league of Peace only by teaching the nations the great lesson of the Fatherhood of God and the Brotherhood of Man.

Every nation must learn that the people of all the nations are children of God and must all share the wealth of the world. You may say that this is impracticable, far away, and can never be accomplished. But this is the work which Universalists are appointed to do. Universalists, sometime, somehow, somewhere, must ever teach this great lesson.

We are not alone. There is always an unseen power working for righteousness. The Infinite is behind us. The eternal years of God are ours.

And that is the message which I bring to you to-day. Stand by this great faith which the world needs and which you are called to proclaim.

It is not necessary to go far away to tell the story of God's love or even to win the nations. God has given us the heathen for an inheritance. Here they come to our own city from far away countries and from the islands of the ocean. And here in Racine we may illustrate the great principles of our faith by our charity, by our kindliness and consideration for all. We shall speak the language of Universal love and it will be heard and the message will be carried far and wide.

What signifies that your numbers are few to-day when you are inspired by truths that are everlasting and have before you ever the vision of final victory, the assurance of the salvation of all souls?

Universalism shall at last win the world.

Dear Friends, stand by this faith. Work for it and sacrifice for it. There is nothing in all the world so important to you as to be loyal to this faith which has placed before you the loftiest ideals which has comforted you in sorrow, strengthened you for noble duty and made the world beautiful for you. Do not demand immediate results but rejoice that you are worthy to be entrusted with this great message and that you are strong enough to work for a great true principle without counting the cost. Go on finding ever new applications of these truths and new enjoyments in their contemplation, always trusting in the one God which ever lives and loves. "One God, one law, one element, and one far-off divine event to which the whole creation moves."

✤ ✤ Press Notices ✤ ✤

NORMAL SIGNAL, West Farmington, Ohio:
Rev. Olympia Brown preached from the latter part of the XVII Psalm, "I shall be satisfied when I awake with Thy likeness." There was a large audience present and they were held spell-bound until the close, when all pronounced it grand.

DULUTH DAILY NEWS:
Mrs. Brown is a woman of force and makes her points in a fearless, witty and independent fashion.

LA CROSSE MORNING CHRONICLE:
The lecture throughout was filled with eloquent and inspiring passages. It was varied with telling anecdotes, happy turns and witty suggestions. Mrs. Brown's articulation is unusually distinct and her voice is clear and resonant. She is not exactly handsome, but she is so entirely engrossed in and possessed by her subject that her personality is forgotten and one thinks only of the great theme which inspires her.

THE ROCKFORD MORNING STAR:
HEAVENLY HASH AND BETTER BABIES
Is What we will Have When the Ladies can Vote,
Says Rev. Olympia Brown.
The lady's remarks were more or less enlivened with facetious stories and were interesting throughout; and the real solid facts and arguments she presented were often applauded.

THE SUPERIOR DAILY LEADER:
A FAULTLESS ORATOR.
Rev. Mrs. Olympia Brown Delivered a Polished Address
at the Wigwam Last Night.
The address at the Wigwam last evening was a treat of the first order when the presentation of a public address in strict harmony with the rules of finished elocution, of perfect enunciation, and the graces of good oratory are considered. Her audience involuntarily awarded a tribute of admiration in response to the well trained voice, in its varying inflection and

modulation, the very music of the art elocutional, not less than to the self-poised, erect and confident presence, whose animated countenance reflected so eloquently the qualities of intellect, culture and conviction. The speaker was Rev. Olympia Brown, of Racine, who may be styled the female Beecher of the rostrum. Mrs. Brown's address was humorously illustrated by timely and taking anecdotes.

THE CHRONICLE, Warren, Ohio:
The principal speaker at the suffragist meeting last night, was Rev. Olympia Brown, of Wisconsin. She is a fluent and eloquent talker and presents her points with enlivening vim and a "thus saith the Lord" positiveness. On occasions she is a bit of moral earthquake and her oratorical shakings up are, on the whole, likely to be more healthful than hurtful.

FAULK COUNTY TIMES, Faulkton, Dak.:
Susan B. Anthony and Rev. Olympia Brown addressed the people of Faulk County at the M.E. church Saturday afternoon and evening, and Rev. Brown preached from the M.E. pulpit Sunday morning and from the Congregational pulpit in the evening. The presentation of the question of impartial suffrage was practical and able. Rev. Brown was more eloquent and more powerful to move and persuade the masses of mankind to vote for the enfranchisement of woman.

THE MENOMONIE TIMES:
Rev. Olympia Brown, of Racine, was eloquent, persuasive, convincing and eminently practical, as ever. To those who know Mrs. Brown best, she seems to constantly gain in power, and her character warms and mellows and ripens with years. Her impassioned plea for motherhood's rights to protect the home will be long remembered as one of the many eloquent appeals uttered at the convention. Frequent and deserved applause interrupted her speech, and was prolonged at the close.

ASHLAND NEWS:
Thursday's train brought to our city a lady whom all should have been glad to honor, Rev. Olympia Brown. A rare intellectual treat was enjoyed by those who could spare time from their pressing duties to listen. The higher aims of women and men were held before us in such a light that no one listening could go away unconvinced. Looking into the bright intellectual and determined face of Mrs. Brown, one feels that with such a guide woman can not fail to sooner or later reach the goal for which they run, equality for all.

ADDRESS OF REV. OLYMPIA BROWN RACINE, WISCONSIN.

Delivered Feb. 1, 1906, before the Woman's Suffrage Committee of the United States Senate.

Gentlemen of the Committee:

The subject of woman's suffrage is not new nor is it strange. It has been set before the people in all its phases for forty years. It has been argued on the floor of Congress by some of the ablest men that ever represented the people in that body of great statesmen; it has year after year been presented before your Honorable Committee by distinguished and consecrated women with an eloquence that ought to have moved the very stones; it has been on trial in Wyoming for between thirty and forty years and in Colorado, Idaho and Utah for many years; it has been adopted by most of the countries of Europe and been endorsed by the best thinkers and the most distinguished men in the civilized world. Statesmen, historians and literary men agree that there is no ground upon which men hold their right of suffrage that does not apply with equal force to women. Therefore it is not necessary to urge before this intelligent woman's suffrage committee the justice of our claim to the right of suffrage; no man with ordinary thinking power doubts it for a moment.

The question which now presents itself is the practical one of how to remove those barriers which stand between women and the exercise of this right of the United States citizen. The changing of the Constitution by means of a Sixteenth Amendment prohibiting States from disfranchising citizens on account of sex would of course settle the whole question and for many years we have sought such an amendment; the late Mrs. E. Cady Stanton the most statesmanlike woman we have ever had insisted upon this as the only solution of the problem and as a citizen she appealed to that great body, the Congress of the United States, which has been entrusted with the guardianship of the liberties of the whole people, and she scorned to make her appeal to any inferior body.

But the years pass and nothing is done in this direction. Indeed we are told by eminent authorities that amending the Constitution is a thing so difficult as to be practically impossible. Therefore we seek other means which if not so radical and effective will, in part, remove those disabilities which prevent us from exercising the citizen's right of suffrage.

The election of Federal officers, from the very nature of the case, ought to be under the control of the Federal Government. That the election of officers of the larger body should be wholly controlled by men in a more limited organization, is in itself an incongruity and in the formation of the Constitution it was so recognized by the framers and the power was given to Congress to intervene, if necessary, to protect the rights of citizens in such elections. That power was given in Section 4, of Article one of the Constitution, which provides that "Congress may at any time by law make or alter such regulations," meaning regulations made by State Legislatures for the election of representatives. This clause was not passed inadvertently but was fully considered and discussed; and in the debates in the Virginia Convention called to ratify the Federal Constitution, this very point was made subject of inquiry and was fully elucidated by James Madison, the man who, perhaps more than any other, carefully followed all the debates and fully understood all the conclusions of the Constitutional Convention. During this debate in answer to a question as to the meaning of this clause, he said: "Should the people of any State by any means be deprived of the right of suffrage it was deemed proper that it should be remedied by the general Government"; showing that the framers of the Constitution fully intended that Congress should have the power in the interest of the people to interfere if necessary with State regulations; indeed the office of Representative in Congress is a Federal office dependent upon the Constitution of the United States for its existence. In the Yarbrough case, 110 U.S. Rep. the Court said:

"But it is not correct to say that the right to vote for a member of Congress does not depend on the Constitution of the United States. The office, if it be properly called an office, is created by the Constitution, and by that alone. It also declares how it shall be filled, namely, by election."

"It is not true, therefore, that the electors for members of Congress owe their right to vote to the State law in any sense which makes the exercise of the right to depend exclusively on the law of the State. This new constitutional right was mainly designed for citizens of African descent. The principle, however, that the protection of the exercise of the right is within the power of Congress is as necessary to the right of other citizens to vote as to the colored citizens, and to the right to vote in general, as to be protected against discrimination."

President Roosevelt in his message of 1904 said:

"The power of Congress to protect the integrity of the elections of its own officials is inherent and has been recognized and affirmed by repeated declarations of the Supreme Court."

And this office of Representative provided for by the Constitution is to be filled by a vote of the "people". That women are people no one can deny. The dictionary definition of people is first—"all human beings—under the same government; speaking the same language; being of the same blood; same tribe of the same state." Woman possesses every attribute of the human being, in the language of Shylock, "Have we not eyes, have we not hands, organs, dimensions, senses, affections, passions; fed with the same food, hurt with the same weapons, subject to the same diseases, healed by the same remedies, warmed and cooled by the same winter and summer; if you prick us do we not bleed: If you amuse us do we not laugh: If you poison us do we not die?" Women have the same ambitions and aspirations as men. Like men we rebel against being "cabined, cribbed, confined", and we seek the largest liberty of the human. Women then are people, and as such entitled to vote according to the Constitution for Members of the House of Representatives.

Still farther the Constitution of the United States provides that "each House shall be the judge of elections and returns and qualifications of its own members." Of what value would this power be if the House had no right to interfere with or change the regulations made by the Legislatures of the different States in this election: The purpose of this section was evidently to secure to the Congress of the United States the ultimate control of the election of federal officers to the end that the right of suffrage might be preserved to the "people". And this is necessary to the integrity, the dignity, and the permanent existence of this branch of the government. A government without citizens, a citizen without a vote, a legislative body without power over the election of its own members, are absurdities which were never contemplated by the framers of our government.

The recognition of the right of suffrage as inherent in the citizenship of the United States would give new meaning to citizenship, add strength to our government and ultimately secure a larger degree of respect from foreign powers; then, to be a United States citizen would be an honor, for it would stand for independence, freedom, power, and all the world pays tribute to these; not only this but each individual representative would receive added respect and be able to stand on the floor of Congress on an equality with every other member, at present such is not the case. Talking the other day with a plain man I mentioned the fact that women vote in four States. "Not for national officers", said he. "Yes," said I. "Impossible", said he, "it would not be fair to the other States." I have met that same statement hundreds of times. It is the first thing that strikes the average man. And it is true, it is not fair. It is the very condition described by James Madison in the Virginia debates where he said: "Some States might regulate the elections on principles of equality and others might regulate them otherwise. This diversity would be obviously unjust," said Mr. Madison.

Our Colorado Representative stands here supported by the intelligent men and women citizens of Colorado. The home-interests, the best intellect, the culture of that great State are ready to back him up in any step he may take for progress. On the other hand the Representative from Michigan or Dakota must pay his respects to an ignorant constituency composed largely of unnaturalized men, immigrants who have within the year been imported from the shores of the Mediterranean or the slums of European cities. What can such a man do in Congress: His intentions are good but his constituency is the trouble. He does not represent the intelligence nor the best interests of his State. It is not fair.

Why not by a uniform Federal suffrage law put all the members of the House of Representatives on an equal footing: Congress can do this as I have shown. Some men claim that Congress has no such power but those very men demand of Congress to fix railroad rates, manage insurance companies, take care of the peoples' money in postal savings banks, collect bad debts for foreign nations, take care of the Islands of the ocean, and they have even asked Congress to establish a baby bureau! Can a body do all this when it is not even able to decide on the election of its own Members?

As well ask the baby in the cradle, held down by its swaddling bands, to assume all the duties and responsibilities of mature manhood as to ask Congress to manage all the business and domestic affairs of this country, settle the birth rate and take care of the babies, when it cannot even secure a uniform suffrage law for the election of its Members! How helpless in self protection, yet called upon to bear such burdens of responsibility!

But it is not true, Congress is in no such helpless condition as these men would have us believe. It has the power "by law to make or alter" the regulations of the states in regard to federal elections, it can protect the "integrity of the elections of its own officials". It can secure an election by the "people" according to the Constitution, and I believe it has the moral stamina necessary to do it.

In conclusion, Mr. Chairman, and Members of the Committee, I urge for the sake of the dignity of the House of Representatives, for the sake of fairness to its individual members, in order to place United States citizenship in its true position before the world, to secure better legislation and especially to "establish justice and ensure DOMESTIC TRANQUILLITY" that at this session a uniform federal suffrage law be passed providing for the election of the members of the House of Representatives by the people, including women; and to that end I ask this Committee to make a report to the Senate on this bill and secure a discussion of the subject and a vote upon it. The bill was presented by a Senator from a State where women have voted for many years. He knew of what he spoke when he presented that bill, it has been approved by many of the best thinkers of the United States, Rev. W.H. Thomas, one of the most noted men and clearest thinkers in this country, said the other day, in speaking of the hearing before this Committee last year: "The arguments of Mrs. Clara Bewick Colby before the committee of the United States Senate on Woman Suffrage, FROM THE CONSTITUTIONAL STANDPOINT, AND THE DECISIONS OF THE SUPREME COURT, ARE UNANSWERABLE. Women are 'People', are 'Citizens', and as such have their legal rights, and it is clearly within the authority of the National Government to affirm and make effective the right of women to vote for members of Congress."

"The fact of sex should have no more to do with the right to vote than should the color of the hair, or the eyes; qualified citizenship is the only question. The egotism, the assumed superiority of men, is both amusing and pathetic. Not till the equality of woman,—mothers, wives, sisters,—is recognized and her help in the great problems of the social order is welcomed, can the world reach the higher."

Other testimonies might be given. When once you have taken a stand on this question you will be astonished at the number of people that will be with you and at the power that will come to you. A cloud of witnesses are looking on waiting to help you in this work.

REV. OLYMPIA BROWN,
OF RACINE, WIS.

SUBJECTS OF LECTURES:

WOMAN AND EDUCATION.

THE WOMANHOOD OF AMERICA.

SCHOOL MATTERS.

THE SYMBOL OF LIBERTY.

THE FIFTH OF APRIL.

THE TRUE LABOR REFORM.

As a Preacher and Lecturer, Mrs. Brown is well known throughout the United States. She was one of the first women in this country to take a full collegiate and professional course of study. She was ordained to the Christian ministry in 1863, and has thus been a preacher and pastor of a church for twenty-four years. She canvassed the state of Kansas in the summer of '67, when Woman's Suffrage was for the first time in the history of the world submitted to the vote of any people. At that time she visited every part of the then new state, making 205 speeches between the fourth of July and the fifth of November, and as a result, gaining for her cause one-third of all the votes cast in the state.

She is at present occupied in speaking throughout Wisconsin on the various subjects in which women as well as men are interested—education, temperence, labor reform and human equality—all claiming a share of her attention. The following are a few out of a multitude of press notices that might be quoted:

"Rev. Olympia Brown spoke at the Congregational church on Wednesday evening to a large audience. Her subject, "The Womanhood of America," was treated in a manner and style that would do credit to the ablest orator and logician. She spoke as one having authority, and not as one not possessing right and justice in her soul. She is an earnest advocate of breaking the bonds with which woman is bound, as a menial slave in regard to the exercise of her political rights. Mrs. Brown is one of the most interesting speakers of the day."—*Palmyra Enterprise*.

A writer in the *Madison State Journal* says:

"The writer has had the privilege of hearing Susan B. Anthony, Julia Ward Howe, Elizabeth Cady Stanton and Mrs. Livermore on similar subjects, and for comprehensive, logical and masterly treatment of her subject Mrs. Brown is fully their equal."

"Rev. Olympia Brown, of Racine, president of the Woman's Suffrage Association of Wisconsin, delivered her lectures,"Symbol of Liberty" and "The Womanhood of America," in Goodrich Hall, on Wednesday and Thursday evenings of last week, and it is clearly evident to the people of Milton that this gifted lady has been here, for wherever she goes she leaves behind her the convictions of an intellectual treat that is not usual to Milton audiences."—*The Milton Telephone*

"Rev. Olympia Brown, of Racine, President of the Woman's Suffrage Association of Wisconsin, delivered a lecture at the Grange Hall in this place Monday evening to a well filled house. This distinguished lady gave her hearers an intellectual treat, such as they have not had for many a day. The audience at once became interested in what she said and listened to her throughout with marked attention; her logic was clear and her reasoning sound. The ladies of this place, and especially the Albany Equal Suffrage and Literary Society, may well feel proud to have such a gifted lady come among them to plead their cause for political rights."—*The Albany Vindicator*

Persons desiring a Lecture should write at once to REV. OLYMPIA BROWN, Racine, Wis. Lectures in the interests of Woman's Suffrage are given without definite charge, if entertainment and place of meeting are furnished, as the Association which she represents is desirous of making an extended canvass of the state.

The Marseillaise of the Women

A song for Suffrage
by Philip Green Wright*
(Sung to the tune of the French Marseillaise)

Around the world there runs a murmur,
  The sound of voices rising clear;
From China's plains, from distant Burma,
  From English town, from Russian mir,
  It grows, it swells upon the ear.
It is the cry of all earth's daughters,
  Arousing from the sleep of years;
  It drowns opposing taunts and jeers
Like the gathering flood of rushing waters.
  "Awake in every land.
   Join forces, hand in hand.
March on, march on, full in our sight,
  The blessed morning light!

"Too long we've held the ignoble station
  Which man in his indulgence gave,
Now fawned upon in adulation,
  Now thrust aside, his drudge and slave;
  "Tis equal comradeship we crave.
Before our eyes, we see, outspreading,
  The wide domain of human work;
  Its arduous heights we do not shirk;
Its depths our eager feet are treading.
  Oh, hear our trumpet call,
   For you, for us, for all.
March on, march on, we take our place,
  Your comrades in the race!

"Our ranks increase; from every region
   New eager throats take up our song;
New eager eyes—oh, countless legion!
   New eager feet fall in along
   Our new crusade 'gainst ancient wrong.
The children in the factories hear us,
   The women toilers' faces shine;
   They cheer us in our cause divine;
It is only the oppressors fear us.
   Awake in every land.
   Join forces, hand in hand.
March on, march on, full in our sight,
   The blessed morning light!

"In civic life, in state, in nation,
   Our vote must weigh as well as man's.
In science, art, and education,
   Our brain the same horizon scans,
   The same unfolding cosmic plans.
With him the ills of life subduing,
   With him the good day pressing on,
   With glowing eyes, the rising sun
We front, with him our path pursuing.
   Oh, hear our trumpet call,
   For you, for us, for all.
March on, march on, perfect the plan,
   The woman with the man!"

* National Woman Suffrage Pub. Co., Inc.
  505 Fifth Avenue, New York City

From a post card in the Schlesinger Library, vertical files.

Index

Greeley, Horace 40, 99
Greene, Frances R. 175
Grimke sisters 21
Gwendolen (see Willis, Gwendolen Brown)
Hale, Edward Everett 40
Hanaford, Pheobe 89, 121, 122,141
Harper, Ida Husted 165, 166, 167, 171
Hay, Mary Garrett 166
Haymarket Square 120
Higginson, T. W. 100
History of Woman Suffrage 165, 166, 172
Holmes, Marcella 170
Hooker, Isabella Beecher 171
Hooton, Katharine Willis 169
Howe, Julia Ward 121
Howland, Emily 166
Hudson, Major 129
Humboldt Union 89
Hutchinson, John 87, 134
Indians 18, 83
Irving house 69
Irwin, Inez Haynes 158
Jackson , Andrew 174
James, Ada 149
James, State Senator David, 148
James, State Senator Norman 125
Jones, Mrs. J. E. 51
Journal-Times 120
Kalamazoo, Michigan 5, 62, 139
Kansas 73, 74, 75, 76, 77, 78, 81, 149, 170, 174
Kansas Pacific Railroad 83
Kansas State Journal 89
Kendall, Anna Norris 158
LaCrosse, Wisconsin 121
Lafayette Park, Washington, D. C. 2, 163
Langston, Charles 88, 95
League of Nations 173
League of Women Voters 173
Leavenworth, Kansas 78
Lee, J. L. 60
Leonard, T. F. 64
Lewis, Dr. Dio 63
Lincoln, President Abraham 67
liquor interests 80, 91, 93
Livermore, Mary A. 121

211

214

Like Olympia Brown, **Charlotte Coté** has been a feminist since child-hood. She grew up in Nebraska in a number of diverse households where she learned that she had to fight to gain equal rights and consideration. She graduated cum laude from high school with a scholarship in drama. Married, she raised four children, then continued her college education with majors in English and communication leading to a master's degree in English from the University of Wisconsin-Milwaukee.

She has won several poetry awards and has published poems in anthologies with the Root River Poets and the Wisconsin Fellowship of Poets.

She is a member of Olympia Brown's former church in Racine, Wisconsin, where she met Olympia Brown's daughter, Gwendolen Willis. That acquaintanceship and Olympia Brown's unsung heroism in the battle for equality, justice and voting rights for women, inspired her to write this biography.